APR 12 2017

Where on Earth

Round Valley Library
23925 Howard St.
Covelo, CA 95428

A Guide to Specialty Nurseries and Gardens in California

Nancy Conner, Demi Bowles Lathrop, and Barbara Stevens

Where on Earth

Fifth Edition

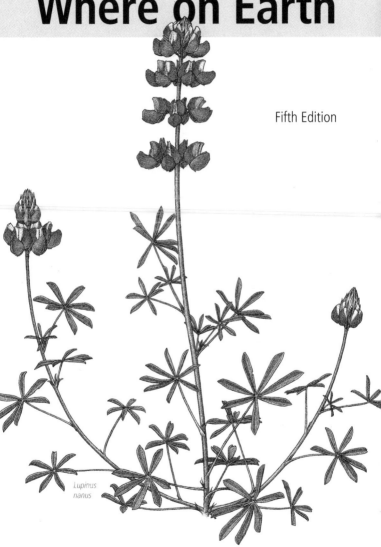

Lupinus nanus

Heyday • Berkeley, California

© 2017 by Nancy Conner, Demi Bowles Lathrop, and Barbara Stevens

All rights reserved. No portion of this work may be reproduced or transmitted in any form or by any means, electronic or mechanical, including photocopying and recording, or by any information storage or retrieval system, without permission in writing from Heyday.

Library of Congress Cataloging-in-Publication Data

Names: Conner, Nancy, author. | Lathrop, Demi Bowles, author.
  | Stevens, Barbara, author.
Title: Where on earth : a guide to specialty nurseries and gardens in
  California / Nancy Conner, Demi Bowles Lathrop, and Barbara Stevens.
Description: Fifth edition. | Berkeley, California : Heyday, [2017] |
  Includes index.
Identifiers: LCCN 2016044528 | ISBN 9781597143943 (pbk. : alk. paper)
Subjects: LCSH: Nurseries (Horticulture)—California—Directories. |
  Ornamental plant industry—California—Directories. | Gardens—
  California—Directories. | Horticulture—California—Directories.
Classification: LCC SB118.487.C2 C66 2017 | DDC 635.9/152025794—dc23
LC record available at https://lccn.loc.gov/2016044528

Cover Design: Ashley Ingram
Illustrations: Kristin Jakob
Maps: Ben Pease Cartography
Interior Design/Typesetting: Leigh McLellan Design
Printed in East Peoria, IL by Versa Press, Inc.

Orders, inquiries, and correspondence
should be addressed to:
    Heyday
    P.O. Box 9145, Berkeley, CA 94709
    (510) 549-3564, Fax (510) 549-1889
    www.heydaybooks.com

10 9 8 7 6 5 4 3 2 1

MIX
Paper from
responsible sources
FSC® C005010
www.fsc.org

Contents

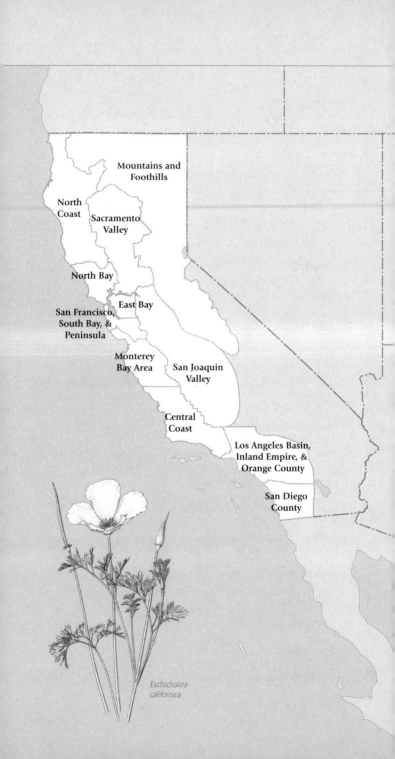

Mountains and
Foothills

North
Coast

Sacramento
Valley

North Bay

East Bay

San Francisco,
South Bay, &
Peninsula

Monterey
Bay Area

San Joaquin
Valley

Central
Coast

Los Angeles Basin,
Inland Empire, &
Orange County

San Diego
County

Eschscholzia
californica

Preface

This is a pivotal time for California horticulture. There has been a shift of attitude in the garden world from giddy excitement about what we *can* grow to a more somber reflection about what we *should* grow. The number-one issue is water. Five years of drought, the diminution of coastal fog, and shrinking aquifers have affected horticulture, as well as habitat and agriculture. California's horticultural world has led the charge for responsible gardening, introducing and supplying plants that are "water wise," "California friendly," "drought tolerant," "Mediterranean climate"—call it what you will—and plants that are appropriate to our many microclimates.

Economics has also put a squeeze on the horticultural world. As more people discover the pleasures of living in California, land and water costs rise. The scarcity of affordable land makes it difficult for small specialty growers to survive. Big box stores undercut pricing. Big growers in Oregon, where land is cheaper, have almost eliminated the commercial cultivation of rhododendrons in the northern part of the state. And then there are natural pests. Just as the pine pitch canker and *Phytophthora ramorus*, which causes sudden oak death, have taken their toll on our natural world, the Asian citrus psyllid and the apple moth, among others, affect the nursery world and the movement of plants throughout the state.

That California horticulture is always evolving is part of its allure. Nurseries offering California native plants are on the rise due to public funding for habitat-restoration projects and the growing realization that native plants make great garden plants. Small-scale "habitat gardening" has caught on. Likewise, the popularity of cacti and succulents in both public and private spaces has encouraged more growers of these. Edibles, too, are a success story, as heirloom fruits and vegetables are made more available.

This book celebrates those passionate individuals and institutions who have expanded and refined California horticulture, despite the current hurdles. We still live where most anything can grow, and this is seductive. It is said that Vista has the most salubrious mean temperature (40°F–80°F) for growing most plants. We have a community and state college system where the best garden technologies and practices are taught, spawning fresh and knowledgeable land stewards each year. Our landscapes have been enhanced by a long history of plant introductions by dedicated horticulturists, starting with whoever planted the first Mission grape. Their stories are told here.

This book is a resource tool for gardeners and garden lovers, a guide to see, savor, and shop for plants. Because we believe in the sensory pleasures of plants, this book is organized to encourage trips to nurseries and horticultural hot spots. We have divided the state into geographic regions, organized north to south and then moving inland. Each region starts with a descriptive essay, followed by listings of specialty nurseries and growers, of notable garden centers, and of horticultural attractions. A specialty nursery is one that specializes in one plant (e.g., Japanese maple) or one category of plant (e.g., California native plants) and one that grows or propagates most of what it sells. A grower is usually a wholesale producer of a wide variety of plants, included here because of their large influence on California horticulture. A notable garden center is one that offers a broad selection of plants, often combined with other garden products and accessories. We see specialty nurseries and growers as plant producers and garden centers as plant distributors. A horticultural attraction is a public destination that merits a visit. A section on mail-order nurseries lists California nurseries from whom you can order but not visit.

Needless to say, there are exceptions to every rule. Several horticultural attractions sell plants and some specialty nurseries propagate but do not specialize. Likewise, the determination of retail or wholesale can be a bit arbitrary, since there are wholesale nurseries open to the public and retail nurseries offering special discounts to the trade. If a nursery is listed as wholesale only, it is by request, meaning that the nursery has neither the staff nor the time to deal with individual retail customers. Please respect this request. For most specialty nurseries, it makes sense to call first to make sure someone will be there when you arrive.

Short thematic essays are included throughout to give gardeners a deeper understanding of how and why some plants are well suited for California gardens and others are not. We hope that good plant selection combined with good garden practices will make your garden thrive.

We have benefited from the wisdom and advice of many generous and knowledgeable people. This book began as a love letter to the plant people who helped launch the San Francisco Landscape Garden Show in 1985 and remains dedicated to the talent and dedication of the amazing folks who shape California horticulture. Special thanks for the fifth edition go to Richard Turner, Jr., Patrick Anderson, Valerie Arelt, Carol Bornstein, Arthur Conner, Lynette Evans, Dave Fross, Kirsten Honeyman, Virginia Hopper, Jennifer Jewell, Glenn Keator, Simar Khanna, Ted Kipping, Sara Malone, Luen Miller, Kathy Musial, Bart O'Brien, Robin Parer, Betsy Reniers, Nevin Smith, Nicholas Staddon, Nan Sterman, Kate Timberlake, Deb Wandell, Richard Ward, Ernie Wasson, Ernest Wertheim, Stewart Winchester, Barbara Worl, and our families for all of their support.

● ● ●

Thank you to the work of Peter R. Dallman, *Plant Life in the World's Mediterranean Climates*; Carol Bornstein, David Fross, and Bart O'Brien, *California Native Plants for the Garden*; Phyllis M. Faber, *California's Wild Gardens*; Nora Harlow, ed., *Plants and Landscapes for Summer Dry Climates of the San Francisco Bay Region*; and Christopher Thomas, *Water-Wise Gardening*. I am indebted. DBL

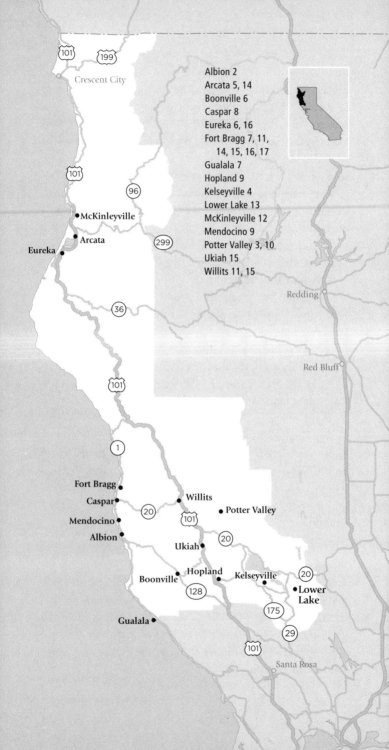

Albion 2
Arcata 5, 14
Boonville 6
Caspar 8
Eureka 6, 16
Fort Bragg 7, 11,
   14, 15, 16, 17
Gualala 7
Hopland 9
Kelseyville 4
Lower Lake 13
McKinleyville 12
Mendocino 9
Potter Valley 3, 10
Ukiah 15
Willits 11, 15

Trillium ovatum

Chapter 1

North Coast

Counties: Del Norte, Humboldt, Lake, Mendocino
Elevational range: Sea level to 6,411 feet at Bear Mountain on the Del Norte–Siskiyou County border
Sunset climate zones: 4, 14, 15, 17
Annual rainfall: This is the wettest region of the state, with 25 to 80 inches of annual rain.
Winter temperatures: Average lows from 34°F down to 21°F; dips down to 8°F to 0°F in high coastal mountains.
Summer temperatures: Temperatures range from 60°F to 75°F; average highs from 75°F to 78°F in Lake County.

The Pacific Ocean defines weather along the northern coast, the stretch of land from Crescent City in Del Norte County at the Oregon border down to Annapolis in Sonoma County. Summers are cool and foggy, while winters are chilly and wet. Ocean upwellings disperse as marine air, modifying the state's characteristic Mediterranean climate, with its dry summers and wet winters. Warm inland air makes up the balance.

One belt of the north Coast Range parallel to the coast juts from the state's northern end down to San Francisco. A long system of valleys separates it from its counterpart, an interior belt. Its low mountain contour creates microclimates with cold air basins and warm thermal pockets. Climate, temperatures, and growing conditions for plant life vary from the open, rolling hills of Potter and Anderson Valleys to the strips of moist, coastal redwood forests along the Navarro and other northern rivers.

Logging is a major industry in Mendocino and Humboldt counties; another large crop is marijuana, currently permitted for medicinal use in the state. The Anderson Valley's cool nights and mornings and sunny days allow thin-skinned Pinot noir grapes to mature slowly for optimal development of flavor.

Majestic among native flora is the coast redwood (*Sequoia sempervirens*), a tree with deeply furrowed red-brown bark and a conic, irregular, and open crown; coast redwoods can soar to 360 feet tall with the pitch of a cathedral spire. At the other end of the flora spectrum is spring-flowering Pacific trillium (*Trillium ovatum*), a tuberous woodland plant, distinctive for its single flower of three white, handkerchief-like petals that ages to deep rose on eight- to ten-inch stems. It grows in wooded canyons from Del Norte down to Monterey counties.

Specialty Nurseries and Growers

Digging Dog Nursery

31101 Middle Ridge Road, Albion 95410
(707) 937-1130 (nursery); (707) 937-1235 (office)
www.diggingdog.com
Email: business@diggingdog.com
Gary Ratway, Deborah Whigham
Retail and mail/online order
Open spring and summer until late October, Tuesday through
    Saturday, 10 a.m.–4 p.m. Always best to call first.

Plant specialties: Top select perennials (especially late-summer and fall bloomers), shrubs, trees, ground covers, ornamental grasses, and deer-resistant and drought-tolerant plants. Significant collections of heaths and heathers (*Erica, Calluna*),

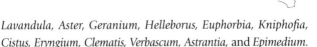

Lavandula, Aster, Geranium, Helleborus, Euphorbia, Kniphofia, Cistus, Eryngium, Clematis, Verbascum, Astrantia, and *Epimedium.*

History/description: After his studies in landscape architecture at UC Davis, Gary Ratway started a small nursery to supply his projects, located next door to the Mendocino Coast Botanical Gardens. The nursery moved and prospered after he and his wife, Deborah, then a textile designer, found this exquisite property in 1984 on a ridgetop clearing in the coastal redwood forest. Deborah, also a horticulturist, switched her full attention to the nursery, selecting plants to propagate that provide year-round intrigue via blossoms, berries, and branches. To promote backyard gardening as an important source of habitat, she selects plants that are bird and pollinator friendly. She believes that "plants give back more than you give them." Gary designed the nursery's extraordinary display gardens, which have graced the cover of *Martha Stewart Living* and have been featured on the Garden Conservancy's Open Days tours. Within the discipline of his arranged beds and crushed-granite pathways erupts a profusion of color-coordinated perennials and shrubs, in peak bloom from June to October. Together the couple have traveled the world looking for interesting plants and are credited with the introduction of *Heuchera x brizoides* 'Weston Pink' and *Cistus* 'John Catterson'. Their lavender plants helped fuel the trend for lavender fields in the late 1990s. Custom growing and design services are available.

Essence of the Tree

P. O. Box 323, Potter Valley 95469
(707) 743-1633; (888) 489-1886 (toll-free)
www.essenceofthetree.com
Email: contactus@essenceofthetree.com
Tricia Smyth
Mail order, retail, and wholesale
Open by appointment only.

Plant specialties: Over 300 cultivars of *Acer palmatum;* selected cultivars of other *Acer* species; other trees suitable for container gardening and bonsai, such as *Malus* and other flowering and fruiting trees; and companion plants of compatible size and cultural requirements for maples in containers, such as dwarf hostas, irises, and azaleas. Selection of distinctive containers.

History/description: As a fourth-generation horticulturist and the daughter of the late Nancy Fiers, whose Mountain Maples Nursery was well regarded for its plant selections and community-education efforts, Tricia Smyth succumbed to destiny. Well trained in her own right, she headed her own landscaping company in California and northern Florida for 15 years; the next 10 years were spent under the tutelage of her mother. The five-acre nursery is located on the fertile floor of the Potter Valley, an old-time agricultural valley that is now the heart of Mendocino's wine country. Essence of the Tree outsources its grafting to an Oregon grower, supplying it with choice scions. Maple fanciers are a passionate lot. Tricia attributes their—and her—passion to the fact that maples have perhaps the most diverse forms possible in the plant world. They mutate easily, and grafting can perpetuate the best of these mutations. For a true plant person, this can be addicting. Mail-order details are available online or through the nursery's full-color, biannual catalog.

Evergreen Gardenworks

P. O. Box 537, Kelseyville 95451
www.evergreengardenworks.com
Email: bonsai@pacific.net
Brent Walston, Susan Meier
Mail/online order
Open by email appointment only.

Plant specialties: Bonsai, including collections of *Acer, Carpinus, Cedrus, Chaenomeles, Cotoneaster, Juniperus, Malus, Pinus, Prunus, Punica, Quercus,* and *Ulmus.* Introductions by Evergreen include *Acer buergerianum* 'Evergreen's Rough Bark', *Chaenomeles* 'Not Minerva', and *C.* 'Contorted Salmon Pink'.

History/description: This nursery was started in 1987 to provide choice plants for Brent Walston's landscape maintenance, construction, and design business. Gradually, his interest shifted to bonsai—first as a means to hone his pruning skills, then as an end in itself. In 1999, the nursery moved to its present location on 10 acres near Clear Lake. Brent Walston does all the propagating and growing, occasionally offers classes in bonsai design, and has an impressive collection of bonsai articles on the nursery's website.

Fickle Hill Old Rose Nursery

282 Fickle Hill Road, Arcata 95521
(707) 826-0708
Facebook: Fickle Hill Old Rose Nursery
Email: ficklehillrose@gmail.com
Cindy Graebner
Retail
Open by appointment only.

Plant specialties: Antique rose varieties suitable for the foggy North Coast; some perennials and shrubs; and unusual fuchsias (non-hybridized, and therefore mite-resistant).

History/description: In the 1980s, Cindy Graebner, working as a landscaper, became frustrated with the availability of plants suitable to the North Coast climate, particularly roses. Hybrid tea roses proved to be a disaster here, prone to all sorts of diseases. Increasingly, she became interested in several non-hybrid plants for their disease tolerance and reliable performance. She propagates from a mature selection of mother stock, garnered over her 25-plus years in the nursery business. Her one-acre site is part nursery and part rambling English-style garden "with Mediterranean accents." She also sells plants at the farmers' market in Arcata, open Saturdays from 9 a.m. to 2 p.m.

Glenmar Heather Nursery, Inc.

7430 Myrtle Avenue, Eureka 95503
P. O. Box 479, Bayside 95524-0479
(707) 268-5560
Email: glenmarheather@yahoo.com
Maria and Tom Krenek
Retail and wholesale
Open by appointment only.

Plant specialties: Over 600 varieties of heaths and heathers (*Calluna, Daboecia,* and *Erica* primarily), with new additions all the time.

History/description: Inspired by the Thompson Heather Garden in Manchester, California, and the Heather Enthusiasts of the Redwood Empire (the local chapter of the North American Heather Society), Maria and Tom Krenek started a nursery business on their home property. The nursery and display gardens are sited next to a 1906-era redwood barn (a remnant of an old dairy farm), surrounded by redwoods and an occasional ocean mist. Deer resistance, drought tolerance, and easy maintenance make these plants a great choice for many coastal gardens.

Goodness Grows

11201 Anderson Valley Way, Boonville 95415
(707) 895-3125
Facebook: @goodnessgrowsnursery
Email: goodnessgrowsnursery@yahoo.com
Sarah Larkin
Retail and wholesale
Open every day but Thursday, 10 a.m.–5 p.m.
    (winter close at 4 p.m.).

Plant specialties: Trees, shrubs, medicinal herbs, flowering perennials, ornamental edibles, and some California native plants.

History/description: Sarah Larkin worked for Wendy and Greg Ludwig for six years at their nursery on this site before buying it in 2013. The idyllic, rural setting, surrounded by vineyards and rolling hills, was once the Tin Man Apple Juice property, and a few heritage apple trees still remain. The old juice-tasting room, a wooden yurt, is now used for propagation. Lovely display gardens with weeping plums, salvias, lavenders, and other Mediterranean-climate plants illustrate many interesting plant combinations.

Gualala Nursery and Trading Co.

38660 South Highway 1, Gualala 95445
P. O. Box 957, Gualala 95445
(707) 884-9633
Facebook: @GualalaNurseryCA
Email: ventrellat@aol.com
Tony and Susan Ventrella
Retail and wholesale
Open Monday through Saturday, 10 a.m.–5 p.m.

Plant specialties: California native plants suited to coastal mountain regions, hardy perennials, Australian plants, and Mediterranean-climate plants.

History/description: Tony Ventrella's passion for plants was sparked by classes taken at Descanso Gardens when he was just a first grader. After college he started a landscape business and converted his grandmother's yard into a wholesale nursery. The nursery relocated to Sepulveda, selling mostly general landscape plants. Then, in 1988, Tony and his wife, Susan, moved north, starting a larger nursery in Gualala. Climate has definitely affected the nursery's plant selection and it now features California natives and hardy perennials. An eclectic garden and home furnishings gift shop is on site.

Heartwood Nursery

20000 Summers Lane, Fort Bragg 95437
(707) 964-7990
Email: dancharvet@gmail.com
Dan and Patty Charvet

Wholesale, some retail
Open by appointment only.

Plant specialties: *Camellia* species (*reticulata, lutchuensis, lapida,* and *transnokoensis*) and *Camellia* hybrids, especially *reticulata* hybrids.

History/description: After college, both Dan and Patty Charvet worked at Berkeley Horticultural Nursery. In 1983, they bought an existing nursery business, which they expanded, relocated, and sold, retaining the nursery's name and camellia collections. A camellia breeder for 45 years, Dan's passion is hybridizing *Camellia reticulata*, breeding primarily for disease resistance and better landscape habit. Some of his successful introductions include *Camellia* 'Bolero', *C.* 'Shelter Cove', and *C.* 'Kwan Yuen'.

Jug Handle Creek Farm and Nature Center

15501 North Highway 1, Caspar 95420
(707) 937-3498 (nursery); (707) 964-4630 (lodging)
www.jughandlecreekfarm.com
Helene Chalfin, director of education and native plant nursery
Retail and wholesale
Open by appointment only.

Plant specialties: California native plants suited to the northern coast that are overstock plants from the farm's restoration projects.

History/description: The old Tregoning Ranch was bought by the nonprofit California Institute of Man in Nature in the 1970s to save it from development and to foster the institute's mission of environmental stewardship. In 1994, buildings on the 33-acre site were upgraded to include a nursery and education center under the aegis of a sister nonprofit, Jug Handle Creek Farm and Nature Center. During the week, groups of schoolchildren from kindergarten through college stay here, do site-specific seed collection, and work in the nursery and at various restoration projects under contract (34 projects to date). Kindergartners, for example, hammer seeds from cones and return a year later to see the sprouts. On weekends, the cabins and lodging are rented out to help pay for all this good work. There are miles of hiking trails through forests and meadows, and nearby is the Pygmy Forest Ecological Staircase in Jug Handle State Reserve, a focal point of the nature center's interpretative walks. The center hosts spring and fall plant sales.

Mendocino Maples

41569 Little Lake Road, Mendocino 95460
(707) 397-5731
www.mendocinomaples.com
Email: info@mendocinomaples.com
Robert Jamgochian and family
Retail, wholesale, online order, and custom grafting
Open by appointment only.

Plant specialties: Maples, including 35 species and 260 cultivars of those species, with over 200 varieties of *Acer palmatum*.

History/description: Robert Jamgochian was introduced to Japanese maples by his father-in-law's collection, but it was his fascination with experimentation as a biology teacher that turned a passing fancy into an enduring fixation. Since 1992, he has been collecting rare and unusual maple species and varieties that prosper along the North Coast. With seed from the International Maple Society, this retired scientist grows and grafts an ever-increasing supply of interesting maples. The one-acre home nursery features a small koi pond surrounded by a lovely tableau of maples. The online catalog includes planting and pruning information.

Oracle Oak Nursery

3001 County Road 110, Hopland 95449
(415) 225-5567
www.oracleoaknursery.com

Email: larryoracleoak@me.com
Larry and Mary Costello
Wholesale and contract growing
Open by appointment only.

Plant specialties: Trees, especially California native oaks. Other California native species include California buckeye, California sycamore, ponderosa pine, and coast redwood. All trees are sold in 24-inch boxes, 15-gallon cans, or 24-inch fabric bags in the ground.

History/description: After thirty years as the Environmental Horticultural Advisor of the UC Cooperative Extension program for San Francisco and San Mateo counties, Larry Costello opened Oracle Oaks as his retirement project. As well as wanting to remain active in the field, he wanted to test various nursery production practices. For instance, he has found that root pruning early in production creates a branched root system that enables a tree to establish itself more quickly in the landscape. Larry is also the author of *Oaks in the Urban Landscape* (2011).

Red Tail Farms

9000 Busch Lane, Potter Valley 95469
(707) 743-2734
www.redtailfarmsofcali.com
Email: info@redtailfarmsofcali.com
Alfredo Belcore
Wholesale and online order
Open to landscape professionals only, Monday through Friday,
     9 a.m.–5 p.m., and Saturday, 9 a.m.–4 p.m.

Plant specialties: California native plants for coastal and foothill regions, perennials, deer-resistant plants, drought-tolerant plants, vines, and vegetables.

History/description: Alfredo Belcore bought this nursery in 2013 from the Gervases, who launched it in 1989. Fourteen greenhouses and a sea of potted plants occupy two acres in the coastal hills.

Sanhedrin Nursery

1094 Locust Street, Willits 95490
(707) 459-9009
www.sanhedrinnursery.com
Email: plants@sanhedrinnursery.com
Dave and Jenny Watts
Retail and mail/online order
January through June, open Monday and Wednesday through
    Saturday, 9 a.m.–5 p.m., and Sunday, 10 a.m.–4 p.m.
    July through December, open Wednesday through Saturday,
    9 a.m.–5 p.m., and Sunday, 10 a.m.–4 p.m.

Plant specialties: Perennials and vegetables, including 30 varieties of tomatoes and peppers and a large selection of organically grown potato varieties in season; trees, shrubs, and vines; bulbs in season; roses, camellias, and azaleas; California native and Mediterranean shrubs; and flower, grass, and cover crop seeds. A large selection of fruit trees is sold online during bare-root season.

History/description: Sanhedrin Nursery started in 1981, when Dave and Jenny Watts decided to move out of the Bay Area to raise their children in a rural area. Finding a small house on Locust Street in Willits, they soon built a store attached to the house and transformed the backyard into a thriving nursery. After a couple of years, they began growing their own bedding plants and vegetable starts, which now make up an important part of their business. Dave's focus is on fruit trees, and his expertise in pruning and orchard development has helped people from all over the county. This mom-and-pop nursery, tucked away on the back streets of Willits, is named for the nearby Sanhedrin Mountain, one of the most imposing peaks in the Mendocino National Forest.

Simply Succulents

31250 Highway 20, Fort Bragg 95437
(707) 357-1541 (cell)
Email: rellasplants@comcast.net

Rella Gadulka
Retail and wholesale
March through September, open every day, 10 a.m.–4 p.m.;
   October through February, open Friday through Monday,
   10 a.m.–4 p.m., unless storming. Best to call ahead.

Plant specialties: Succulents and companion plants, including palms and perennials, especially those that provide habitat for insects and birds; a good collection of *Epiphyllum, Agave* (40 types), and *Aloe* (50 types); and lawn-alternative materials, such as water-wise grasses and ground-cover herbs.

History/description: Detroit-born Rella Gadulka wandered off as a toddler and, after an anxious search, was found contentedly staring at a succulent. Thus began a lifelong fascination with these drought-tolerant plants. As Rella remarks, she likes plants like she likes people—low maintenance, but with spunk and vigor. No stranger to business, she opened a fruit stand at age four and later sold vegetables to supplement her school tuition. The nursery, opened in the late 1980s, is on the back acre of a two-acre lot and features long lanes of plants, in sizes from 3-inch to 25-gallon containers. Now a 45-year resident of Fort Bragg, Rella propagates 90 percent of her plants from seed and from plant exchanges with the Cactus and Succulent Society of America and the International Sedum Society.

Singing Tree Gardens

5225 Dow's Prairie Road, McKinleyville 95519
(707) 839-8777
www.singtree.com
Email: sales@singtree.com or donw@singtree.com
Ryan Scott, Don Wallace
Retail and mail/online order
Open Wednesday through Saturday, 9 a.m.–5 p.m.

Plant specialties: 200-plus hybrids and many species of *Rhododendron,* particularly new hybrids and fragrant varieties; dwarf, rare, and unique conifers; heaths and heathers; hydrangeas; and unique shrubs and trees.

History/description: Singing Tree Gardens was launched in 1993, a direct result of Don Wallace's rhododendron hobby. From the start, his goal was to educate his customers about the galaxy of rhododendron possibilities and to make the best of these available. Singing Tree offers many of the newest hybrids, including *R.* 'Seaview Sunset' and *R.* 'Naselle', and introduced the exotic and fragrant *R.* 'Patricia Marie' to the trade. The 10-acre site includes extensive "vignette gardens" illustrating many plant combinations for year-round color and interest.

Specialty Oaks, Inc.

12552 Highway 29, Lower Lake 95457
(707) 995-2275
www.specialtyoaks.com
Email: info@specialtyoaks.com
John McCarthy
Wholesale
Open by appointment only.

Plant specialties: California native oak trees, including *Quercus agrifolia* (coast live oak), *Q. douglasii* (blue oak), *Q. kelloggii* (black oak), *Q. lobata* (valley oak), and *Q. wislizenii* (interior live oak). Each year, 2,500 choice examples are selected from approximately 9,000 seedlings. Each is shaped, root pruned, and field grown for five years, and the result is a well-proportioned oak with a 10- to 12-inch caliper and a well-developed root ball.

History/description: As the owner of McCarthy Tree Specialties, a San Francisco Peninsula tree-care service, John McCarthy noticed the difficulty of replacing the many oaks falling victim to age, disease, and suburban encroachment. Seizing the opportunity, he went into nursery production in 1985. As an arborist certified by the International Society of Arboriculture, he still gives tree-care consultations.

Notable Garden Centers

Fiddler's Green Nursery

525 South Franklin Street, Fort Bragg 95437
(707) 964-3555
Email: fgn@att.net

Wanda Johansen bought this former location of Heartwood Nursery, transforming it into a small garden center with a large selection of plants from local growers and 700 to 1,000 varieties of roses brought in each year.

Harecreek Nursery and Power Equipment

32461 State Highway 20, Fort Bragg 95437
(707) 964-4648
www.harecreeknurseryandpower.com

Opened by Sandy Babcock in 1977, this nursery is owned today by Sandy's niece Kathy Babcock and Kathy's husband, Steve Welter. The power-tool business was brought in by Kathy's father, a retired logger. The nursery specializes in large quantities of a large variety of plants, a boon for landscapers.

Mad River Gardens

3384 Janes Road, Arcata 95521
(707) 822-7049
www.madrivergardens.com

Since the 1980s, Jack and Gloria Stewart have supplied an assortment of indoor and landscape plants that are selected to prosper in the temperate climate here. Located on the outskirts of town, Mad River Gardens offers bonsai, edibles, fruit trees, perennials, herbs, and drought-tolerant plants.

North Star Nursery

17901 North Highway 1, Fort Bragg 95437
(707) 961-1074
www.northstarnursery.com

John Vitale bought this 25-year-old nursery six years ago and has been expanding its propagation of old-time garden favorites that have fallen from favor since the dawn of patented plant material. The nursery offers a wide range of plants, from natives to succulents and everything in between, as well as funky rusted treasures in its home and garden décor section.

Sparetime Supply

208 East San Francisco Avenue, Willits 95490
(707) 459-6791
www.sparetimesupply.com

Owned by the Griggs family since 1983, this nursery features a broad selection of plants that thrive in North Coast climates, including native plants, arrayed in a large yard. The nursery's online store sells everything you need for gardening except the plants.

Whispering Winds Nursery

3301 South State Street, Ukiah 95482
(707) 462-0422
www.whisperingwindsnursery.com

Unusual varieties of a broad selection of plants. Started in 2010, this nursery occupies one acre on an old ranch property, with display gardens highlighted with quirky collectibles.

Horticultural Attractions

Humboldt Botanical Garden

7351 Tompkins Hill Road, Eureka 95501
P. O. Box 6117, Eureka 95502
www.hbgf.org
Email: hbgf@hbgf.org
(707) 442-5139

The nonprofit Humboldt Botanical Gardens Foundation was formed in 1991 to create a major botanical garden of plants appropriate to the North Coast. The garden itself opened its doors in 2012. The 44-acre site, next to the College of the Redwoods, is located at the juncture of Pacific marine and Mediterranean climates, which enables a wide spectrum of plants to grow here. Still in the process of being developed, Humboldt Botanical Garden includes a native plant garden, a natural riparian area, an ornamental terrace garden, and a temperate woodland garden. It is the center of the area's horticultural activity, with ongoing volunteer programs, special events, and tours. Open Wednesday through Sunday. A spring plant sale usually occurs during the first weekend in May.

Mendocino Coast Botanical Gardens

18220 North Highway 1, Fort Bragg 95437
www.gardenbythesea.org
Email: info@gardenbythesea.org
(707) 964-4352

Mendocino Coast Botanical Gardens was founded in 1961 by retired nurseryman Ernest Schoefer and his wife, Betty. Since then, it has grown to include several nationally recognized collections. Located in the moist, coastal woodlands, the specialties here offer something of interest in every season. Bulbs, camellias, and rhododendrons highlight a winter stroll. The

perennial garden is in peak bloom during the summer, and the dahlia collection explodes with color in the fall. The topography is varied, ranging from breathtaking coastal bluffs to fern-filled canyon trails. The gardens serve as a haven for more than 150 species of birds and a harbor for rare and endangered plants. Educational programs and volunteer opportunities abound. The Nursery on the Plaza is open all year (no charge to shop) and sells unusual perennials and plants as seen in the gardens. Biannual plant sales take place in September and April. Open every day (excluding major holidays), November through February, 9 a.m.–4 p.m., and March through October, 9 a.m.–5 p.m. Well-behaved dogs are allowed on leash, and an electric cart is available for those with special needs. Admission fee.

Trillium Lane

18855 Trillium Lane, Fort Bragg 95437
(707) 964-3282

The private garden of the doyenne of rhododendron culture, Eleanor Philip, is now tended by her husband, Bruce. Open by appointment only, from April through June.

California Native Plants

I n California, 6,000 species, subspecies, and varieties of plants are native, having evolved to suit the climate, the topography, and fellow flora and fauna. Though there are more natives here than in any other state, accounting for nearly one-quarter of plants found north of the Mexican border in North America, many have fallen or are in danger of falling victim to development.

In our Mediterranean climate, many native plants live with intense heat and no precipitation for a good part of the year, replenished only by winter rains. Plants adapt to this cycle through mechanisms that cool leaves and reduce water loss. For example, many plants' colors reflect sunlight: muted gray, gray-green, silver, and tawny brown shades dominate Mediterranean-climate landscapes. Others have developed tough, leathery leaves with smaller stomata, or surface pores, to guard against water loss and to slow photosynthesis, thereby fostering summer dormancy. Plants known as geophytes store their foods in underground bulbs, tubers, corms, and rhizomes; autumn rains and cool temperatures wake and replenish them so that they sprout into growth. Hairy or waxy plant surfaces also guard against water loss. Drought-deciduous plants drop their leaves and go dormant in summer to avoid losing water; others develop two types of leaves, one for winter and another for summer. Some plants hold their leaves upright to lessen sun exposure. Mediterranean-climate shrubs and trees can also develop dual root systems, with a deep taproot and fine surface roots to best capture water.

Wildfires break out frequently in Mediterranean-climate regions, and plants have evolved survival strategies in response. Some shrubs resprout from their root crowns, or burls, while others bear seeds that need intense fire heat to break dormancy and sprout.

Natives by Habitat

The key plant habitats of this long and geographically diverse state are: chaparral, coastal scrub, oak woodland, and redwood forest.

Chaparral, or "place of scrub oak"—a dense and widespread vegetation—provides many garden-worthy shrubs. These include manzanita (*Arctostaphylos*), California lilac (*Ceanothus*), chamise (*Adenostoma fasciculatum*), and coast silk tassel (*Garrya elliptica*).

In the scruffy **coastal scrub** you will find sages (*Salvia*), buckwheats (*Eriogonum*), coyote brush (*Baccharis pilularis*), and California sagebrush (*Artemisia californica*).

There are 18 species of **oaks** that grow throughout the state, from scrub oaks to majestic broadleaf trees. These include scrub (*Quercus dumosa*), coast live (*Q. agrifolia*), canyon (*Q. chrysolepis*), and valley oaks (*Q. lobata*).

Coast **redwoods** (*Sequoia sempervirens*) thrive in coastal fogbelt forests, often with associates Douglas fir (*Pseudotsuga menziesii*), madrone (*Arbutus menziesii*), and California bay (*Umbellularia californica*).

Two other fine conifers from this habitat are Monterey pine (*Pinus radiata*) and Monterey cypress (*Hesperocyparis macrocarpa*).

Natives by Type

Trees: California buckeye (*Aesculus californica*), oaks (*Quercus*—many species), Pacific dogwood (*Cornus nuttallii*), coast redwood (*Sequoia sempervirens*).

Shrubs: wild lilac (*Ceanothus*), Western redbud (*Cercis occidentalis*), bush anemone (*Carpenteria californica*), manzanita (*Arctostaphylos*—many species), red-flowering currant (*Ribes sanguineum*) and fuchsia-flowered gooseberry (*R. speciosum*), wild rose (*Rosa californica*), purple sage and Cleveland sage (*Salvia leucophylla* and *S. clevelandii*), wild mock orange (*Philadelphus lewisii*), and Western azalea (*Rhododendron occidentale*).

Ground covers and perennials: Western columbine (*Aquilegia formosa*), wild ginger (*Asarum caudatum*), bleeding heart (*Dicentra formosa*), Saint Catherine's lace (*Eriogonum giganteum*), Coulter's Matilija poppy (*Romneya coulteri*), blue-eyed grass (*Sisyrinchium bellum*), western meadow rue (*Thalictrum occidentale*), and California fuchsia (*Epilobium canum*).

Bulbs: one leaf onion (*Allium unifolium*), California brodiaea (*Brodiaea californica*), harvest brodiaea (*B. elegans*), mariposa lilies (*Calochortus* species), fairy lanterns (*Calochortus* species), wild hyacinth (*Dichelostemma capitatum*), Douglas iris (*Iris douglasiana*), *Lilium* species, and Ithuriel's spear (*Triteleia laxa* and other species).

Annuals: red sand verbena (*Abronia maritima*), chicalote (*Argemone munita*), farewell-to-spring (*Clarkia amoena, C. rubicunda,* and other *Clarkia*), California poppy (*Eschscholzia californica*), blue field gilia (*Gilia capitata*), tidy tips (*Layia platyglossa*), sky lupine (*Lupinus nanus*), monkey flower (*Mimulus* species), baby blue eyes (*Nemophila menziesii*), wild heliotrope (*Phacelia distans*), and California buttercup (*Ranunculus californicus*).

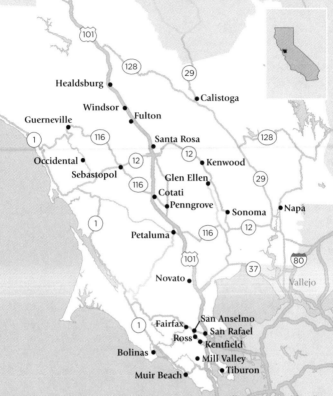

Chapter 2

North Bay

*Aesculus
californica*

Counties: Marin, Napa, Solano, Sonoma
Elevational range: Sea level to 2,574 feet at Mount Tamalpais
(Marin County); 1,600 feet at Mount Burdell (flanks in Napa,
Sonoma, and Lake counties); and 4,342 feet at Mount St. Helena
Sunset climate zones: 7, 9, 14, 15, 16, 17
Annual rainfall: Kentfield has the highest amount of annual pre-
cipitation, 47 inches, due to its location: it is located on the eastern
slopes of Mt. Tamalpais. Average rainfall in Sonoma: 29 inches;
Napa: 24 inches; and Solano: 25 inches.
Winter temperatures: Lows 18°F to 0°F
Summer temperatures: Highs 86°F to 93°F

The North Bay, a broad reach of land from Annapolis
near the coast east through the wine country of Napa
County to Isleton in Solano County, provides mountain-
to-valley terrains and prime agricultural land. Climates here
vary with geography and proximity to the ocean, from mild
climates along the coast and San Pablo and San Francisco bays
to cold air basins where chilly winters prevail along Coast
Range mountaintops. The region's broad inland valleys of
Sonoma and Napa counties often register hotter summers and
colder winters than along the coast or in the bayside regions.
Occasional frost hits both valley bottoms and hilltops.

With its benign climate and open, rolling rural land, the North Bay has long supported agriculture. It is not unusual to see cattle grazing for dairy farming and ranching. The Napa Valley is known for Cabernet Sauvignon and Chardonnay grapes, hosting some 400 wineries within its boundaries, while to its west lies Sonoma County, home to the widely planted Chardonnay grape. Distinct microclimates mark both of these regions, where temperatures can vary 10 degrees from one vineyard to the next. Along the western fringe of Solano County stretches a thermal belt, and prune, apricot, pear, and apple orchards once thrived there. With growth, many orchards gave way to industrial parks.

Native plants abound in the North Bay, including Tiburon mariposa lily (*Calochortus tiburonensis*). This rare form of mariposa lily, or fairy lantern bulb, grows on a Tiburon hillside, where its greenish petals mottled purple brown blend in with companion grasses and make a natural meadow. Stalwart California buckeye or horse chestnut (*Aesculus californica*), a native shrub or tree with silvery bark, grows on Mount Tamalpais. On fall hikes along Mount Tam's trails, deep chestnut-brown seeds collect on the ground, and in the spring, scented, snowy white flowers crown it.

Specialty Nurseries and Growers

Aztec Dahlias

2478 East Washington Street, Petaluma 94954
(707) 799-5635
www.aztecdahlias.com
Email: customer.service@aztecdahlias.com
Jamie and Rosa O'Brien
Retail, wholesale, and mail/online order
Open mid-May for plants and mid-June for flowers until early November, every day except Monday, 10 a.m.–5 p.m.

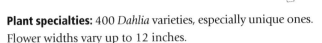

Plant specialties: 400 *Dahlia* varieties, especially unique ones. Flower widths vary up to 12 inches.

History/description: Jamie O'Brien had never met a dahlia until the re-landscaping of his parents' yard. This love-at-first-sight encounter led to a booming hobby, and soon his garden had over 100 varieties, at which point his wife, Rosa, said it was time to make something of this or stop. Named for the first cultivator of the Mexican dahlia, the nursery opened in 1999. Each year Jamie and Rosa plant 5,000 tubers on their two-acre field, all varieties registered by the American Dahlia Society. Plants and flowers are sold on site and at farmers' markets in Napa, Sonoma, Santa Rosa, and San Francisco. Tubers are sold online.

Bamboo Sourcery Nursery and Gardens

666 Wagnon Road, Sebastopol 95472
(707) 823-5866
www.bamboosourcery.com
Email: bamboo@bamboosourcery.com
Jennifer York, Joe Ruffatto
Retail and wholesale
Open Tuesday through Saturday, 9 a.m.–4 p.m.
Appointments are recommended, but drop-ins are welcome.

Plant specialties: Bamboo (almost 300 species)—both running and clumping types from all over the world—and effective containment methods. The bamboos offered display an amazing array of variation, from culm and leaf color and variegation to differing textures, shapes, sizes, and forms. Bamboo Sourcery has everything from giant timber types to small lawn-like ground covers, distinctive bamboos for garden highlights, and bamboos that are excellent for privacy screens.

History/description: Like many specialty nurseries, Bamboo Sourcery finds its origins in the plant-collecting passion of one exceptional individual. Bamboo Sourcery is the inspiration of

Gerald Bol, whose untimely death in 1996 was a tragic loss to horticulturists worldwide. He made myriad trips to South and Central America and the Far East, making important contributions to the understanding and classification of bamboo while amassing this amazing collection. The nursery, which opened in 1984, is itself a demonstration garden of mature bamboo species located on seven terraced acres nestled in the coastal forest. Bol's daughter Jennifer York and her husband, Joe Ruffatto, now run the nursery. With her background in environmental education and his background as an artist and general contractor, they have expanded the nursery's offerings and initiated a number of sustainability initiatives, including producing all of their own energy (solar). In 2010, Bamboo Sourcery received the Environmental Business Alliance's Best Practices Award. Bamboo installations, consultations, and maintenance services are offered. Good information about bamboo is available on the nursery's website.

Las Baulines

150 Olema-Bolinas Road, Bolinas 94924
(415) 868-0808
Michael Bernsohn
Retail
Open every day, 10 a.m.–5 p.m.

Plant specialties: Plants for Bay Area coastal climates, including many California natives.

History/description: Michael Bernsohn started the nursery in 1973 with Bryan Hale, backed by a combined 30 years of horticultural experience in the field. Originally an old horse pasture, the 3.5-acre site slightly slopes down to a creek and exudes the wood-timbered, organic wholesomeness of Bolinas, which lies just a bit farther down the road. Many impressive specimen plants give the nursery a well-deserved sense of age. Michael is still very active in landscape design and construction.

California Carnivores

2833 Old Gravenstein Highway South, Sebastopol 95472
(707) 824-0433
www.californiacarnivores.com
Email: info@californiacarnivores.com
Peter D'Amato; Damon Collingsworth, manager
Retail and mail/online order
Open Thursday through Monday, 10 a.m.–4 p.m.

Plant specialties: Over 1,000 varieties of carnivorous and bog plants, specializing in *Sarracenia* (American pitcher plants), *Drosera* (sundews), *Dionaea* (Venus flytraps), *Pinguicula* (butterworts), *Utricularia* (bladderworts), and *Nepenthes* (tropical pitcher plants).

History/description: Grower Peter D'Amato developed an interest in insect-eating plants at the age of 12, growing up near the New Jersey Pine Barrens, where these plants thrive. He opened California Carnivores after his successful display at the 1989 San Francisco Landscape Garden Show. The nursery now houses the largest collection of carnivorous plants in the United States. Some are exotics, but most are US natives. The nursery's relocation to Sebastopol in 2001 enabled an expansion of its growing, display, and retail areas. Peter continues to be impassioned and engaging, and his expertise is widely sought by botanical gardens and national network gardening programs. His book *The Savage Garden: Cultivating Carnivorous Plants* (Ten Speed Press, 1998) has won two book awards and is still the top-selling title on the subject.

California Flora Nursery

2990 Somers Street, Fulton 95439
P. O. Box 3, Fulton 95439
(707) 528-8813
www.calfloranursery.com
Philip Van Soelen, Sherrie Althouse
Retail and wholesale
Open times vary by season. Call or check the website.

Plant specialties: A wide diversity of California native plants and habitat plants recommended for greater Bay Area climates, including perennials, shade plants, ornamental grasses, and Mediterranean-climate, drought-tolerant, deer-resistant, and habitat-friendly plants.

History/description: After running the nonprofit Circuit Riders' revegetation nursery, Sherrie Althouse and Philip Van Soelen started California Flora Nursery in 1981 to make wider selections of native plants available to the public. Both are past presidents of the local chapter (Milo Baker) of the California Native Plant Society. Phil's background in environmental studies combined with his engaging artistry produced a children's ecology book, *Cricket in the Grass,* now regrettably out of print. Sherrie and Phil have discovered and introduced *Achillea millefolium* 'Sonoma Coast', *Ceanothus* 'Hearts Desire' and *C.* 'Coronado', *Monardella villosa* 'Russian River', *Oxalis oregana* 'Smith River White', and *Vitis californica* 'Russian River'. A list of the nursery's inventory and plant and habitat information is available online.

California Orchids

515 Aspen Road, Bolinas 94924
(415) 868-0203
www.californiaorchids.com
Email: mnisbet@pacbell.net
Mary Nisbet
Retail
Open only during biannual sales.

Plant specialties: Over 1,000 indoor and outdoor species of orchids.

History/description: Mary Nisbet grew indoor plants in Oregon, then moved to the Bay Area to work with the Rod McLellan Company. In 1987, she launched her own orchid-boarding business, based on the model at McLellan's. This remains the core of her business, though her plant sales in the spring and fall attract a crowd of orchid fanciers. Sign up on the website to be notified about exact dates.

The Center for Social and Environmental Stewardship

9619 Old Redwood Highway, Windsor 95492
(707) 838-6641 ext. 2
www.cfses.org
Retail and wholesale
Open by appointment only.

Plant specialties: Site-specific collections of oaks and other drought-tolerant California native plants for restoration of disturbed or developed areas. Most are sold in super-cel tubes to encourage deep root development.

History/description: This nonprofit organization, formerly known as Circuit Rider Productions, Inc., has a win-win philosophy, intending to solve both the problems of the earth and the problems of its people. It runs social and environmental programs to improve the fundamental quality of life in Northern California. The nursery was established in 1978 as its primary environmental program, originally to propagate site-specific native plants for revegetation of disturbed areas. Profits from this now-expanded enterprise are used to address human-resource needs, funding job training, employment counseling, drug prevention, and summer youth employment.

Cottage Gardens of Petaluma

3995 Emerald Drive, Petaluma 94952
(707) 778-8025
www.cottagegardensofpet.com
Email: info@cottagegardensofpet.com
Bruce Shanks
Retail and wholesale
Open every day, 9 a.m.–5 p.m.

Plant specialties: More than 600 varieties of perennials, *Clematis* (57 varieties), shrubs, succulents, ornamental grasses, herbs and seasonal vegetable starts, fruit trees, vines, and old and new roses. A large variety of drought-tolerant, shade-tolerant, Mediterranean-climate, and deer-resistant plants.

History/description: This family business opened in 1991 on an enchanting hillside setting overlooking the Petaluma Valley. A cascade of fieldstone terraces covers the 1.5-acre nursery site, where perennials mingle with staked clematis vines. Informative signage takes the guesswork out of creating a perennial border or growing a vegetable garden. Farther up the hill are 2.5 acres of sustainably managed growing grounds, which supply almost all of the plants for sale. All of the nursery's herb and vegetable starts are grown from seed. Pollinators of all kinds are encouraged and protected in this environment-friendly nursery. The nursery also crafts whimsical concrete stepping stones called tuffits.

Emerisa Gardens

555 Irwin Lane, Santa Rosa 95401
(707) 525-9644 (retail); (707) 525-9600 (wholesale)
www.emerisa.com
Email: retail@emerisa.com
Muchtar and Rohana Salzmann
Retail and wholesale
Retail open Tuesday through Saturday, 9 a.m.–5 p.m. (winter close at 4 p.m.), and Sunday, 10 a.m.–4 p.m. Wholesale open weekdays, 9 a.m.–5 p.m. (winter close at 4 p.m.), and Saturday, 9 a.m.–1 p.m.

Plant specialties: Over 2,500 different varieties of hardy and unusual perennials, shrubs, grasses, vines, and herbs, including *Lavandula, Salvia, Campanula, Geranium, Clematis, Penstemon, Achillea, Festuca,* and *Heuchera,* to name just a few.

History/description: After raising eight children and having a variety of jobs, Muchtar Salzmann returned to school at Cal Poly, earned a degree in crop science, and, in 1990, purchased a small wholesale nursery in Sebastopol. In 1996, having outgrown that space, he moved to the current 20-acre site, and the following year he added a retail component, the Nursery at Emerisa Gardens, to respond to growing public demand for his plant material. In 2014, Muchtar handed the reins over to his children. The wholesale nursery is entirely a family affair, with four of his children, his brother, his son-in-law, his daughter-in-law, and his niece all working there. Emerisa Gardens was named to honor Muchtar's parents, Emerson and Marisa.

Forni-Brown Gardens

1214 Pine Street, Calistoga 94515
(707) 942-6123
Lynn Brown, Peter Forni, Barney Welsh
Retail open selected days in April and May.

Plant specialties: An extensive collection of heirloom and unusual varieties of vegetables, particularly tomatoes (85 varieties) and peppers (60); culinary herbs.

History/description: This partnership started in 1980, when organic farmer Lynn Brown asked his early-rising, grape-growing friend Peter Forni to help harvest his zucchini blossoms, which required predawn attention. Vineyard owner Barney Welsh joined a few years later, supplying the farm with its permanent location. Primarily growing produce for Bay Area restaurants, Forni, Brown, and Welsh have been true pioneers in the locavore, organic, and heirloom movements, among the first to popularize arugula and mesclun. Stories abound about Forni-Brown's reintroductions of lapsed patented vegetables and preservation of old varieties, such as the early-ripening, black-skinned 'Black Russian' tomato, whose seed was given to him by a 90-year-old Russian Orthodox nun to preserve her culinary heritage. Forni-Brown Gardens is a preeminent cultural resource for edible gardening.

Garden Delights Nursery

2115 Adobe Road, Petaluma 94954
(707) 775-5008 (cell)
www.hanascape.com
Email: hanascape@aol.com
Erik Hagiwara-Nagata
Wholesale and retail
Open by appointment only.

Plant specialties: Unusual ornamental trees and shrubs, including Japanese maples, dogwoods (new hybrids and evergreen cultivars), and magnolias and michelias, with selections of weeping and contorted forms; winter-flowering, low-maintenance, drought-tolerant, and California native plants; fruit trees, blueberries, and other edibles.

History/description: Erik Hagiwara-Nagata is the great-great-grandson of Makoto Hagiwara, who created the Japanese Village exhibit at the 1894 California Midwinter International Exposition, which became the Japanese Tea Garden in Golden Gate Park. As the exhibits were being removed, Makota Hagiwara got the permission of Superintendent John McLaren to expand the Japanese Village into a five-acre garden and tea garden, which he did at his own expense and on his own time over a great number of years. In honor of the Japanese Tea Garden's 100th anniversary, Erik donated a collection of cherry blossom trees to Arlington National Cemetery in Virginia and the Golden Gate National Cemetery in San Bruno, California. A landscape architect, he offers design consultations through his firm HaNaScapes. In 2005, he started Garden Delights Nursery in response to repeated requests from friends and clients for plants used in his landscaping efforts.

Garden Valley Ranch Nursery

498 Pepper Road, Petaluma 94952
(707) 795-0919
www.gardenvalley.com
Email: info@gardenvalley.com

Mark Grim
Retail, wholesale, and mail/online order (for bare-root roses)
Open Wednesday through Sunday, 10 a.m.–4 p.m. Earlier close
November to mid-January.

Plant specialties: Roses—including hybrid tea, floribunda, English, heirloom, climbers, miniatures, and tree roses.

History/description: Garden Valley Ranch, originally an old dairy ranch owned by one of General Vallejo's lieutenants, is a genuine destination location. Eight and a half acres of roses are organized into various sections and gardens, including pergolas, fountains, a pond, a fragrance garden, and a Gertrude Jekyll–inspired perennial border. The nursery was started in 1981, when rose aficionado Rayford Reddell planted fields of roses for the cut-flower market; better colors and a longer-lived flower result when roses are not grown in hothouses. In 2005, Mark Grim moved north from Fresno to "retire" in Sonoma County after 30 years in the trucking business, but retirement was cut short by the opportunity to buy this nursery he had long admired during visits north. Not willing to rest on past laurels, the nursery adds 50 to 60 new rose varieties each year.

Geraniaceae

122 Hillcrest Avenue, Kentfield 94904
(415) 461-4168; (415) 269-4168 (cell)
www.geraniaceae.com
Email: geraniac@pacbell.net
Robin Parer
Retail and online order
Open by appointment only, from early spring to late fall.

Plant specialties: Over 500 selected forms of *Geranium,* as well as *Erodium* and *Pelargonium* (scented-leaf, angel and pansy face, ivies, regal, rosebud, species, primary hybrids, and uniques).

History/description: Robin Parer is a delight and unquestionably the number-one fan of the hardy geranium. Her indefatigable efforts as lecturer, collector, propagator, and exhibitor have made the once-lowly geranium a garden favorite. She has collected plants on trips to remote areas of Australia, Europe, and the Andes and continues to track down new resources in the United Kingdom, Europe, and Australia. With 500 species and selected forms of hardy geraniums, her one-acre garden/nursery and her 11,000-square-foot greenhouse contain the largest collection of pelargoniums, geraniums, and erodiums in the country. The garden has mixed perennial and shrub borders and a woodland section, illustrative of the versatility and landscape use of the family *Geraniaceae.*

Greencraft Studio

8270 Petaluma Hill Road, Penngrove 94951
405 Kains Avenue, Suite 106, Albany 94706 (mailing address)
(707) 567-5877
www.greencraftstudio.com
Email: info@greencraftstudio.com
Chien Wu
Retail and wholesale
Open by appointment only.

Plant specialties: Wisteria and fig trees whose stems and trunks are interwoven in a variety of patterns.

History/description: In 2005, landscape architect Chien Wu stayed home to care for his ailing wife and started weaving a backyard wisteria. Fascinated by the possibilities of forming woven-stemmed topiaries, he started to experiment with a variety of techniques. In 2007, he began production on a two-acre organic farm in Sebastopol, testing different patterns and plants. Figs were added to his repertoire, then table grapes, and climbing roses will soon be in the mix. All of his plants are woven over a frame of his designing, and it takes at least two years for plants to be trained for a finished product. His original intent was to market these for use in the high-end hotel landscapes that he was designing, but public interest in these stunning creations prompted retail sales.

Greenman Nursery

2833 Old Gravenstein Highway, Sebastopol 95472
(415) 710-2562
www.greenmannurseryca.com
Email: cam@greenmannurseryca.com
Cam and Texie Teter
Retail, with discounts to the trade
Open Friday through Monday, 10 a.m.–5 p.m. (call first)
or by appointment.

Plant specialties: Fruit trees, berry bushes, roses, vegetable starts (including 30 varieties of tomatoes and 25 varieties of peppers), cacti and succulents, California natives, and aquatic plants—"a little bit of everything, and lots of somethings."

History/description: Instead of selling lemonade as a kid, Cam Teter sold wildflowers and homegrown tomatoes. Years working in nurseries in Virginia and here (Sloat Garden Center), followed by more years of work as a landscaper, more than qualify Cam to know which plants work well where. The nursery is synergistic to his landscape business and reflects 20 years of plant collecting and propagating. The almost two-acre nursery, opened in 2006, has character and wholesomeness—a reflection of its owners. Roses here are propagated from the specimen roses left in the ground when Vintage Roses vacated the property some years ago.

Harmony Farm Supply and Nursery

3244 Gravenstein Highway North, Sebastopol 95472
P. O. Box 460, Graton 95444
(707) 823-9125
www.harmonyfarm.com
Email: rick@harmonyfarm.com
Rick Williams
Retail and online order
Open Monday through Saturday, 7:30 a.m.–6 p.m.
(winter close at 5 p.m.), and Sunday, 9 a.m.–5 p.m.

Plant specialties: Fruit and nut trees, berry bushes, and organic vegetable starts; drought-tolerant landscape plants.

History/description: This has been a headquarters for bio-intensive and organic gardening since 1980, when the business started as a supplier of organic fertilizers and natural pest controls. It was bought in 2007 by Rick Williams, and practically all the employees have been there from the start, committed to spreading the word about good land-stewardship practices, including drip irrigation and rainwater harvesting. The nursery's five-acre site includes orchards and greenhouses, where they propagate all their own CCOF (California Certified Organic Farmers)–certified organically grown vegetable starts. To help preserve and promote local crop culture, Harmony's online bare-root catalog identifies which fruit cultivars are Sonoma County heirlooms. Classes are offered most Saturdays, on topics such as edible landscaping, gardening for wildlife, and grafting.

Jungle Bamboo and Palm Nursery

503 West Railroad Avenue, Cotati 94931
(707) 794-8292
www.instantjunglenorcal.com
Email: kimes90@pacbell.net
Andrew Kimes, manager
Retail and wholesale
Open Monday through Friday, 8 a.m.–4:30 p.m.,
and Saturday by appointment.

Plant specialties: Cold-hardy, specimen-quality bamboo (50 varieties) and palms (12 genera); fruiting and non-fruiting olive trees.

(See Instant Jungle listing in chapter 7 for history/description.)

Larner Seeds

235 Grove Road, Bolinas
P. O. Box 407, Bolinas 94924
(415) 868-9407

www.larnerseeds.com
Email: info@larnerseeds.com
Judith Lowry
Retail, wholesale, and online order
Open Tuesday and Thursday, 10 a.m.–5 p.m.,
and Saturday, noon–4 p.m.

Plant specialties: California native plants and seeds, especially those suited to the coast, including wildflowers, grasses, trees, vines, and shrubs. *Limnanthes douglasii* var. (Point Reyes meadowfoam), *Calandrinia ciliata* (red maids), and *Eschscholzia californica* var. *maritima* (coastal California poppy) are uniquely offered here.

History/description: Judith Lowry went into the seed business in 1977 to perpetuate the horticultural gene pool for the restoration of West Marin and North Coast flora. She opened the Larner Seeds nursery in 1986 in response to requests by landscapers for actual plants grown from her wide variety of native seeds. In addition to seeds, plants, tools, and books, the nursery sells a point of view—that gardening and restoration ecology can find a meeting place in California's backyards. The nursery also features a one-acre demonstration garden focused on edible native species. Judith's books, *Gardening with a Wild Heart: Restoring California's Landscapes at Home, The Landscaping Ideas of Jays,* and *California Foraging,* inspire readers to think of their gardens as places connected to the natural world. Workshops and classes are held on site, and there are open houses in May and July. The nursery also offers custom collecting, growing, and seed-packing services. Consultations are offered to homeowners wishing to restore their native landscape, and the "Quail House" cottage in the middle of the demonstration garden is available to rent.

Lone Pine Gardens

6450 Lone Pine Road, Sebastopol 95472
(707) 823-5024 (retail); (707) 823-5060 (wholesale)
www.lonepinegardens.com

Janet Price and Steve Price
Retail and wholesale
Open Thursday through Saturday, 10 a.m.–5 p.m.

Plant specialties: Cacti, succulents, and bonsai (seedlings and cuttings for bonsai starters and field-grown, larger pre-bonsai stock); unusual perennials.

History/description: Educated in botany and horticulture in the United Kingdom and United States (specializing in desert plants), Janet Price and her late husband, Ian, returned to England to operate a nursery there. A nostalgia for the ability to grow desert plants outdoors brought them back to the American West. In 1975, they opened this four-acre nursery to have ample room for their growing ambitions and large cactus and succulent garden. Janet now works with her son Steve, offering good advice about which succulents you can safely grow outdoors. The nursery has a spectacular panoramic view of the coastal mountains.

Momiji Nursery— Exclusively Japanese Maples

2765 Stony Point Road, Santa Rosa 95407
(707) 528-2917
www.momijinursery.com
Email: momijinursery@yahoo.com
Sachiko and Mike Umehara
Retail, mail order, and custom grafting
Open every day, 9 a.m.–4 p.m., by appointment only.

Plant specialties: Grafted varieties of Japanese maples (250-plus *Acer palmatum* cultivars) in a complete range of sizes (dwarf, semidwarf, and standard) and colors (bright red, burgundy, variegated, and green); good selection of *A. palmatum dissectum* (cascading form). All trees are grafted and grown in Sonoma County, slowly and in the traditional way, to develop good fibrous root systems for better absorption of nutrients. Available in 1-gallon to 32-inch box containers.

History/description: Mike Umehara grew up developing a sensitivity for Japanese horticulture under the tutelage of his father, Mitsuo, who was the bonsai master and curator of the original Japanese Tea Garden in San Mateo's Central Park. Mike went on to study horticulture at Cal Poly and became a landscape contractor. With Sachi's interest in the arts and the encouragement of J. D. Vertrees, a lifelong love of *momiji* (Japanese maples) was launched in 1979. The Umeharas grow their own understock seedlings and graft their maples to produce unique and hard-to-find selections. The large specimen plants on their three-acre property are exquisite.

Napa Country Iris Garden

9087 Steele Canyon Road, Napa 94558
(707) 255-7880
www.napairis.com
Email: irises@napairis.com
John and Lesley Painter
Retail and mail/online order
Open during bloom season, usually mid-April to mid-May, Friday through Sunday, 10 a.m.–5 p.m.

Plant specialties: Tall-bearded irises (over 500 varieties) and peonies.

History/description: The iris virus caught up with Lesley Painter in the late 1980s, and she is still enamored by the beauty of its flower, the huge variety of color possibilities, and the ease of its growth. The Napa County Iris Garden business grew incrementally, from farmers' markets to selling some potted irises to shops in Napa, to a mail-order business, to the retail open days. Both Painters discovered the delight of hybridizing in the mid-1990s, and they now introduce about seven varieties each year. Still collecting, they add about 60–100 new varieties to their collection yearly, while eliminating others for a fresh spring showing. Their fields of flowers sit on sloping land in a picturesque valley.

Nature's Acres

Penngrove
1628 Lake Street, San Francisco 94121 (mailing address)
(415) 317-3978
www.naturesacresnursery.com
Email: naturesacresnursery@gmail.com
Josiah Clark
Retail, wholesale, and contract growing
Open by appointment only.

Plant specialties: California native plants—trees, grasses, shrubs, annuals, ground covers, and riparian/wetland plants.

History/description: The nursery, started in 2008 in Sebastopol by Josiah Clark and two friends, was relocated recently to an old chicken ranch in Penngrove, where it is painstakingly being "re-wilded." The mission here is to be a "force of nature" by supplying site-specific plants for the coastal San Francisco region to foster habitat for wildlife. The collection ranges from Santa Cruz to Mendocino, though it is focused on the San Francisco Peninsula and Marin County. Josiah is a consulting ecologist and wildlife monitor and has worked with the Golden Gate National Recreation Area (GGNRA) and San Francisco's Natural Areas Program.

O'Donnell & Son's Fairfax Nursery

1700 Sir Francis Drake, Fairfax 94930
(415) 453-0372
www.odonnellsnursery.com
Email: info@odonnellsnursery.com
Paul O'Donnell
Retail
Open every day, 9 a.m.–5:30 p.m.; best to call first on weekends.

Plant specialties: California native plants, organic fruit trees, berry bushes, vines, seeds, vegetables, and herbs.

History/description: After graduating from college in the East in 1982, Paul O'Donnell hopped into a VW van and headed west. On the recommendation of a Golden Gate Bridge toll taker, he headed for Samuel P. Taylor State Park to camp. En route, he stopped in Fairfax to do his laundry and noticed this nursery across the street. He walked over to meet the owner and was hired on the spot. After working there for a year, he did landscaping and habitat restoration until he was able to buy the nursery in 1990. By then he was fervent in his belief in the principle of "all organic, all the time" and in the importance of growing plants with genetic integrity to the area. He wild-collects seeds from specific habitats to match up with the ecology of a client's yard. As a licensed landscape contractor, general contractor, arborist, and restoration specialist, he offers a wealth of services. His third-acre site here contains vignettes and companion planting displays. His patented vermicomposting system is beneficial for gardeners, and he hopes it will someday make a dent in the landfill.

Peacock Horticultural Nursery

4296 Gravenstein Highway South, Sebastopol 95472
(707) 291-0547
www.peacockhorticulturalnursery.com
Email: peahortnursery@comcast.net
Robert Peacock
Retail
Seasonal open times; check website or Facebook.

Plant specialties: Hard-to-find plants for the collector and home gardener, especially those with unusual or interesting form or foliage. Featured plants include conifers (*Agathis* to *Wollemia*); shade plants (*Acer, Arisaema, Beesia, Disporum, Podophyllum, Polygonatum, Uvularia, Zantedeschia*); plants with variegated, chartreuse, black, or really weird foliage (*Acanthus* to *Zelkova*); dry-garden plants, including succulents (*Agave, Aloe, Echeveria, Jovibarba, Yucca*); and plants from the Southern Hemisphere (*Acacia, Leucadendron*, restios, *Xanthorrhea*).

History/description: Robert Peacock's quest for finding unusual specimens, especially those that tolerate shade, became an obsession during his years of work as a landscaper grown weary of planting the same old plants. In the early 1990s he began collecting seeds, cuttings, and plants acquired from botanical gardens, overseas sources, and other specialty growers. He is now a full-time plant collector and nurseryman. In 2001, Robert and his partner, Marty Waldron, found a beautiful early nineteenth-century farm property adjacent to the Laguna de Santa Rosa Open Space Preserve east of Sebastopol. The unique two-acre nursery, with meandering paths, garden rooms, and planted beds, allows visitors to visualize interesting plant combinations as they might appear in one's own garden.

Pond and Garden Nursery

6225 Stony Point Road, Cotati 94931
(707) 792-9141
www.pondandgardennursery.com
Email: info@pondandgardennursery.com
Scott Wilson
Retail
Open Thursday through Tuesday, 9 a.m.–5 p.m.

Plant specialties: Extensive collection of dwarf conifers, as well as aquatic plants, Japanese maples, hostas, koi, and pond supplies.

History/description: Scott Wilson's long involvement with plants began during high school, with his first job as a "hydraulic engineer"—a.k.a. water boy—at a Novato nursery. In 1976, he bought the nursery he then worked for in Ignacio, running it until he lost his lease. The next 15 years he worked as a landscaper, always collecting plants, especially conifers and maples, until this aquatic plant nursery came up for sale in 1996. He propagates his aquatic plants on site and buys everything else from specialty growers up north, always looking for unusual selections.

Russian River Rose Company

1685 Magnolia Drive, Healdsburg 95448
(707) 433-7455
www.russian-river-rose.com
Email: info@russian-river-rose.com
Jan and Michael Tolmasoff
Retail, with discounts to the trade
Open weekends in April and May, 10 a.m.–5 p.m.
(with special themes each weekend),
for special garden events in the fall, or by appointment.

Plant specialties: Roses (650 varieties, all types), irises (150 varieties), and perennials that attract butterflies, bees, and hummingbirds, such as *Salvia, Abutilon, Fuchsia, Penstemon, Scabiosa,* and *Gaillardia.*

History/description: In 1976, the Tolmasoffs bought a 15-acre prune orchard just a mile from downtown Healdsburg, which they slowly began converting to a vineyard. With a $100 gift from her grandmother, Jan bought some roses for the ends of her grape rows, thus starting something grand. Inspired by the catalog of Roses of Yesterday and Today, with its poetic plant descriptions, she began tracking down old rose varieties and those that thrive in the northern Bay Area. The garden is worth a visit by itself, with its 500-foot-long allée of arching, rambling roses. A self-guided tour leads visitors past a hummingbird wall, through a fragrance garden, and along a "rose history trail" that traces the evolution of different rose types, from old species roses to the most recent All-American Rose introductions. The garden nursery is located in the lower Dry Creek Valley, surrounded by vineyards and hills.

Sonoma Horticultural Nursery

3970 Azalea Lane, Sebastopol 95472
(707) 823-6832
www.sonomahort.com
Email: sonomahort@comcast.net

Polo de Lorenzo; Armando Garcia, manager
Retail and wholesale
Open Thursday through Monday, 9 a.m.–5 p.m.

Plant specialties: Rhododendrons (1,200 kinds), azaleas (600), shade-loving trees (*Cornus, Laburnum,* and *Acer*), shrubs, and companion plants.

History/description: Polo de Lorenzo, working in a nursery in Oakland, looked around for a nursery to buy and found for sale the Sonoma Horticultural Nursery, which was started in 1964 by the Barber family mainly to grow Exbury azaleas. De Lorenzo and his partner bought the nursery in 1976 and set out to build a remarkable garden. Anyone looking for a real springtime show (at its peak in mid-April) should plan a visit to Sonoma Hort's eight acres of gardens and shade houses. In addition to the fields of rhododendrons, azaleas, and other ericaceous blossoms, there is an impressive laburnum walk, maple allée, and birch woodland. Visitors will also enjoy the owner's 40-plus years of accumulated knowledge.

Urban Tree Farm Nursery

3010 Fulton Road, Fulton 95439
(707) 544-4446
www.urbantreefarm.com
Email: sales@urbantreefarm.com
Ruthie Martin, Travis Woodard
Retail
Open Monday and Wednesday through Saturday, 8 a.m.–5 p.m., and Sunday, 10 a.m.–5 p.m.

Plant specialties: Big trees, broad evergreens, flowering trees, fruit trees, palms, conifers, and shrubs in 5-gallon up to 48-inch boxes; grasses, vines, and perennials.

History/description: Former farmer Stanley Bradbury worked for years for the Sonoma County Agricultural Department while growing Christmas trees at home for sale. Originally more of a hobby than an enterprise, his growing of conifers expanded to include broad-leaved trees. After his retirement from the ag department, he opened a retail nursery in 1971. By 1990, he was ready to either grow the business or retire. Enter Ruthie, an old friend, who urged him to do the former and became an equal partner and then his wife. In 1991, Urban Tree Farm expanded to this new location and now grows 80,000 trees in containers on 20 acres with a featured display garden. It claims to be the largest single-location nursery open to the public in California. Sadly, Stanley has since died, but Ruthie's nursery manager since 1996, grandson Travis Woodward, became a partner in 2004.

West County Oasis Bamboo Garden

3525 Stony Point Road, Santa Rosa 95407
(707) 585-7415
www.westcountybamboo.com
Email: westcountybamboo@gmail.com
Jesus Mora
Retail, some mail order
Open Monday through Saturday, 9 a.m.–5 p.m.

Plant specialties: Bamboo (250 kinds, both runners and clumpers) and palms.

History/description: For 10 years, Jesus Mora worked with Gerald Bol at Bamboo Sourcery, and after Gerald's untimely death, he stayed on as nursery manager there for 15 more years. There could be no better tutorial on or tutor in the subject of bamboo. Jesus is now the go-to guy for bamboo identification and on the board of the American Bamboo Society. He started this five-acre nursery in the flats just south of Santa Rosa in 2010, propagated from his lifelong collection of plants. A pleasant stroll can be had beneath the shade of timber bamboo and mature palms, and there is a small display garden. Rhizome barriers and custom-built bamboo planter boxes are also available.

Wild Garden Farm

2710 Chileno Valley Road, Petaluma 94952
(707) 769-9114
www.wildgardenfarm.com
Email: sales@wildgardenfarm.com
Roanne Kaplow
Retail and wholesale
Call for seasonal hours.

Plant specialties: California native trees, shrubs, grasses, and flowering perennials for backyard habitat gardening, natural landscaping, pollinator forage, and insectary hedgerows. Emphasis on plants with multiple functions or cultural significance, such as those grown for basketry, botanical dye, edible landscaping, both Western and Asian healing and health support, and water conservation and biofiltration, among other practical uses.

History/description: As the successor to North Coast Native Nursery, Wild Garden Farm builds on three decades of dedication and expertise growing a reliable palette of native species that public agencies, ecologists, and landscape professionals depend on to achieve their restoration and landscaping goals. Backyard habitat gardeners with a love of native flora and fauna and individuals wishing to transform thirsty lawns and landscapes into productive, edible, and drought-tolerant gardens are most welcome here. Custom propagation, horticultural and ecological restoration, and design and maintenance services are available.

Wild Toad Nursery

3525 Stony Point Road, Santa Rosa 95407
(707) 529-5261
www.wildtoadnursery.com
Email: sabrina@wildtoadnursery.com
Sabrina Howell
Retail
Open Monday through Saturday, 9 a.m.–5 p.m.

Plant specialties: Aquatic plants, including water lilies, and "cheery" drought-tolerant plants.

History/description: Sabrina Howell, a self-described "office goddess," believes in the intersection of education and nature. A gardener, naturalist, and school garden teacher with a host of degrees and certificates, Sabrina launched Wild Toad Nursery in 2015 within the grounds of West County Oasis Bamboo Garden, where she also works. As her tagline—"plants for ponds, pollinators, and people"—suggests, she advocates for the importance of including a water feature in backyards as a water source for wildlife, especially in drought years.

Wildwood Nursery

10300 Sonoma Highway, Kenwood 95452
(707) 833-1161; (888) 833-4181 (toll-free)
www.wildwoodmaples.com
Email: sales@wildwoodmaples.com
Ricardo and Sara Monte
Retail and mail order
Open March through October, Tuesday, 9 a.m.–3 p.m.,
and Wednesday through Sunday, 9 a.m.–4 p.m.
Winter hours are seasonal; call ahead.

Plant specialties: Trees, including Japanese maples (150 cultivars), *Cornus* (40 varieties), *Ginkgo* (including dwarf and semi-dwarf forms), *Cotinus,* and *Davidia;* conifers; habitat plants; and ornamental shrubs.

History/description: Driving north from Marin County in 1975, looking for ample and affordable land on which to start a nursery, the Montes found these rural 12 acres, the former site of an old dairy. The nursery is a family-run affair. Plantsman Ric nurtures the plants, Sara nurtures Ric, and their son Joseph helps out, time permitting (he also has his own landscaping, design, and tree-shaping business, Joe Monte Landscapes). The four-acre nursery site includes growing grounds and display gardens surrounded by vineyards, grazing land, and marsh.

Notable Garden Centers

Armstrong Garden Centers

1430 South Novato Boulevard, Novato, (415) 878-0493
130 Sir Francis Drake Boulevard, San Anselmo, (415) 453-2701
www.armstronggarden.com

(See listing in chapter 8.)

Green Jeans Garden Supply

690 Redwood Highway, Mill Valley 94941
(415) 389-8333
www.greenjeansgardensupply.com

Kevin Sadlier and Xander Wessells opened Green Jeans in 1996 on an empty site on the frontage road of Highway 101. Because they propagate some of their plants from cuttings supplied by local and international sources, you may find rare plants here that you can find nowhere else. Perennials, orchids, vegetables, trees, shrubs, and sculpture are for sale, and design services are available.

Sloat Garden Center

www.sloatgardens.com
700 Sir Francis Drake Boulevard, Kentfield, (415) 454-0262
657 East Blithedale Avenue, Mill Valley, (415) 388-0102
401 Miller Avenue, Mill Valley, (415) 388-0365
2000 Novato Boulevard, Novato, (415) 897-2169
1580 Lincoln Avenue, San Rafael, (415) 453-3977

(See listing in chapter 4.)

Sonoma Mission Gardens Nursery

851 Craig Avenue, Sonoma 95476
(707) 938-5775
www.sonomamissiongardens.com

The nursery's four-plus acres enable a large assortment of annuals, perennials, Japanese maples, bamboo, cacti, succulents, shade plants, aquatic plants, vegetables, and fruit trees. It has some of everything, with an emphasis on the rare and unusual. Dave Fazio started the nursery in the mid-1970s on the grounds of the old Mission gardens in downtown Sonoma, moving soon thereafter to this location. The nursery features impressive hanging baskets, as well as display gardens, an aviary, and the occasional goat.

Horticultural Attractions

Luther Burbank Home and Gardens

Corner of Santa Rosa & Sonoma Avenues, Santa Rosa
P. O. Box 1678, Santa Rosa 95402
(707) 524-5445
www.lutherburbank.org

Hybridizing wizard Luther Burbank (1849–1926) slept here. This pioneer of plant introduction put Mother Nature into fast forward. His home and garden were given by his widow to the City of Santa Rosa and are now managed by the nonprofit Luther Burbank Home and Gardens Association. The 1.5-acre gardens that showcase his introductions were revitalized in 1991. Areas are devoted to medicinal herbs, cutting flowers, roses, wildlife habitats, and ornamental grasses, and the gardens are worth a visit even when the home is closed. California's plant maestro introduced about 800 plant varieties, including the Shasta daisy, Elberta peach, plumcot, Santa Rosa plum, and Burbank potato. The gardens include the greenhouse that Burbank designed and built in 1889, as well as his grave. Plants are sold on site. The gardens are open every day, 8 a.m.–sunset. Tours of the home and museum are given Tuesday through Sunday, April to October, 10 a.m.–4 p.m. Garden visits are free; there is an admission charge for house tours.

The Luther Burbank Experiment Farm (Gold Ridge Farm)

7777 Bodega Avenue, Sebastopol 95472
(707) 829-6711
www.wschsgrf.org

Operated by the Western Sonoma County Historical Society, this is a three-acre remainder of Luther Burbank's Gold Ridge Farm, now dedicated to his living legacies, among which are the Santa Rosa plum, the fast-growing Paradox walnut, the spineless cactus, and the Shasta daisy. Open all year for self-guided tours. Group docent-led tours, which include a visit to Burbank's cottage, are available by appointment. Plant sales are held every Wednesday, 9 a.m.–noon, and a spring plant sale takes place each year on Mother's Day weekend.

Cornerstone Sunset Gardens

23570 Arnold Drive (Highway 121), Sonoma 95476
(707) 933-3010
www.cornerstonesonoma.com

After attending the International Garden Festival in the Loire Valley, Theresa and Chris Hougie became inspired by the blending of art and nature and decided to try something similar back in the Bay Area, where they grew up. The result is a six-acre rotating gallery of garden installations by local and nationally prominent landscape architects and garden designers, such as James Van Sweden, Walter Hood, Roger Raiche, David McCrory, and John Greenlee. In 2016, *Sunset Magazine* moved its test gardens and kitchens here from Menlo Park. It is worth noting that since 2013, *Sunset* has been testing a variety of plants each year, supplied to them by their worldwide network of plant breeders from summer dry climates. Three or four of the best are introduced each year. The gardens are open every day, 10 a.m.–5 p.m. Call ahead on weekends in case the gardens are closed for a private event. Free admission.

Ferrari-Carano Winery

8761 Dry Creek Road, Healdsburg 95448
(707) 433-6700
www.ferrari-carano.com

Five acres of gardens, including annual beds for seasonal show (featuring 6,000 tulips and 12,000 daffodils), a series of mixed California borders, a rose garden, a formal courtyard, and a meandering stream with ponds and waterfall.

The Friends of Vintage Roses

3003 Pleasant Hill Road, Sebastopol 95472
(707) 829-5342
www.thefriendsofvintageroses.org

In the 1980s, Gregg Lowery and Phillip Robinson amassed "one of the most comprehensive multiple-class collections of old roses ever assembled" and sold them through their nursery, Vintage Gardens. Their two-acre garden showcasing the collection of 3,500 species of old and rare roses is now owned and being cataloged by the nonprofit Friends of Vintage Roses. The garden is not currently open to visitors as the nonprofit works to revitalize the collection of roses; however, volunteers are welcome on "Dirt Days" and on the first Saturday after Mothers' Day, when specimens are cut for the Celebration of Old Roses in El Cerrito.

Green Gulch Farm Zen Center

Off Highway 1, between Mill Valley and Muir Beach
1601 Shoreline Highway, Muir Beach 94965
(415) 354-0420 (farm and garden)
www.sfzc.org/green-gulch

Green Gulch is a Buddhist practice center and organic farm and garden. Produce from the eight-acre farm is available at farmers' markets and at the farm. The smaller garden, separating the living quarters from the farm and sea beyond, includes rose arbors, a formal herbal circle, espaliered fruit trees, and masses of flowers. Classes on organic gardening are offered some Saturdays. A robust garden apprenticeship program gives everyone a chance to be part of this serene and successful tending of the earth. Green Gulch's big plant sale is in April and occasionally there is a sale in the fall, although some plants well suited for coastal climates are always available for self-service sales. Open every day, 9 a.m.–3 p.m.

Korbel Champagne Cellars Garden

13250 River Road, Guerneville 95446
(707) 824-7316
www.korbel.com

This century-old garden was beautifully restored in 1979 by horticulturist Phillip Robinson under the guidance of Valerie Heck, a member of the family who bought the cellars from the Korbels in the 1950s. Situated on a hillside surrounding the historic Korbel family home, the garden overlooks majestic redwood forests and vineyards in the Russian River Valley. The Antique Rose Garden features antique roses originally planted by the Korbel family and companion plants arranged to suggest different parts of the world. Garden tours are offered Tuesday through Sunday, mid-April through October (weather permitting).

Marin Art and Garden Center

30 Sir Francis Drake Boulevard, Ross 94957
(415) 455-5260
www.magc.org

Incorporating this site as a nonprofit organization in 1945, Marin conservationists Caroline Livermore and Gladys Smith protected the estate property from development. It is now dedicated to the arts, horticulture, and environmental conservation and stands as a living memorial to those who served in World War II. Eleven acres of heritage trees, flowering shrubs, and seasonal plantings provide a backdrop for cultural programs, classes, and celebrations.

Matanzas Creek Winery

6097 Bennett Valley Road, Santa Rosa 95404
(800) 590-6464
www.matanzascreek.com

The winery is surrounded by an acre and a half of terraced lavender fields and a large strolling garden through a naturalized landscape of perennials, ornamental grasses, herbs, and natives. Open during daylight hours for self-guided tours.

McEvoy Ranch

5935 Red Hill Road, Petaluma 94952
(707) 778-2307
www.mcevoyranch.com
Email: visit@mcevoyranch.com

The ranch, on 80 acres of coastal hills studded with more than 18,000 olive trees, serves as a legacy for the late Nan McEvoy, a newspaper maven turned olive oil heroine. Worth a drive-by.

Old St. Hilary's Church and
John Thomas Howell Wildflower Preserve

210 Esperanza Street, Tiburon 94920
www.landmarkssociety.com

A rare example of Carpenter Gothic, St. Hilary's Church, built in 1888, was deconsecrated in 1959 and now serves as a venue for events. It graces a grassy, serpentine-rock mound with great Bay Area views that is host to profuse wildflowers in spring, including some rare and endangered species.

Quarryhill Botanical Garden

12841 Sonoma Highway, Glen Ellen 95442
P. O. Box 232, Glen Ellen 95442
(707) 996-3166 (office); (707) 996-3802 (tours)
www.quarryhillbg.org

Jane Davenport Jansen bought this 40-acre madrone/oak woodland and abandoned quarry in the Mayacamas foothills in 1968 to start a vineyard. A chance encounter with Lord Charles Howick forged a joint endeavor with England's Kew Gardens to sponsor a plant-collecting trip in 1988 to southwest China to preserve endangered native flora there. Despite climate differences between Sonoma and Sichuan Province, seeds collected in China germinated well here. Jane sponsored 14 more collecting trips, founded a propagation facility, and started a 25-acre garden to showcase East Asian flora before her untimely death in 2000. The woodland garden today features many favorites of Asian origin, such as dogwoods, lilies, and maples. A Chinese heritage rose garden highlights the important influence Chinese roses have had on the development of modern roses. A plant sale is held during the garden's annual Earth Day celebration. The garden is open every day, 9 a.m.–4 p.m., for self-guided tours, and is closed on major holidays. Docent tours are available by reservation.

Western Hills Garden

16250 Coleman Valley Road, Occidental 95465
(707) 872-5463
www.westernhillsgarden.com

This iconic garden of horticultural wizards Marshall Olbrich and Lester Hawkins was preserved after their deaths by a cadre of volunteers until its purchase by Chris and Tim Szybalski in 2010. Begun in 1960, the magical three-acre strolling garden contains the plant collection of Olbrich and Hawkins, who were among the first to introduce Mediterranean and Australian plants and whose knowledge spawned a generation of specialty growers and plant hobbyists. The garden, chock-full of mature specimens of rare and unusual plants, is located in the coastal redwood country, 60 miles north of San Francisco. Now, with its infrastructure repaired and its old "bones" revealed, the garden is open Saturdays, 10 a.m.–4 p.m., and Tuesdays and Thursdays by appointment. A garden boutique sells plants propagated from those on the property.

Invasive Plants

An invasive plant is a nonnative species that, when introduced to a new land where it is unchecked by its natural predators, flourishes and ends up harming local wildlife and even human health. In general, invasive plants are fast growers, producing abundant seed and maturing quickly. Resistant to pests and disease, they spread and crowd out and displace native species. They can increase wildfire and flood danger, diminish water supply, and even alter soil chemistry. Pampas grass, cape ivy, giant reed, highway ice plant, and select mustards and brooms are a few examples.

These plants differ from "naturalized plants," or nonnatives that adapt to local environments but do not necessarily spread, and "weeds," or nonnative plants that spread to agricultural, urban, or other disturbed lands but require tillage and irrigation to survive.

How do invasives get here? Major culprits are the horticulture and aquarium trades, as well as international travel and shipping. Nurseries sometimes sell invasives that unwitting gardeners plant. Many invasives are garden runaways, exotic ornamentals that have escaped the confines of the garden. Once there is one of them, wind, clothing and cars, and birds and mammals carry their seeds elsewhere. Plant fragments might break off and regrow into new plants.

Pampas grass (*Cortaderia selloana*) is an Argentine native that was introduced to Europe in the early 1800s by a Scottish horticulturist, then by nurserymen to Santa Barbara, where commercial production began in 1874. It has since colonized California roadsides; as late as 1946, soil conservation services in Ventura and Los Angeles counties were planting pampas grass to prevent erosion and supplement dryland forage. At Stinson Beach, in San Diego, and in other locales, it has caused problems by choking out native species, thereby threatening plant diversity and depriving native bees, birds, and butterflies of food and shelter.

Cape ivy or German ivy (*Delairea odorata*), likewise introduced by the nursery trade as an ornamental, first arrived in the eastern United States and came to California in the 1950s. It has now invaded 500,000 acres of the state. This perennial vine climbs over other plants to form a solid cover, blocking out their light and smothering them.

Giant reed (*Arundo donax*) can divert a stream corridor from its natural flow by growing across it. It forces dammed water to travel around it and increases the potential for erosion, flooding, and even fire damage. It also gives fire a "bridge" to cross from one side of a stream to the other.

Highway ice plant (*Carpobrotus edulis*) hinders shore birds, such as the endangered snowy plover, from nesting in dunes.

Mustards and brooms can change the soil's very chemistry. Bacteria that live in small growth nodules on their roots fix nitrogen, boosting soil nutrient levels and threatening native plants' health.

What can a gardener do?

- Don't plant invasives. Educate yourself about which plants are invasive in your climate zone: some threaten one climate zone more than another. (Highway ice plant, for instance, is invasive in the south, north, and central coasts and Delta zones, but not in the desert, the Central Valley, or the Sierra and coastal mountains.)

- Plant noninvasive alternatives instead. As opposed to pampas grass, plant these attractive and plumed alternatives: California native deer grass (*Muhlenbergia rigens*) or noninvasive hybrid Foerster's reed grass (*Calamagrostis x acutiflora* 'Karl Foerster').

- Buy from educated nurseries.

- Spread the word to others. If there is a question about whether a plant is invasive or potentially so, both the California-based organization PlantRight (plantright.org) and the California Invasive Plant Council (cal-ipc.org) can help.

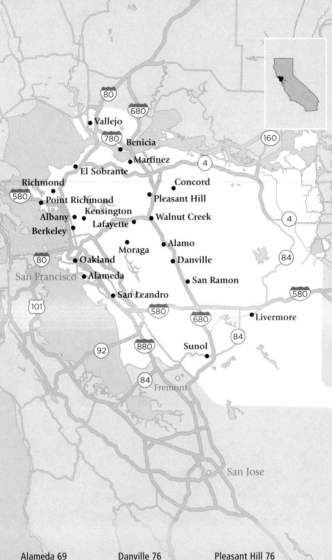

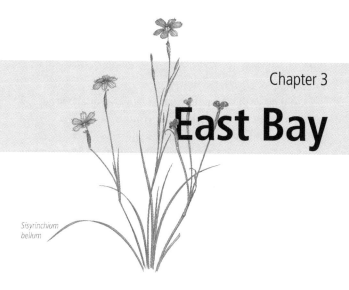

Chapter 3

East Bay

Sisyrinchium
bellum

Counties: Alameda and Contra Costa
Elevational range: Sea level to 3,849 feet at Mount Diablo
(Contra Costa County)
Sunset climate zones: 14, 15, 16, 17
Annual rainfall: Berkeley (Alameda County), 24 inches; Brentwood
(eastern Contra Costa County), 13 inches
Winter temperatures: Lows range from 26°F to 16°F inland, with
a record low of 11°F. Farther west, lows range from 36°F to 23°F.
Summer temperatures: Average highs vary from 71°F to 97°F.

Alameda and Contra Costa counties make up the East
Bay, once jointly known as "Contra Costa" or the
"opposite coast." The bay, a 1,600-square-mile estuary
rich with wildlife around which these counties grew, separates
them from San Francisco. The inner Coast Range runs through
both counties, setting apart their more urbanized western edge
from the sprawling suburban areas to the east.

Climate zones vary with distance to the ocean and to area
waterways—namely, San Francisco, San Pablo, and Suisun
bays—which add moisture to air and temper local climates.
Communities on bay shorelines share a marine climate with
San Francisco, where persistent summer fog filters light and
cools air. Onshore winds kick up in summer as marine air is

sucked in through the Golden Gate. Winters are mild and wet, and summers are relatively cool.

Cold air drains from higher slopes, so thermal belts enjoy greater warmth than marine zones. Winters around the bay are warmer than farther inland. Hilltops and valley bottoms experience colder winters than either the coast or nearby thermal belts. When marine air spills through the bay openings in the Coast Range it moderates eastern portions of these counties.

Blue-eyed grass (*Sisyrinchium bellum*), a member of the iris family, grows in the wilds throughout the East Bay hills and much of California's grasslands. An herbaceous perennial with green or bluish-green grass-like leaf blades, it bears spring flowers that range from white to deep violet. This diminutive native grows from 12 to 18 inches high by 6 inches wide.

Specialty Nurseries and Growers

Annie's Annuals

740 Market Avenue, Richmond 94805
(888) 266-4370 (toll-free); (510) 215-1326
www.anniesannuals.com
Email: contact@anniesannuals.com
Annie Hayes
Retail, wholesale, and mail order
Open every day, 9 a.m.–5 p.m. (November
    through January, close at 4 p.m.).

Plant specialties: Rare, unusual, and heirloom annuals and perennials (over 2,500 varieties) and California native plants (over 225 species).

History/description: Annie Hayes was lured west during the good times of the folk/rock music era and led a predictably interesting life. She settled in the Bay Area and worked at Berkeley Horticultural Nursery for a number of years. Endlessly fascinated by seed, she started propagating and pretty soon had flats all over her front and back yards. The nursery was inevitable and opened in 1990. Though all plants are grown on site, Annie particularly relishes the challenge of propagating unusual plants from seed; 85 percent of the business is now propagated from seed collected from all over the world through the nursery's extensive connections with botanical gardens, research facilities, and other passionate gardeners. Annie's plants, widely distributed through retail nurseries up and down the state, have had a big impact on what is grown in California gardens. Mail orders are shipped throughout the continental United States, with an availability list and videos on the website.

Ruth Bancroft Garden Nursery

1552 Bancroft Road, Walnut Creek 94598
(925) 944-9352 (office)
www.ruthbancroftgarden.org
Retail
Open Tuesday through Sunday, 10 a.m.–4 p.m.

Plant specialties: Plants that thrive in summer-dry climates, including large collections of succulents, drought-tolerant plants, and California native plants, and the largest collection of members of the protea family in Northern California.

History/description: This three-acre garden is a proud remainder of the once-flourishing 400-acre fruit farm owned by the Bancroft family since the 1880s. In 1972, after the area was rezoned, and with the town encroaching, Philip Bancroft cut down the last bit of his walnut orchard and turned the land over to his wife, Ruth, as a home for her collection of 1,000 succulent plants. Preeminent plantsmith Lester Hawkins laid out the initial design of mounded beds linked by curving pathways. Ruth's mastery of plant combination has created an exquisite garden of 2,000 succulents, cacti, and companion plants, despite the occasional setback of frost and flood. Ruth, now a robust centenarian, can still occasionally be spotted in the garden. The garden was the inspiration for the founding of the Garden Conservancy, a national organization dedicated to the preservation of significant gardens. In 1993, the nonprofit Ruth Bancroft Garden, Inc., was formed to manage and maintain the garden.

Cactus Jungle Nursery and Garden

1509 4th Street, Berkeley 94710
(510) 558-8650
www.cactusjungle.com
Email: store@cactusjungle.com
Peter Lipson, Hap Hollibaugh
Retail, wholesale, and online order
Open Monday through Friday, 9 a.m.–5 p.m.,
    and Saturday and Sunday, 10 a.m.–5 p.m.

Plant specialties: Cacti and succulents; California native plants (grasses, shrubs, perennials); drought-tolerant perennials; shrubs and trees; bamboo; unusual interior plants; terrariums and air plants; and a wide range of carnivorous plants.

History/description: These avid gardeners and plant collectors met in Alaska and started a backyard nursery business in Berkeley in 2002, which moved to this location in West Berkeley, fully appreciating the long history of agriculture and horticulture that had once been in this area before these businesses moved to Richmond. The nursery mixes its own blends of soils and amendments and grows the majority of its plants in West Berkeley on an old railroad right-of-way. Design services and plant classes are offered and the nursery can install large specimens, prune cacti, and repot plants.

Calaveras Nursery

1000 Calaveras Road, Sunol 94586
(925) 862-2286
www.calaverasnursery.com
Email: calaverasnursery@gmail.com
Martin family

Retail and wholesale
Open every day, 9 a.m.–4 p.m.

Plant specialties: Trees, shrubs, perennials, palms, succulents, fruit trees, and vines—"a bit of everything," in a big variety of sizes.

History/description: Bud Martin, a talented grower, opened a wholesale nursery in the mid-1960s called Sunol Nurseries. It expanded to include retail sales in the early 1970s. Today, three generations of Martins are at work here. What distinguishes Calaveras is both the number of different types of plants and the quantities of each lined up in the six acres of sales grounds. Rows upon rows of plants occupy the flatland in the Sunol Valley surrounded by coastal hills.

Devil Mountain Wholesale Nursery

9885 Alcosta Boulevard, San Ramon 94582
(925) 829-6006
www.devilmountainnursery.com
Email: sales@devilmountainnursery.com
Patrick Murphy
Wholesale; public may visit only accompanied by a landscape
    professional
Open Monday through Friday, 7:30 a.m.–3 p.m.,
    and Saturday, 8 a.m.–noon.

Plant specialties: A wide variety of containerized landscape plants, from 4-inch potted perennials to specimen trees. What the nursery does not grow it will try to broker in.

History/description: After school at Cal Poly, Patrick Murphy entered the nursery trade—first in production, then in sales—hitting the road for a few giant nurseries, such as Hines Growers. His frustration grew with being able to sell to landscapers only what was being produced. His dream of being able to serve as a one-stop shop for landscape professionals took root here in 1995. Devil Mountain grows most of what it sells on 100 acres near Lodi, with new sales yards anticipated for Petaluma and Morgan Hill. Its website is worth viewing for its articles and plant lists, especially for the so-called drought devils (3,600 varieties)—tried-and-true, drought-resistant California native and Mediterranean-climate plants.

The Dry Garden

6556 Shattuck Avenue, Oakland 94609
(510) 547-3564
www.thedrygarden.com
Email: thedrygarden@sbcglobal.net
Richard Ward
Retail
Open Tuesday through Saturday, 10 a.m.–5 p.m.,
    and Sunday, 11 a.m.–4 p.m.

Plant specialties: Hard-to-find and "queer" plants, including cacti and succulents for seasonally dry climates, Mediterranean plants, ornamental grasses, and a large collection of bamboo.

History/description: This self-professed plant and garden maniac is having a lot of fun growing and searching for weird and interesting plants. His one-acre garden nursery has enlivened a previously dead corner of North Oakland. Richard opened the nursery with his late partner, Keith Cahoon, in 1987. The two knew each other from their student and early days working in Nashville, and both became obsessed with collecting cacti and succulents. When they reconnected in California many years later, they combined their collections and the nursery was born. The Dry Garden is home base for the Bay Area's most impassioned horticultural group, the Hortisexuals.

East Bay Wilds

2777 Foothill Boulevard, Oakland 94601
(510) 409-5858
www.eastbaywilds.com
Email: pete@eastbaywilds.com
Pete Veilleux

Retail and wholesale
Open by appointment only.

Plant specialties: Hard-to-find California native plants (500–600 species).

History/description: After 17 years in the social services, Pete Veilleux was ready for a change. Having grown up among the creeks and woods of New Hampshire, he was infused early on with a love of the great outdoors and a fascination about the relationship between plants and places. He started a small gardening service in 2002 to reconnect with his early interests on a daily basis. He continued to "explore the wilds" and started propagating some of the things he found, first to give to friends and then to use in projects for his clients. In 2006, the nursery opened to the public, by appointment only. Pete's goal is to inspire people to value and protect the harmony of the natural world that surrounds them. East Bay Wilds also sells garden antiques, sculptures, and used furniture collected from flea markets and yard sales. Garden design, installation, and maintenance services are offered.

Golden Gate Palms & Exotics

425 Cutting Boulevard, Point Richmond 94804
(925) 325-PALM
www.goldengatepalms.com
Email: info@goldengatepalms.com
Gary Gragg
Retail, wholesale, and very limited mail order
Open Monday through Saturday, 9 a.m.–4:30 p.m.,
    except for major holidays and if threat of rain. Call first.

Plant specialties: Cold-hardy, subtropical plants, especially palms; avocados, citrus, succulents, bananas, bromeliads, cycads, cannas, flowering trees, and vines.

History/description: Bay Area–born Gary Gragg's childhood fascination with palms was bolstered by what he saw while a student at San Diego State. During college he started work as a landscaper, and after graduation in 1991 he returned home and opened Exotic Flora Landscape and Nursery, Inc., a design/build landscape business. Among his many projects were several major exhibits at the Oakland Zoo. Soon he was selling the overflow plants propagated for his projects. In 2003, he opened this three-acre Point Richmond nursery, which includes a variety of display gardens, ranging from lush subtropical rain forest to Mediterranean habitat to desert. One of his award-winning displays at the San Francisco Flower and Garden Show, "Livin' Cheap in Baja," is a permanent installation in the gardens. Thirty episodes of his television show, *Superscapes,* aired in 2009 on HGTV.

Green Thumb Works

16276 East 14th Street, San Leandro 94577
(510) 502-0992
www.greenthumbworks.com
Email: contact@greenthumbworks.com
Sandra Nevala-Lee
Retail
Open Saturdays, March through October, 10 a.m.–2 p.m.

Plant specialties: California native plants.

History/description: Merritt College–trained Sandra Nevala-Lee brings native plants to central Alameda County (Hayward, San Leandro, San Lorenzo, and Castro Valley), hoping to increase habitat for wildlife. She is part of the burgeoning urban farming movement in this area, which thrives due to large lot sizes and dedicated individuals. Each Saturday she brings in a different selection of natives from wholesalers to sell from this lot next to a men's clothing store.

Lee's Florist & Nursery

1420 University Avenue, Berkeley 94702
(510) 843-0502
www.leesfloristnursery.com
Email: LeesFlorist1420@gmail.com

Wilton Lee
Retail and online order
Open Monday through Friday, 9 a.m.–5:30 p.m.;
    Saturday, 9 a.m.–5 p.m.; and Sunday, 10 a.m.–3 p.m.

Plant specialties: Unusual Chinese-origin plants, such as *Osmanthus, Michelia,* and *Chloranthus.*

History/description: Wilton Lee's father started a full-service florist business here in 1941. A little while after Wilton took over in 1970, a small plant nursery was added in the back. Still family owned and operated, the third generation is now on site.

Native Here Nursery

101 Golf Course Drive, Tilden Park, Berkeley 94708
(510) 549-0211
www.nativeherenursery.org
Email: nativehere@ebcnps.org
California Native Plant Society; Charli Danielsen, nursery director
Retail and wholesale
Open year round, weather permitting, Tuesdays, noon–3 p.m.;
    Fridays, 9 a.m.–noon; and Saturdays, 10 a.m.–2 p.m.

Plant specialties: California native plant species from Alameda and Contra Costa counties.

History/description: Native Here Nursery was started in 1993 as an outgrowth of an older nursery called D.A.W.N. (Design Associates Working with Nature). Its original purpose was to propagate plants from locally collected seed and cuttings for revegetation projects in Alameda and Contra Costa counties. The nursery is now a major support venture of the East Bay chapter of the California Native Plant Society (CNPS), which encourages customers to restore native plantings in their own yard to provide habitat for wildlife. The nursery's website eloquently advocates for the importance of using locally collected plants in restoration projects to preserve traits of local ecosystems and to promote more successful regeneration. The nursery is administered by Charli Danielsen, an active, long-time leader in CNPS, and is operated with the assistance of many volunteers. Check the website for plant availability lists (updated twice yearly), lists of plants that attract butterflies, and events. The nursery hosts the East Bay CNPS plant fair in October.

Oaktown Native Plant Nursery

702 Channing Way, Berkeley 94710
(510) 387-9744
www.oaktownnativenursery.info
Email: oaktown@oaktownnativenursery.info
Kristin Hopper
Retail, wholesale, and contract growing
Open Thursday and Friday, 10 a.m.–5 p.m.; Saturday,
    10 a.m.–4 p.m.; and other days by appointment.

Plant specialties: California native plants of the greater San Francisco Bay Area, including perennials, trees, shrubs, vines, grasses, sedges, rushes, and bulbs; plants for restoration projects, revegetation, and habitat gardening.

History/description: The Oaktown Nursery began with a handful of native plant enthusiasts propagating natives for fun in a backyard in Oakland. Arriving in California in 1989, Kristin Hopper, an avid hiker, started to learn about native plants in order to feel more at home in her new natural surroundings. This led to restoration work with Friends of Sausal Creek and the GGNRA and, ultimately, to the founding of this nursery in 2004. Kristin grows locally appropriate, drought-tolerant plants from the entire California floristic province.

Planta Seca

300 Miranda Lane, Alamo 94507
(925) 935-5213
Facebook: @plantasecausa
Email: plantaseca@yahoo.com

Bill Munkascy
Retail and email order
Open by appointment only.

Plant specialties: Cacti, especially *Mammillaria, Ariocarpus, Rebutia,* and *Sulcorebutia.*

History/description: This is a story oft told in these pages. A random purchase of a plant—in this case, a saguaro cactus—prompted admiration, then fascination, then unfettered adoration. Abetted by the local plant society in San Jose, connections were made, knowledge was gleaned, and a collection was born. Now, four greenhouses and 30 cold frames later, Bill Munkascy's collection fills his half-acre backyard nursery. Sales of his plants are mostly at plant shows and on eBay (under the seller name "plantaseca"), but retail customers are welcomed by appointment.

Ploughshares Nursery

2701 Main Street, Alameda 94501
(510) 755-1102
www.ploughsharesnursery.com
Email: jbridge@apcollaborative.org
Jeff Bridge, nursery manager
Retail
Open Wednesday, 10 a.m.–5 p.m.; Thursday and
    Friday, 11 a.m.–6:30 p.m.; and weekends, 10 a.m.–5 p.m.

Plant specialties: California native plants, drought-tolerant plants, and edible plants, including a large variety of fruit trees.

History/description: Ploughshares Nursery combines the best of social and environmental practices. It provides job training, and 100 percent of its revenue supports the mission of its parent organization, Alameda Point Collaborative—a supportive housing community for formerly homeless individuals and families. The three-acre nursery follows sustainable/green practices and includes a demonstration garden and free workshops.

Soh-Ju-En Satsuki Bonsai

2254 Tennessee Street, Vallejo 94591 (mailing address)
(707) 315-5492
www.sohjuensatsukibonsai.com
Email: sojuen@aol.com
Darren and Laura Wong
Retail and mail/online order
Open by appointment only.

Plant specialties: Bonsai plants, mostly Satsuki azaleas and white pines; specimen plants and starts (10–15 years old, imported from Japan).

History/description: Looking for a hobby to do together in 1998, dentist Darren Wong and his wife, Laura, came upon a bonsai specimen on the Internet. This led to schooling by bonsai master Tatemori Gondo of the now-defunct El Dorado Bonsai Society. For the past 11 years, the Wongs have gone twice a year to Japan to study under bonsai master Sushil Nakayama in Nara. Although they consider it to still be a "hobby," bonsai occupies increasingly more space in their minds and time in their lives.

Terra Viridis

4726 Hilltop Drive, El Sobrante 94803
(510) 222-9438
Bob Johannessen, Carol Morse
Retail and wholesale
Open on weekends, by appointment only.

Plant specialties: Bamboo (140+ species in the collection, including the genera *Bambusa, Phyllostachys, Fargesia, Sasa,* and *Pleioblastus*); ferns, including *Pyrrosia;* and herbs, California natives, vegetables, and ornamentals.

History/description: Yet again, passionate plant hobbyists discover they can profit from their pleasures. In 1981, Bob Johannessen, influenced in his youth by his mother's fern collection, started his own collection and eventually became president of the San Francisco Fern Society. He then got hooked on bamboo, thanks to a sale by the Northern California chapter of the American Bamboo Society at the San Francisco Botanical Garden. Carol Morse, a botanist by training, has been propagating plants for most of her life. This crowded, quarter-acre backyard nursery reflects their combined interests and their commitment to *terra viridis*, the Latin term for "green earth." Bob and Carol's plants are sold also at the Sunday farmers' market in Oakland's Jack London Square and at the Tuesday farmers' market in Concord.

The Watershed Nursery

601-A Canal Boulevard, Richmond 94804
(510) 234-222
www.thewatershednursery.com
Email: twn@thewatershednursery.com
Laura Hanson, Diana Benner
Retail, wholesale, and custom growing
Open for retail customers Tuesday through Sunday, 10 a.m.–4 p.m.

Plant specialties: Site-specific California native plants from the nine Bay Area counties.

History/description: Diana Benner was doing restoration work and noticed that there was a dearth of site-specific plant material for her projects. Laura Hanson was an independent contractor doing wetland monitoring and had a dream to grow plants. The two found each other and the nursery was born in 2001. It was originally located in Berkeley and later moved to Point Richmond for more space. Diana and Laura now have an acre of city land in front of the water-treatment plant—a good example of smart use of vacant city property. By tracking where each of their plants is from, they are able to provide optimal material for local restoration projects in tidal wetland, riparian, oak woodland, grassland, and chaparral habitats. Over their years in business their inventory has grown, so they now have a robust selection of native plants for local homeowners and landscapers as well. An availability list and information about special sales is on the nursery's website.

Wildheart Gardens

1526 Fairview Street, Berkeley 94703
(510) 368-2811
www.wildheartgardens.com
Email: wildheartgardens@yahoo.com
Christopher Shein
Retail
Open by appointment only.

Plant specialties: Unusual, edible perennial vegetables and California native plants.

History/description: When Chris Shein was a senior in college, he dug in his first community garden. He was well trained there in the philosophy and practice of permaculture, and his life since has been about sustainable human settlement and following permaculture's guiding ethic of "earth care, people care, and fair share." Early on, he practiced "guerrilla gardening," setting up food gardens wherever he could find space, but some time after a particularly fine "farm" in Santa Cruz became a Circuit City, he shifted his focus to a more grounded approach to land tenure. Chris runs a permaculture landscape design/build service and teaches permaculture at Merritt College, where, with his students, he has created a one-acre "food forest," an intensively planted orchard with seven underlayers of food-producing plants. His small backyard nursery produces all sorts of wonders, such as Bolivian sunroot, Egyptian walking onion, tree collards (which can grow 9 to 12 feet tall!), and tree tomatoes from South America—all edible and suited to East Bay climates. California native plants are grown here as well to enhance this backyard ecosystem by attracting beneficial pollinators and predators.

Notable Garden Centers

Alden Lane Nursery

981 Alden Lane, Livermore 94550
(925) 447-0280
www.aldenlane.com

In 1955, town promoter Buck Sharp somehow convinced Jack and Ruth Williams to put up their life savings to buy two 10-acre parcels of walnut orchard that he was sure would make a most desirable nursery. Without their knowing the first thing about plants, and with no money left to get things rolling, the nursery slowly evolved, thanks to nurse Ruth's exceptional sense of nurturing. Today the nursery covers five acres; one acre is filled with shrubs, another half-acre with trees. The nursery's hallmark is the stand of 50 or so valley oaks, each 300 to 400 years old, which provide a dramatic backdrop as well as some welcome, cooling shade. Daughter Jackie was enlisted as a water girl at the age of three and is today in charge. Her husband, Tom Courtright, runs Orchard Nursery in Lafayette. The couple also run Kidz Club, a summer camp to inspire young gardeners. Sue Fordyce (of the old Orchid Ranch) oversees the nursery's orchid collection, and they also offer trees, especially Japanese maples and fruit trees; water-garden plants; indoor plants; edible plants, including a wide selection of heirloom varieties and berries; roses; tropical plants; perennials; shrubs for sun and shade; and seeds.

Berkeley Horticultural Nursery

1310 McGee Avenue, Berkeley 94703
(510) 526-4704
www.berkeleyhort.com

Opened in 1922 and now in its fourth generation of Doty family ownership, Berkeley Hort is known for its large and varied plant selection, with an emphasis on the unusual and appropriate. The Dotys were responsible for the palm plantings at Hearst Castle in San Simeon and have introduced hundreds of *Fuchsia* varieties to the Bay Area, as well as the Vireya rhododendron 'George Budgen'. The nursery, almost two acres in size, has a "tropical" courtyard and rockery display. It offers edibles, fruit shrubs and trees, California natives, annuals, perennials, vines, shrubs, bulbs, ground covers, rock garden plants, cacti and succulents, roses, and aquatic, carnivorous, and shade plants. During daylight savings time, the nursery is open every day but Thursday, 9 a.m.–5:30 p.m.; non–daylight savings hours are 8:30 a.m.–5 p.m.

East Bay Nursery

2332 San Pablo Avenue, Berkeley 94702
(510) 845-6490
www.eastbaynursery.com

Operating at this location since 1926 and owned by the Courtwright/Davis family since 1942, East Bay offers a good selection of large specimen plants, California native plants, drought-tolerant plants from around the world, succulents, fruit trees, grasses, perennials, Japanese maples, shade plants, shrubs, trees, and organically grown vegetables. The nursery also boasts seasonal displays. Fruit trees can be ordered here direct from Dave Wilson Nursery.

Flowerland

1330 Solano Avenue, Albany 94706
(510) 526-3550
www.flowerlandshop.com

Carly Dennett is the third owner of this nursery, which has been in operation since 1937. Since she bought it in 2008, she has transformed the 1950s building into an "urban boutique nursery with a modern aesthetic." All plants are supplied by local growers. Australian plants, South African plants, California native plants, grasses, perennials, and annuals are featured, including many specialty fuchsias.

Moraga Garden Center

1400 Moraga Road, Moraga 94556
(925) 376-1810
www.moragagarden.com

The Moraga Garden Center was started by Ken Murakami's father in 1972 as a sideline to his career as a landscape architect, and Ken started working here full time in 1986. Expanding the nursery's selection, Ken collects plants that are hard to find at the wholesale level. Sharing his finds with other growers, he has helped bring many interesting plants into the trade. Plant specialties include unusual conifers and dwarf conifers, including *Cedrus libani* 'Green Prince', and deciduous trees, especially Japanese maples. The nursery also stocks perennials (500+ varieties), hostas, camellias, bamboo, roses on their own rootstock, daylilies (250 varieties), irises, *Epimedium*, and oddball things, such as *Carpinus koreana*, as well as vegetables and rare fruit trees, such as medlar.

Orchard Nursery & Florist

4010 Mt. Diablo Boulevard, Lafayette 94549
(925) 284-4474
www.orchardnursery.com

Opened in 1946 on the site of an old pear orchard, the nursery was bought and expanded by Tom Courtwright in 1972. The five-acre property with its old ranch house has 2.5 acres of plants for sale and specializes in rare and unusual plants, Japanese maples, perennials, succulents and cacti, and fruit trees. It puts on extravagant holiday displays, and special orders are a specialty. Full florist services are available.

Sloat Garden Center

1555 Kirker Pass Road, Concord, (925) 681-0550
800 Camino Ramon, Danville, (925) 837-9144
828 Diablo Road, Danville, (925) 743-0288
6740 Alhambra Avenue, Martinez, (925) 935-9125
2895 Contra Costa Boulevard, Pleasant Hill, (925) 939-9000
www.sloatgardens.com

(See listing in chapter 4.)

Westbrae Nursery

1272 Gilman Street, Berkeley 94706
(510) 526-5517
www.westbrae-nursery.com

The brother-sister team of Jeff Eckhart and Christine Szybalski, both in the tech business and both avid gardeners and plant lovers, leaped at the chance to buy this garden center when it came up for sale in 2008. Christine and her husband, Tom Szybalski (a cousin of well-regarded Oregon nurseryman Sean Hogan), bought and are restoring the Western Hills Nursery property in Occidental.

Horticultural Attractions

The Ruth Bancroft Garden

1552 Bancroft Road, Walnut Creek 94598
(925) 944-9352 (office); (925) 210-9663 (tour hotline)
www.ruthbancroftgarden.org

(See listing under Specialty Nurseries, above.)

Berkeley Municipal Rose Garden

1200 Euclid Avenue, Berkeley 94708
(510) 981-5150
www.ci.berkeley.ca.us/

This Civil Works Administration project dedicated in 1937 features 3,000 roses (250 varieties) on a terraced amphitheater with redwood pergola. Peak display on Mother's Day.

Bringing Back the Natives Garden Tour

(510) 236-9558
www.bringingbackthenatives.net

The East Bay chapter of the California Native Plant Society organizes this free tour to showcase native plant gardens in the East Bay on the first Sunday in May. There are plant sales at selected native plant nurseries on the day of the tour.

Forrest Deaner Native Plant Botanic Garden

Benicia State Recreation Area
(707) 648-1911
www.parks.ca.gov/

A joint project of the Willis Linn Jepson chapter of the California Native Plant Society and the California State Parks, this 3.5-acre garden was dedicated in 2004 as the first and only native plant garden in Solano County. Early demonstration gardens, made possible with funding from the Coastal Conservancy and the efforts of many volunteers, include sensory/residential, memorial, butterfly/hummingbird, Native American, and wildflower meadow/riparian areas. Biannual plant sales help fund the garden.

Marcia Donohue's Garden

3017 Wheeler Street, Berkeley 94705
(510) 540-8544

A collector's garden, packed with unusual plants and the sculptured art of Marcia Donahue. Open Sunday afternoons, 1 p.m.–5 p.m.

Dunsmuir Hellman Historic Estate

2960 Peralta Oaks Court, Oakland 94605
(510) 615-5555
www.dunsmuir-hellman.com

This 50-acre historic landscape was designed by John McLaren for the I. W. Hellman, Jr., family, who owned the property from 1906 until the late 1950s. A 37-room mansion built in 1878 for Alexander Dunsmuir is available for event rental. Grounds are open Tuesday through Friday, 11 a.m.–4 p.m., free of charge, with a fee for docent-led tours of the house.

Firestorm Memorial Garden

Intersection of Hiller Drive and Tunnel Road, Oakland
(510) 843-3828
www.oaklandlandscapecommittee.org

The Firestorm Memorial Garden of California natives and Mediterranean-climate plants was designed by Ron Lutsko, with memorial sculptures commemorating the devastating 1991 Oakland/Berkeley Hills fire. The energetic nonprofit Oakland Landscape Committee maintains the garden and, with generous support from local nurseries, has added large plantings of roses. The committee has also planted gardens at six public schools in Oakland and created the Frank Ogawa Firescape Garden, at the entrance to the North Oakland Sports Field (6900 Broadway), and the Gateway Garden, at the intersection of Tunnel Road and Caldicott Lane.

The Gardens at Heather Farm

1540 Marchbanks Drive, Walnut Creek 94598
(925) 947-1678
www.gardenshf.org

Heather was a horse and this was her farm, owned by Mr. Marchbanks, a famous breeder of thoroughbreds. Since 1968 it has been a public-education garden, operating as a non-profit organization. Its 24 demonstration gardens, located throughout the six-acre hillside site, include the signature Cowden Rose Garden (1,000 roses, 150 cultivars), as well as a native plant garden, a water-conservation garden, a butterfly garden, and a sensory garden. All the gardens demonstrate sustainable gardening practices. The gardens are open daily from sunrise to sunset, and there are occasional plant sales.

Gardens at Lake Merritt

666 Bellevue, Oakland 94610
www.gardensatlakemerritt.org

Seven acres of themed gardens at the north end of Lake Merritt have made a comeback thanks to Friends of the Gardens at Lake Merritt, under the nonprofit banner of the Oakland–East Bay Garden Center. Gardens include a pollinator garden, a sensory garden, a bay-friendly garden, and a bonsai garden.

Markham Nature Park & Arboretum

1202 La Vista (off Clayton Road), Concord 94521
(925) 681-2968
www.markhamarboretum.org

Both an arboretum and a creekside natural area on 16 acres, the site began development in 1981 through a partnership between the City of Concord and the nonprofit Markham Regional Arboretum Society. The park includes plant displays, a wisteria arbor, and an international garden of plants from all over the world that grow well in the inland Northern California region. Plant sales are held every Tuesday, 9 a.m.–noon. Saturday plant sales and programs also take place on selected dates.

Morcom Rose Garden

700 Jean Street, Oakland 94610
(510) 597-5039
www.friendsofoaklandrose.org

Conceived to lift spirits during the Depression, the Morcom Rose Garden's first rose was planted by Mayor Frank Morcom in 1933. Today, formal plantings of 500 varieties of roses cover seven acres managed by the City of Oakland Recreation and Parks Department and supported by several nonprofit groups, including Friends of the Morcom Rose Garden.

Regional Parks Botanic Garden

Wildcat Canyon Road at foot of South Park Drive,
    Tilden Regional Park, Berkeley 94701
(510) 544-3169
www.ebparks.org/parks/vc/botanic_garden
www.nativeplants.org (Friends of the Regional Parks
    Botanic Garden)

Part of the East Bay Regional Park District, the botanic garden in Tilden Regional Park is devoted exclusively to the growth and preservation of California native flora and includes many rare and endangered plants. There are extensive collections of *Manzanita* and *Ceanothus.* The 10-acre garden on the slopes of Wildcat Canyon is divided into sections, each representing a different California plant community, with a year-round creek running below. The Friends of the Regional Parks Botanic Garden offers docent tours on weekends, plant sales in the spring (third Saturday in April) and fall (first Saturday in October), and talks and slide shows on most Saturdays. The botanic garden celebrated its 75th birthday in 2015. It is open daily, 8:30 a.m.–5:30 p.m., from June through September, and 8:30 a.m.–5 p.m. the rest of the year. Free.

UC Blake Garden

70 Rincon Road, off Arlington, Kensington 94707
(510) 524-2449
www.blakegarden.ced.berkeley.edu

Formerly the home of Mr. and Mrs. Anson Blake, this 11-acre garden and house is the official residence of the president of the University of California system and is used as a teaching lab for the UC Berkeley Department of Landscape Architecture. The garden was designed in the mid-1920s by Mrs. Blake and her sister Mabel Symmes, one of the first UC Berkeley landscape architecture students. The house was situated to take advantage of the spectacular views and to serve as a windbreak for the garden. A great variety of microclimates makes possible a variety of garden rooms, including a redwood canyon, a dry Mediterranean garden, an Italianate formal garden, and an Australian hollow. It is open to visitors Monday through Friday, 8 a.m.–4:30 p.m., and closed on university holidays.

UC Botanical Garden

200 Centennial Drive, Berkeley 94720
(510) 643-2755; (510) 642-3343 (the Plant Deck)
www.botanicalgarden.berkeley.edu

Founded in 1890, the UC Botanical Garden began as a large glass conservatory on campus to serve as a living museum of California native plants. In the 1920s, it was moved to its current location in Strawberry Canyon, where it now occupies 34 acres and hosts one of North America's most diverse plant collections, including 10,000 species of plants from around the world, unique in being mostly wild collected. The garden is organized into geographic sections, highlighting California native, New World desert, Mexican and Central American, South American, Mediterranean, Australasian, South African, Asian, and Eastern North American plants. The California collection, the most diverse anywhere, includes a redwood forest, a serpentine area, vernal pools, a pygmy forest, and alpine rock gardens. There is also a garden of old roses, as well as several greenhouses displaying enormous cactus and succulent collections, orchids, ferns, and tropical and carnivorous plants. The collection is used extensively for research and education, as well as being a rich horticultural resource contributing to plant introductions. Spectacular views toward the Bay and Golden Gate are offered throughout the garden. Plants are available daily at the Plant Deck and at large seasonal plant sales in the fall (September) and spring (April). The garden is open daily, 10 a.m.–5 p.m.; the Plant Deck is open 10:30 a.m.–4:30 p.m.

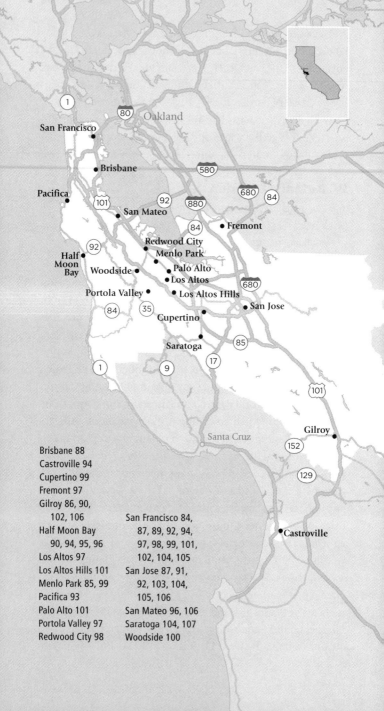

San Francisco

Brisbane

Oakland

Pacifica

San Mateo

Fremont

Redwood City
Menlo Park

Half
Moon
Bay

Woodside

Palo Alto
Los Altos

Portola Valley

Los Altos Hills

San Jose

Cupertino

Saratoga

Santa Cruz

Gilroy

Castroville

Brisbane 88
Castroville 94
Cupertino 99
Fremont 97
Gilroy 86, 90,
    102, 106
Half Moon Bay
    90, 94, 95, 96
Los Altos 97
Los Altos Hills 101
Menlo Park 85, 99
Pacifica 93
Palo Alto 101
Portola Valley 97
Redwood City 98

San Francisco 84,
    87, 89, 92, 94,
    97, 98, 99, 101,
    102, 104, 105
San Jose 87, 91,
    92, 103, 104,
    105, 106
San Mateo 96, 106
Saratoga 104, 107
Woodside 100

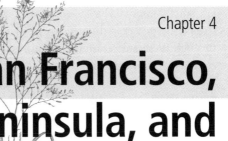

Chapter 4

*Chlorogalum
pomeridianum*

San Francisco, Peninsula, and South Bay

Counties: San Francisco, San Mateo, Santa Clara
Elevational range: Sea level to 4,360 feet at Mount Hamilton
(Santa Clara County), a mountain in the Diablo Range
Sunset climate zones: 14, 15, 16, 17
Annual rainfall: San Francisco, 21 inches; San Mateo, 19 inches;
San Jose, 14 inches
Winter temperatures: 30°F to 20°F
Summer temperatures: Average high temperature in San Francisco,
66°F; temperatures up to 80s°F and 90s°F on the Peninsula and in
the South Bay in September and October.

Thick fog often blankets San Francisco in summer,
making for cool, damp days of gray, filtered light. September and October Indian summers promise the relief
of warm, sunny days. Wet, mild winters offer little if any frost,
and the growing season stretches year round. Climate zones, or
microclimates, vary within the city as warm, sunny pockets rub
shoulders with those bathed in fog and lower light. Heat belts
stretch through the Mission, Bernal Heights, Bayview–Hunters
Point, and Russian and Telegraph hills and give intrepid city
gardeners sun and heat to grow tomatoes and even peaches.

As one travels farther south through the Peninsula and
South Bay, summer temperatures rise and fog lessens, as does

rainfall. In mountain valleys with colder winter climates, fruit trees with greater chill needs thrive. Thermal belts spread through these areas. Summer winds rushing down eastern mountain slopes cool hot days. The Santa Cruz mountain ridge separates coastal and bay communities of the Peninsula. San Mateo County is rich with lakes, creeks, and streams.

The South Bay includes the northern, urbanized end of the Santa Clara Valley. Originally known as the Valley of Heart's Delight for the abundant produce grown there, this valley is now called Silicon Valley for its computer and high-tech industries. The southern part of Santa Clara County still remains rural, with grapes a thriving crop.

Diverse plant communities flourish in this region: redwood forests, oak and pine woodlands, and chaparral. Salt marshes and coastal prairies of exotic annual grasses and native perennial grasses weave their way with coastal scrub down to northern Santa Barbara County. Red buckwheat (*Eriogonum latifolium*), seaside daisy (*Erigeron glaucus*), cliff lettuce (*Dudleya farinosa*), and coyote brush (*Baccharis pilularis*) thrive. Other natives include coast blue blossom (*Ceanothus thyrsiflorus*), scrambling virgin's bower (*Clematis ligusticifolia*), chaparral clematis (*Clematis lasiantha*), and soap plant (*Chlorogalum pomeridianum*), the bulb used for soap by Native American Indians. This lily family member, found on dry, open hills, blooms in July and August. Plants can reach from two to ten feet tall, and delicate white spreading flower clusters emerge from rosettes of gray-green wavy leaves.

Specialty Nurseries and Growers

Bay Natives

10 Cargo Way, San Francisco 94124
(415) 287-6755
www.baynatives.com

Email: info@baynatives.com
Geoffrey Coffey, Paul Furman
Retail, wholesale, and online order
Open weekdays, 7:30 a.m.–5:30 p.m.,
    and weekends, 9:30 a.m.–5:30 p.m.

Plant specialties: California native plants (400 species), including perennials, shrubs, trees, vines, grasses, ferns, bulbs, and annuals.

History/description: Landscape designer Geoffrey Coffey and landscape architect and photographer Paul Furman combined their growing collections of native plants and opened an online nursery in 2005, with growing grounds atop historic terraces west of Twin Peaks (not open to the public). In 2011, they leased this location from the Port of San Francisco's sunny, industrial waterfront at India Basin. In addition to their interest in native plants, they are at the forefront of the effort to encourage local food production in Bayview, an area long short on fresh produce. The nursery's well-organized website provides good descriptions of each plant, along with growing conditions, provenance, and Paul's photographs.

Brookside Orchids

2718 B Alpine Road, Menlo Park 94028
(650) 854-3711; (650) 854-4156 (plant boarding)
www.brookside-orchids.com
Email: orchidsbrookside@gmail.com
Jim Heierle
Retail, wholesale, and mail order
Open Monday through Friday, 7:30 a.m.–3:30 p.m.,
    and Saturday, 10 a.m.–3 p.m.

Plant specialties: Orchid plants (25-plus genera), as well as seedlings and meristems.

History/description: Jim Heierle followed both his father and grandfather into the orchid business, working as they did at Niven Nursery in Marin County. Jim opened his own business in 1981 after studying ornamental horticulture here and in Europe and working for the Orchid House in Los Osos. He has introduced *Miltonia* 'Jim Heierle' and several heat-tolerant *Odontoglossum* hybrids. Occasionally you might catch some of the nursery's newest introductions at a local farmers' market. Information about plant availability, tours and open houses, and boarding services is available on the website.

Carman's Nursery

8470 Pharmer Road, Gilroy 95020
(408) 847-2313
www.carmansnursery.com
Email: carmansnursery@gmail.com
Nancy and Bob Schramm
Retail and some wholesale
Open Thursday, Friday, and Sunday, 10 a.m.–5 p.m.
　　(winter close at 4 p.m.). Best to call first.

Plant specialties: Bonsai starters, dwarf conifers, rock-garden plants, and unusual fruiting plants, such as fig, pomegranate, kiwi, and caper; odd and rare plants from around the world; and plants suitable for the garden railroad hobby.

History/description: Started in 1937 as a bedding-plant nursery by Hugh Carman, Nancy Schramm's grandfather, Carman's Nursery became a leader in plant introductions for California gardens under the visionary leadership of her father, Ed Carman, who ran the nursery from the 1950s until 2002. Ed Carman greatly expanded California horticulture, thanks to his talent for propagation, his worldwide connections with like-minded people, and his encyclopedic knowledge of plants and places. Among his many introductions are the kiwi, *Coprosma* cultivars, *Cupressus* 'Swane's Golden' from New Zealand, and *Rhodohypoxis* and *Dymondia* from South Africa. He was involved in virtually every horticultural organization and was honored as the Pacific Coast Nurseryman of the Year in 1995. Nancy, the youngest of Ed's three daughters, grew up in the nursery. She continues in his footsteps of civic engagement, serving on the board of the Western Horticultural Society, organizing the Hot Plant Picks exhibit at the San Francisco Flower and Garden Show, and writing a monthly column, "A Passion for Plants," for *Out and About* Magazine. In 2005, she moved the nursery to her home in Gilroy. She regularly takes the nursery on the road, attending garden and bonsai shows, Master Gardener events, garden railway events, and the National Heirloom Expo.

Chateau CharMarron Peony Gardens

5335 Sierra Road, San Jose 95132
(408) 251-7048
www.4peonies.com
Email: peonies4u@aol.com
Marcia Reed
Retail and email order
Open during bloom season, Wednesday, Saturday, and Sunday,
9 a.m.–6 p.m.; Thursday and Friday, noon–6 p.m.;
or by email appointment.

Plant specialties: Herbaceous, tree, and Itoh peonies.

History/description: Marcia Reed started out selling irises from her garden overlooking the Calaveras Reservoir, but when customers began admiring her peonies, she switched to selling them in 1996. She is especially fond of the Itoh peony, an intersectional cross between the herbaceous and tree peonies, developed by Toichi Itoh in 1948, which provides the better leaf and color range (yellow) of the tree peony without its woodiness. Her demonstration garden has 1,000 planted peonies, apparently of no interest to deer, gophers, or snails. Rootstock is shipped in the fall; potted plants are available all year.

Golden Gate Orchids

225 Velasco Avenue, San Francisco 94134
(415) 990-1314
www.goldengateorchids.com

tom@goldengateorchids.com
Tom Perlite
Retail and wholesale
Open by appointment only (because his business
   is in a residential area).

Plant specialties: Orchids, particularly *Dendrobium cuthbert-sonii,* and Vireya rhododendrons.

History/description: While a premed student at UC Berkeley, Tom Perlite took a botany class, just because he needed the units and could not get into other sciences. This administrative fluke changed his course of action. Graduating with a degree in botany, he went to work at Rod McLellan Co. to learn the orchid business. He bought an existing azalea nursery with 30,000 square feet of greenhouses in 1981 and opened Golden Gate Orchids. After many years in the orchid business, Tom has downsized greatly, and he now specializes in *Dendrobium cuthbertsonii,* a species from New Guinea, and propagating tropical rhododendrons (Vireyas).

Greenlee and Associates

284 Visitacion Avenue, Brisbane 94005
(415) 468-1961
www.greenleeandassociates.com
Email: greenleeandassociates@gmail.com
John Greenlee
Wholesale, some retail and mail order
Open by appointment only.

Plant specialties: Ornamental grasses and grass-like plants, drought-tolerant plants, ground covers, coastal California natives, and meadow accessories.

History/description: Probably more than anyone, John Greenlee is responsible for the increased interest in ornamental grasses in the West. His first book, *The Encyclopedia of Ornamental Grasses* (1992), introduced California to their many possibilities, with color photographs and comprehensive descriptions of over 300 ornamental grasses. Known as the Grassman, John is an articulate believer in the meadow garden, or "natural" lawn, of low-growing native tufted grasses and compatible flowering plants. His book *The American Meadow Garden* (2009) offers appealing alternatives to the resource-guzzling mowed lawn. He travels widely in search of durable and interesting grasses and plants. An articulate spokesman for the splendors of grass, John has hosted many episodes of the PBS television series *The New Garden*. He has extensive growing grounds in Pomona and Watsonville. Design, installation, and consulting services are available.

Flora Grubb Gardens and The Palm Broker

1634 Jerrold Avenue, San Francisco 94124
(415) 626-7256
www.floragrubb.com
Email: info@floragrubb.com
Flora Grubb, Saul Nadler
Retail and wholesale
Open Monday through Saturday, 9 a.m.–6 p.m., and
    Sunday, 10 a.m.–6 p.m. (winter close at 5 p.m.).

Plant specialties: Drought-tolerant plants for Mediterranean climates, including Australian and New Zealand natives, succulents, and rare palms.

History/description: Garden designer Flora Grubb and Saul Nadler bought The Palm Broker in 2003 and developed the site into a small nursery called Guerrero Street Gardens. Known from the start for dramatic and unusual plants and for the owners' insatiable love of them, the nursery was soon overflowing with plants. In 2007, they moved to this one-acre site in the industrial Third Street corridor, with lofty art/tech nursery buildings designed by Boor Bridges Architecture. The nursery combines a refined sense of design with a passion for plants, especially those with sculptural qualities and a tolerance for drought. A large, hanging succulent wall garden attests to the owners' creativity; they also sell kits to make your own, along with great coffee, designer garden furniture, and pots. Their 40-acre growing grounds in San Diego County, East West Trees (see listing in chapter 8), supply their distinctive palms and some of their succulents and subtropical plants. Check website for information about classes and book events. Tours are available upon request. Garden consultations and design services are offered, and floral arrangements are available through the Cutting Garden.

Highway 92 Succulents

at Pastorino Farms
12511 San Mateo Road, Half Moon Bay 94019
(650) 863-3309
www.highway92succulents.com
Email: info@highway92succulents.com
Therese Smith
Retail
Open Wednesday and Thursday, 11 a.m.–5 p.m.; Friday, 10 a.m.–
    5 p.m.; and Saturday and Sunday, 9 a.m.–5 p.m.

Plant specialties: Succulents: large collections of *Echeveria* and *Aloe,* some hard-to-find varieties such as variegated *Coltyledon* 'Kitten Paws'; grafted cacti. 2-inch to 15-gallon pots.

History/description: After retiring from the National Park Service, Therese Smith began a joint venture with a succulent-collecting partner to create "hanging succulent walls." The partner exited, but Therese was captivated by the possibilities of these plants and continued the business as a succulent and cactus nursery, abandoning the creation of walls. The nursery occupies two greenhouses at Pastorino Farms. Clients bringing their own containers can pot up their purchases at the Potting Bench.

Menlo Growers

11605 New Avenue, Gilroy 95021

P. O. Box 1234, Gilroy 95021
(408) 683-4862
www.menlogrowers.com
Email: menlogrowers1@aol.com
Mike and Helena Vogel
Retail and wholesale
Open Monday through Friday, 8 a.m.–4 p.m.,
    and Saturday, 8 a.m.–11:30 a.m.

Plant specialties: Citrus (over 50 varieties, especially dwarf); tropical fruit trees; avocado and other subtropical fruit trees; deciduous fruit and nut trees.

History/description: Trained in pomology at Cal Poly, San Luis Obispo, Mike Vogel figured he had done something right when he found this 20-year-old nursery for sale in 1995. He has established a reputation for innovative work and plans to keep adding new, proven varieties. The nursery propagates about 40,000 plants each year on the six-acre site.

Middlebrook Gardens Design Studio/Lab Native Plant Nursery

76 Race Street, San Jose 95126
(408) 292-9993
www.middlebrook-gardens.com
Email: info@middlebrook-gardens.com
Alrie Middlebrook
Retail
Open Monday through Friday, 7 a.m.–3 p.m.,
    and Saturday, 10 a.m.–4 p.m.

Plant specialties: California native plants.

History/description: This small nursery in downtown San Jose is packed with difficult-to-find native plants and is part of Alrie Middlebrook's landscape design/build/maintenance company. Her book, *Designing California Native Gardens,* coauthored with Glenn Keator, introduces California's plants according to their specific plant community, which is how she organizes the nursery's display garden to give visitors an idea of sensible plantings. With an emphasis on education, the nursery also displays edible gardens, living roofs, vertical gardens, gray-water systems, and aquaponics systems (which use fish-tank water as fertilizer for plants).

Nature's Acres

1628 Lake Street, San Francisco 94121 (mailing address)
(415) 317-3978
www.naturesacresnursery.com

(See listing in chapter 2.)

Nola's Iris Garden

at Prevost Ranch and Gardens
4195 Sierra Road, San Jose 95132
(408) 929-6307
www.walking-p-bar.com
orders@walking-p-bar.com
Nola and Gary Prevost
Retail and mail/online order
Open during peak bloom season, April and May.

Plant specialties: *Iris germanica*, bearded iris (2,000 varieties).

History/description: Looking for their dream place, the Prevosts found this beautiful 43-acre ranch in the foothills of the Mount Diablo Range, where they board horses, run cattle, and grow five acres of irises. When they first moved in, Gary's mother gave them a present of 300 rhizomes, which they planted along the driveway and sort of forgot about. Several years later, when they were trying to decide what the agricultural use of their land should be, they noticed that the irises were thriving. With Maryott's Iris Garden having just closed, they saw an opportunity. The nursery opened in 2004 and continues to introduce new varieties hybridized by their many friends.

Shelldance Orchid Gardens

2000 Highway 1, Pacifica 94044
(650) 355-4845
www.shelldance.com
Email: nancyvictoriadavis@hotmail.com
Michael Rothenberg, Nancy Victoria Davis
Retail and wholesale
Open for retail sales Saturday and Sunday, 10 a.m.–5 p.m.;
    wholesale by appointment only.

Plant specialties: Orchids—such as *Phalaenopsis, Oncidium, Dendrobium, Paphiopedilum, Odontoglossum, Miltonia,* and *Cattleya*—and both species and hybrid bromeliads—including two of their introductions, *Aechmea* 'Shelldancer' and *A.* 'Pacifica'.

History/description: It really was a case of starting out "selling seashells down by the seashore." As hard as it is to believe, this incredible business began on San Francisco's Union Street selling tillandsias in shells. In 1976, artist Michael Rothenberg and poet Nancy Victoria Davis leased this multiple-greenhouse site in Pacifica, formerly Herb Hagar's Vallemar Orchids, and acquired a portion of his orchid collection. Around the same time they met an orchid grower from Florida and went with him on collecting expeditions to tropical rainforests. They sold off a good portion of their bromeliad collection to the City of Singapore to be placed in the National Botanical Gardens there. Michael and Nancy's plants appear in the San Francisco Academy of Sciences Rain Forest exhibit, the South American Aviary exhibit at the San Francisco Zoo, and a Star Trek movie. One of their Historic Landmark–certified greenhouses has been transformed into a magnificent tropical rain forest, reflecting the couple's artistic sensibilities. The nursery operates at Sweeney Ridge, part of the Golden Gate National Recreation Area, under an agricultural use lease with the GGNRA. The National Park Service and Shelldance share a commitment to preserving natural resources for the benefit of future generations.

Sobralias

at Bruce Rogers Orchids
225 Velasco Street, San Francisco 94134
(415) 235-4819
and at the Orchid Zone
15819 Del Monte Farms Road, Castroville 95012
(831) 776-1242
Bruce Rogers, John Chant
Wholesale
Open by appointment only.

Plant specialties: *Sobralia* orchid hybrids and species, both seedlings and mature plants.

History/description: This partnership between Bruce Rogers and John Chant began as a breeding program in 2002 to popularize and develop new *Sobralia* orchid hybrids. Although *Sobralia* orchids are among the tallest ("they grow like bamboo," says Bruce—with species growing from 1 to 44 feet, and new hybrids ranging from 1 to 6 feet) and largest-blooming (6- to 8-inch) orchids in the world, they were not previously available in plant markets. Native to Central America and tropical South America, these orchids can be grown outdoors in our coastal, Mediterranean climate. Bruce Rogers serves on the advisory committee for the Conservatory of Flowers in Golden Gate Park and is the author of *The Orchid Whisperer* (2012).

World's Rare Plants

at Pastorino Farms
12511 San Mateo Road, Half Moon Bay 94019
(650) 454-9002
www.worldsrareplants.com
Email: worldsrareplants@gmail.com
Mary and Richard Wuydts, Jan and Phillip Small
Retail
Open Monday through Thursday, 10 a.m.–4 p.m.,
    and Friday through Sunday, 10 a.m.–5 p.m.

Plant specialties: Carnivorous plants, especially sundews, pitcher plants, Venus flytraps, and nepenthes; also tillandsias.

History/description: Landscaper Richard Wuydts had been collecting carnivorous plants for over 30 years and got the bright idea that sisters Mary and Jan should start a business selling them. What started out on a table in a parking lot on weekends in 2010 now occupies three greenhouses, thanks to Richard's knowledge and the sisters' gung ho spirit. Everything you need is here to create your own fairy garden.

Yerba Buena Nursery

at Pastorino Farms
12511 San Mateo Road (Highway 92), Half Moon Bay 94019
(650) 851-1668
www.yerbabuenanursery.com
Email: inquiry@yerbabuenanursery.com
Kathy and Anya Crane
Retail
Open Tuesday through Saturday, 9 a.m.–5 p.m.

Plant specialties: California native plants (more than 600 species) and native ferns.

History/description: This grandmother of all native plant nurseries was started in 1960 by Gerda Isenberg, who became fascinated with the native plants growing on her property in a Woodside canyon, site of the original nursery. In 1996, at the age of 94, she sold the nursery to Kathy Crane. Seeking a more accessible location, Kathy moved about 20,000 plants to Pastorino Farms, a charming complex of small specialty growers right on Highway 92. Several greenhouses are fronted by demonstration beds that include some descendants of Gerda's mother stock. Garden design services here can help you select native plants for small spaces or lawn replacement.

Notable Garden Centers

Bongard's Treescape Nursery

12460 San Mateo Road, Half Moon Bay 94019
(650) 726-4568

Ron Bongard comes from a family of growers; his grandfather grew coastal vegetables, and his father, with whom he opened the business in 1975, grew cut flowers. Their 10-acre site includes growing grounds and a good assortment of bedding plants, trees, shrubs, and perennials. Open every day except holidays, 9 a.m.–5 p.m.

Golden Nursery

1122 2nd Street, San Mateo 94401
(650) 348-5525
www.goldennursery.com

This family-owned and -operated nursery was started by George Takemori in 1976 and remains a hidden gem in San Mateo County. The emphasis here is on the rare and unique, with noteworthy collections of Japanese maples, fruit trees, and rose varieties.

Half Moon Bay Nursery

11691 San Mateo Road, Half Moon Bay 94019
(650) 726-5392
www.hmbnursery.com

Ron Mickelsen started the nursery right after his service in the Korean War as a specialty nursery selling fuchsias. Then he added tuberous begonias, geraniums, and cyclamens. Today, Half Moon Bay offers a full range of interesting garden plants and organic supplies. Ron grows about half of what he sells on location. Offerings include a California native plants section and a camellia/rhododendron/azalea section.

Hortica

566 Castro, San Francisco 94114
(415) 863-4697

David Gray's small backyard nursery is filled with his personal selection of interesting plants, including orchids and houseplants.

Ladera Garden and Gifts

3130 Alpine Road, Suite 380, Portola Valley 94028
(650) 854-3850

Juan and Mercedes Navarro offer a nice variety of maples, dogwoods, rare trees and shrubs, and perennials and a large collection of California native plants. They have been at it for 30 years and are still enthusiastic, believing that there is something new to learn each day.

Los Altos Nursery

245 Hawthorne Avenue, Los Altos 94022
(650) 948-1421
www.losaltosnursery.com

Three generations of the Faruchi family have worked here since two brothers started this nursery on the old family farm in 1947. Known especially for their vegetables and fruit trees, they offer good-quality general nursery stock as well. A demonstration vegetable garden and a pond area with Japanese-style plantings inspire a love of gardening. The nursery is closed October 31 until March 1.

Regan Nursery

4268 Decoto Road, Fremont 94555
(510) 797-3222
www.regannursery.com

In 1995, Marsha Hildebrand bought this nursery from the Regan family, who started it in 1958. It is known primarily for its vast assortment (1,000 varieties) of roses—floribundas, grandifloras, hybrid teas, landscapes, minis, and climber and patio trees—which are sold bare root in January and February and in pots the rest of the year. The nursery has a full selection of general nursery stock—annuals, perennials, vines, shrubs, and trees—featuring fruit trees, vegetables, and Japanese maples. They handpick specific plants from a network of local and national growers that they have developed over the years.

Sloat Garden Center

3237 Pierce Street, San Francisco, (415) 440-1000
2700 Sloat Boulevard, San Francisco, (415) 566-4415
327 3rd Avenue, San Francisco, (415) 752-1614
www.sloatgardens.com

Dave Geller started this nursery in 1958 to take advantage of an empty lot on Sloat Street. Once part of GET Department Store, then a small independent outlet, Sloat's horizons have expanded since the arrival of Dave Straus, a longtime employee here bought into the business in 1968. With a full and interesting selection of plants, the nursery has a knack for spotting horticultural trends and is very community oriented. Workshops and seminars are listed on the website.

Wegman's Nursery

492 Woodside Road, Redwood City 94061
(650) 368-5908
www.wegmansnursery.com

Swiss-born nurseryman Rudy Wegman opened this business in 1960, and his family has been involved ever since, with son Mark managing the nursery today. The full-service nursery covers two acres and has large sections of color plants (annuals and perennials), vegetables, trees and shrubs, aquatic plants, and cacti. Wegman's will special order for customers and holds periodic workshops and seminars.

Yamagami's Nursery

1361 South DeAnza Boulevard, Cupertino 95014
(408) 252-3347
www.yamagamisnursery.com

Tradition counts, even in the transformed Silicon Valley. In 1948, Taro Yamagami bought two acres surrounded by orchards and opened a fruit stand. Earning a degree in landscape architecture, he started a design/build business and started to grow plants as a means to supply his business. Slowly, plants supplanted fruit and the stand became a nursery. Taro sold the nursery in 1963 to his longtime nursery manager, Mas Oka, and Mas's wife, Betty. Upon Mas and Betty's retirement in 1983, son Preston took over, followed in 2013 by Preston's daughter, Brittany, and her husband, Mike Sheade. The offerings here are encyclopedic, from sod to Tibetan wonderberry and *Murraya koenigii* (curry leaf). The website is full of plant care guides and other useful information.

Horticultural Attractions

Allied Arts Guild

75 Arbor Road, Menlo Park 94025
(650) 325-3259
www.alliedartsguild.org

A Gardner Dailey–designed complex of Spanish Colonial–style studios and courtyards created in the 1920s to foster the arts. Featured gardens include the Garden of Delight, the Court of Abundance, and the Rose Allée.

Conservatory of Flowers

100 John F. Kennedy Drive, Golden Gate Park, San Francisco 94118
(415) 831-2093
www.conservatoryofflowers.org

Built in 1879, this is the oldest public wood-and-glass conservatory in North America, filled to profusion with more than 17,000 species of plants. Plants are arranged in galleries reflective of their native habitat, such as tropical jungle, highland tropics, and aquatic (where the first US blooming of a *Victoria amazonia* was recorded). A potted-plant gallery pays tribute to the conservatory's Victorian past. The conservatory also has an exhibition gallery. Open Tuesday through Sunday, 10 a.m.–4:30 p.m. Admission fee.

Filoli Center

86 Cañada Road, Woodside 94062
(650) 364-8300, ext. 507 (tours), ext. 509 (visitor information)
www.filoli.org

Filoli is one of few remaining grand country estates in California. Now a National Trust for Historic Preservation property, Filoli was built from 1915 to 1917 by William Bourne, who inherited the Empire Mine at age 17. He plowed the same Western energy into his garden as he did into the mine, when he made it the deepest in the country. Filoli's 16-acre garden is distinctly Californian, with grand views of the coastal range, although it borrows from European garden tradition. Organized as a series of outdoor rooms, Filoli includes a woodland garden, a rose garden, impeccably maintained formal gardens, and colorful seasonal displays. There are miles of woodland trails throughout the 654-acre estate. Friends of Filoli, the membership support group, organizes lectures and a series of special events. Plants propagated at the garden are offered for sale in the courtyard next to the garden and gift shop. Open from early February to the end of October, Tuesday through Saturday, 10 a.m.–3:30 p.m., and Sunday, 11 a.m.–3:30 p.m. Tours can be arranged by emailing tours@filoli.org. The center also has an active volunteer program, classes, exhibits, and workshops.

Foothill College Bamboo Garden

12345 El Monte Road, Los Altos Hills 94022

This garden boasts 70 varieties of bamboo, first planted in 1989 to study the adaptability of bamboo varieties for Bay Area climates, on a two-acre hillside below the Japanese Cultural Center.

Elizabeth F. Gamble Garden

1431 Waverley Street, Palo Alto 94301
(650) 329-1356
www.gamblegarden.org

This turn-of-the-century Colonial/Georgian Revival–style home was built by Edwin Percy Gamble, a banker and son of the cofounder of Procter & Gamble. He and his family moved to Palo Alto to be near Stanford University, where their four children went to study. Today this 2.3-acre estate is a community horticultural foundation. Garden highlights include a wisteria garden, a rose garden, a cherry allée, an herb garden, and demonstration gardens. Regularly scheduled classes are held in the historic carriage house on such topics as soil amending, container gardening, and flower arranging. Plant sales are scheduled periodically throughout the year. The gardens are open during daylight hours. The office and reference library are open weekdays, 9 a.m.–2 p.m. Entrance to the garden is free; docent tours are available by reservation for a fee.

Garden for the Environment

7th Avenue at Lawton Street, San Francisco
(415) 558-8246
www.gardenfortheenvironment.org

A splendid one-acre demonstration garden offering environmental education programs about water conservation, organic gardening, urban composting, and sustainable food systems.

The Gardens of Alcatraz

Alcatraz Island, San Francisco Bay
(415) 981-7625 (tour tickets)
www.alcatrazgardens.org

A partnership between the Garden Conservancy, the Golden Gate National Parks Conservancy, and the National Park Service restored the historical gardens that clung to this rocky island from the 1860s until 1963, when it was first a US military fort, then a federal penitentiary, and then abandoned. That any plants grew here at all is a testimonial to the efforts of wardens, wives, and inmates. Today, heirloom roses bloom, the foundations of officer's cottages are filled with fuchsias and calla lilies, and the plantings on Cell House Slope sparkle in the sun.

Gilroy Gardens Family Theme Park

3050 Hecker Pass Highway (Highway 152), Gilroy 95020
(408) 840-7100
www.gilroygardens.org

The brainchild of Michael and Claudia Bonfante, this horticultural theme park is now run by a nonprofit to educate the public about the importance of trees. Rides and attractions move among six gardens, filled with more than 200 topiary trees and the famous Circus Trees, trained and grafted into amazing shapes.

Golden Gate Park

From Stanyan Street to the ocean,
    between Fulton Street and Lincoln Avenue
(415) 831-2700 (San Francisco Recreation and Park Department)
www.parks.sfgov.org

The transformation of this strip of wind-whipped, desolate sand dunes into lush parkland was a horticultural tour de force. Engineer William Hammond Hall planned and started the project by stabilizing the sand dunes in the 1880s, but it was Scotsman John McLaren, park superintendent from 1890 to 1943, who was able to create an English-style landscape park using Mediterranean-climate plants. Using street droppings to enrich the soil, he introduced plants from around the world, including *Sparrmannia africana* and *Leptospermum laevigatum*. He was the park's number-one advocate for 53 years during sometimes cantankerous times, always vigilant to protect the park from commerce and commemorative statues, though not the one that honors him. Golden Gate Park is the largest (1,017 acres) manmade municipal park in America, host to a myriad of activities. In addition to the San Francisco Botanical Garden and Conservatory of Flowers, special gardens include the Japanese Tea Garden, Rhododendron Dell, National AIDS Memorial Grove, Dahlia Garden, and Shakespeare Garden. Both the California Academy of Sciences and the DeYoung Museum are located alongside the park's historic Music Concourse, created for the California Midwinter International Exposition in 1894. The Golden Gate Park Nursery, located at 100 Martin Luther King Drive, often holds plant sales on the third Saturday of each month (best to call first, [415] 242-6370). The park is open every day.

Guadalupe River Park and Gardens

715 Spring Street at Taylor Street, San Jose 95161
(408) 298-7657 (conservancy)
www.grpg.org

Part of a three-mile-long, 450-acre park project being developed along the Guadalupe River by the Guadalupe River Park Conservancy. Featured gardens include a historic orchard and heritage rose garden (with 3,400 varieties of roses, it is the largest collection in the United States and the third largest in the world).

Hakone Gardens

21000 Big Basin Way, Saratoga 95070
(408) 741-4994
www.hakone.com

Formerly the private garden of the Stine family, created by a
court gardener of the Emperor of Japan in 1918 and renovated
in 1966. Zen gardens on 18 acres feature camellias, shaped
trees, wisteria, bamboo, iris, and azaleas. Hakone also holds
lectures and demonstrations and is the meeting place for several plant societies.

Overfelt Gardens

368 Educational Park Drive, San Jose 95133
(408) 251-3323
www.sjparks.org

This 33-acre park incorporates a natural sanctuary, a fragrance
garden, and the Chinese Cultural Garden.
(www.chineseculturalgarden.org)

Presidio Tunnel Tops

Presidio of San Francisco
Golden Gate National Recreation Area
Between Lincoln Boulevard and Mason Street
(415) 561-5300
www.presidio.gov

Coming soon (2018). Fourteen acres of new parkland atop
the Doyle Drive tunnels connect the Presidio's Main Post with
Crissy Field via a series of gardens, meadows, a woodland,
and a coastal bluff that cascade down to dunes and a children's learning landscape. Designed by James Corner Field
Operations, the park promotes ecological and horticultural
wonder while affording amazing views of the Golden Gate
and San Francisco Bay.

Emma Prusch Farm Park

647 South King, San Jose 95116
(408) 264-9654 (foundation)
www.pruschfarmpark.org

This small farm-style park with animals, a fruit orchard, and community gardens has the mission "to help keep... a sense of country atmosphere alive here in San Jose."

San Francisco Botanical Garden

Ninth Avenue and Lincoln Way, Golden Gate Park,
    San Francisco 94122
(415) 661-1316
www.sfbotanicalgarden.org

Officially opened in 1940, the San Francisco Botanical Garden today has 55 acres containing over 8,000 different kinds of plants from around the world. Plants are arranged in a series of gardens to educate and delight visitors, including the Garden of Fragrance, the Succulent Garden, the Zellerbach Garden of Perennials, the South African Garden, and the Cloud Forests. Three areas showcase California native plants: the Arthur L. Menzies Garden of California Native Plants, the Redwood Grove Trail, and the John Muir Nature Trail. There are important collections of Asiatic magnolias (considered the most significant collection for conservation purposes outside of China) and plants from Australia and New Zealand. The San Francisco Botanical Garden Society, the garden's support group, maintains the Helen Crocker Russell Library of Horticulture and has a very active education program, with lectures, workshops, tours, gardening clinics, ethnobotany programs, children's activities, and daily free docent tours. A big annual plant sale is held the first weekend in May; specialized plant sales take place on second Saturdays (but not in January, February, August, or December). Plants are available daily at the arbor next to the garden bookstore. For information on plant sales, call the nursery at (415) 661-3090.

San Jose Municipal Rose Garden

Naglee Avenue at Dana, San Jose 95126
(408) 277-5422
www.sjparks.org

An official All America Rose Selections Test Garden, the San Jose Municipal Rose Garden boasts 3,500 colorful and fragrant roses covering 5.5 acres on an old prune orchard site, supported by Friends of the San Jose Rose Garden.

San Mateo Garden Center

605 Parkside Way, San Mateo 94403
(650) 574-1506
www.sanmateogardencenter.org

Over 40 horticultural groups hold their meetings, shows, sales, benefits, classes, and workshops here. The garden shop sells plants on Monday, Wednesday, and Friday mornings.

San Mateo Japanese Tea Garden

605 Parkside Way, Central Park, San Mateo 94403
www.cityofsanmateo.org

This Japanese garden features meandering paths through serene plantings with a koi pond, a granite pagoda, and a tea house.

Syngenta Flowers

2280 Hecker Pass Highway (Highway 152 West), Gilroy 95020
(408) 847-7333
www.syngenta-us.com

In 2008, Syngenta Flowers, a global, wholesale producer of flower seeds, bought Goldsmith Seeds, which had operated here for many years. Six acres of growing grounds are used to field-test new flower selections each year. In bloom from June through September, this floriferous wallop has been known to cause traffic jams along the highway. Interested motorists are now encouraged to stop by for a closer look at tomorrow's flowers in the fields and in Syngenta's two-acre public display garden.

Villa Montalvo (Montalvo Arts Center)

15400 Montalvo Road, Saratoga 95070
(408) 961-5800
www.montalvoarts.org

This large (175-acre) Italian-style country estate owned by San Francisco mayor and US senator James Phelan in the middle of the Santa Cruz Mountains is now a venue for performances and the arts, run as a nonprofit and managed by Santa Clara County Parks. The gardens, originally designed by John McLaren, include formal gardens, lawns, an arboretum, a botanical garden, and natural areas with hiking trails.

Plant Suitability

For a plant to succeed in a garden, it must be suited to the site. To determine what is suitable for your garden, you'll need to do some sleuthing.

Look around to see what thrives in your area, in your neighbors' gardens, and in local parks and botanical gardens. These plants likely will grow in your garden. What looks weak, spindly, or withered? Steer away from these, which are probably poor choices for your garden. Learn about your garden's climate, soil, light, and rainfall. The right plants for your garden should look healthy and require little maintenance (including water and pesticides) once they are established.

Climate

Climate zone maps, such as those in the *Sunset Western Garden Book,* help determine your garden climate's basic character. For example, proximity to the ocean affects a garden, moderating temperature extremes. Familiarizing yourself with seasonal rainfall patterns is critical to understanding your garden's water needs.

Soil

Minerals with particles of different sizes and shapes make up soil. Clay soil has flat, small particles that your eye cannot single out. This type of soil drains slowly but retains nutrients. Silt particles are larger and not flat, so they don't pack together as tightly; these soils fall between clay and sandy with regard to drainage and nutrient retention. Sand has even larger particles, easy to discern. Sandy soils drain quickly but do not hold nutrients. Most succulents and cacti thrive in sandier soils. Plants such as roses need some clay to give soil heft and retain nutrients.

Soil pH measures soil acidity or alkalinity. On a scale of 0 to 11, neutral soil has a pH of 7, alkaline soil a pH higher than 7, and acid soil a pH less than 7. The pH of most garden soils ranges between 5 and 9. Certain pH levels accompany soil types: California's northern coastal region, where rain falls heavily, has acid soils, whereas areas with scant rainfall are more alkaline. Once a gardener knows his or her soil pH, it becomes easier to determine suitable plants. For example, woodlanders such as rhododendrons, camellias, and azaleas thrive in acid soils, whereas many hellebores prefer alkaline soils.

Light

How many hours of sunlight does your garden get each day? Select plants for the kind and degree of light the garden receives. Plants for shady areas include Torrey pine (*Pinus torreyana*), shrubs like creek dogwood (*Cornus sericea*), fuchsia-flower gooseberry (*Ribes speciosum*), Nootka rose (*Rosa nutkana*), wild ginger (*Asarum caudatum*), virgin's bower (*Clematis ligusticifolia*), sword fern (*Polystichum munitum*), bleeding heart (*Dicentra formosa*), and other woodlanders. Those suited to full sun include redbud (*Cercis occidentalis*), bush anemone (*Carpenteria californica*), Coulter's Matilija poppy (*Romneya coulteri*), chalk dudleya (*Dudleya pulverulenta*), buckwheat (*Eriogonum*), wild lilac (*Ceanothus*), and sage (*Salvia*).

Water

How much rain falls in your garden? Do you want to use supplemental irrigation? Some plants have lower water needs than others. Plants native to California and other Mediterranean-climate regions adapt to dry summers with little or no additional water. Plants native to regions that receive summer rainfall will need plenty of water during California's dry summers.

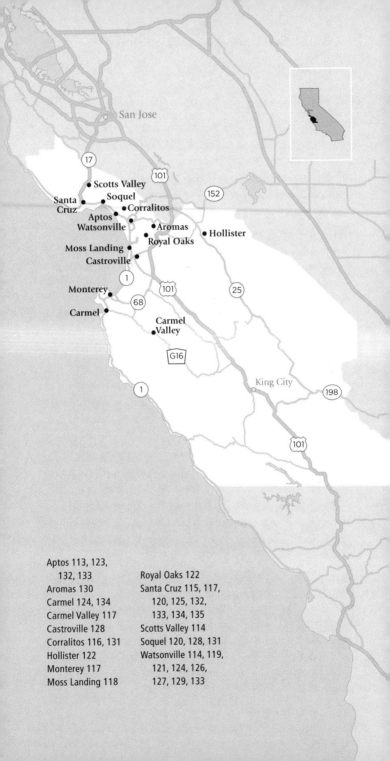

Chapter 5

Monterey Bay Area

Iris douglasiana

Counties: Monterey, San Benito, Santa Cruz
Elevational range: Sea level to 3,455 feet at Fremont Peak in the Gabilan Mountains (San Benito and Monterey counties) and 5,853 feet at Junipero Serra Peak in the Santa Lucia Mountains (Monterey County)
Sunset climate zones: 7, 14, 15, 16, 17
Annual rainfall: Santa Cruz, 31 inches; Monterey, 20 inches; Hollister (San Benito County), 13 inches
Winter temperatures: Lows average 28°F to 21°F. Extreme lows from 18°F to 0°F.
Summer temperatures: Average highs range from 60°F to 72°F.

From Santa Cruz, the coastline curves south toward Monterey Peninsula, enclosing a wide, open-mouthed bay once a thriving center for the fishing industry until its decline in the 1950s due to overfishing. Proximity to the ocean defines this region's climate, and as in San Francisco and along the North Coast, damp marine air moderates temperatures, filters light, cools summer air, and makes for mild winters.

The Salinas River Valley, some of the most fertile agricultural land in the state, lies inland between Santa Lucia and the Gabilan mountains, along the Salinas River in Monterey County. The Salinas is the region's longest river (155 miles),

111

and for the most part it runs underground. Lettuce, spinach, and strawberries flourish here. Nearby Castroville has been crowned artichoke capital of the world. Vineyards also stud the valley landscape. Inland, at mid and higher mountain elevations, patches of gray pine (*Pinus sabiniana*) dot the landscape, along with plants that need winter chill, such as bulbs, peonies, pears, apples, and cherries.

Coastal communities range from forest, coastal scrub, and chaparral to grasslands and dunes. Closed-cone pine forests, whose seed-bearing cones need fire to open, thrive in the marine fog, forming natural windbreaks to buffer persistent onshore winds. Monterey pine (*Pinus radiata*), bishop pine (*Pinus muricata*), and lodgepole pine (*Pinus contorta),* as well as Gowen cypress (*Cupressus goveniana*) and Monterey cypress (*Hesperocyparis macrocarpa*), populate this terrain. Growing with them may be beach strawberry (*Fragaria chiloensis*), yerba buena (*Clinopodium douglasii,* formerly *Satureja douglasii*), monkey flower (*Mimulus aurantiacus*), and wild roses. Manzanitas and California lilacs dominated this coastal chaparral until real estate development displaced plant life. Farther inland, dramatic coast gives way to bucolic valleys of chaparral and grasslands.

Among wild iris, the coast iris, *Iris douglasiana,* discovered by and named for nineteenth-century Scottish botanist and plant collector David Douglas, grows here. For centuries its knee-high, sword-shaped leaves provided strong fibers for fishnets and ropes, and its blooms, true to the meaning of the Greek word from which it derives its name, come in a rainbow of colors from purplish-red to blue, light lavender to creamy white. On its yellow-and-white blaze, painted signal patches guide butterfly and bee pollinators. These perennials bloom in spring and slowly spread, forming clumps.

Specialty Nurseries and Growers

Astone's Protea

7160 Freedom Boulevard, Aptos 95003
(831) 662-3735
www.astonesprotea.com
Mike and Bettina Astone
Retail and wholesale (to florists)
Open by appointment only.

Plant specialties: South African and Australian *Proteaceae*, including *Leucospermum, Leucodendron, Banksia,* and *Protea*.

History/description: The Astones have been in business since 1985 and have grown proteas at this four-acre location since 1990. Still very much a mom-and-pop business, Astone's sells one-gallon potted plants and cut flowers at local farmers' markets in Menlo Park and at Cabrillo College and Monterey Bay Junior College. All plants are grown on site, watered only during the first two summers after planting. During the holidays Astone's offers protea wreaths.

Bamboo Giant, Inc.

5601 Freedom Boulevard, Aptos 95003
(831) 687-0100
www.bamboogiant.com
www.bamboo4sale.com (online store)
Email: sales@bamboogiant.com
Larry Gullman; Daniel Gullman, manager
Retail and wholesale
Open every day, 9 a.m.–4 p.m.

Plant specialties: Bamboo (50 varieties), especially *Phyllostachys* species.

History/description: In 1999, when foul weather forced Larry Gullman to leave his sailboat in Santa Cruz, he happened upon a sales notice for this magnificent 31-acre property at an old quarry site. Previously developed as a weekend hobby for a family group of arborists and horticulturists, the garden now has 15 acres of lofty bamboo planted in the dramatic old stone quarry and includes redwood groves, deciduous magnolias, ponds, and water plants. The property inspired Larry Gullman's passion for bamboo. Privacy screens are a specialty.

Bay Laurel Nursery

1554 Bean Creek Road, Scotts Valley
P. O. Box 66595, Scotts Valley 95067
(831) 438-3999
www.baylaurelnursery.org
Email: baylaurelnurserysv@gmail.com
Peter and Laurie Moerdyke
Wholesale
Open by appointment only.

Plant specialties: 100 varieties of rhododendrons and companion plants, such as *Pieris* and *Camellia*.

History/description: Peter Moerdyke has always been a plant lover. After studies at Cal Poly, he purchased Boulevard Garden Rhododendron Nursery in Palo Alto in 1977 and moved it to Scotts Valley. The nursery and display garden are on the Moerdykes' 12-acre property in the coastal hills. They sell in large lots and suggest that home gardeners shop for their product in their local retail nursery.

Bay West Nursery

84 Wheelock Road, Watsonville 95076
(831) 768-9218
www.baywestnursery.org
Email: baywestnsy@gmail.com
Henrique Martinez
Wholesale, some retail
Open Monday through Saturday, 8:00 a.m.–4:30 p.m.

Plant specialties: Trees and shrubs, with many available in larger sizes (15-gallon and 24-inch boxes); perennials and grasses; and drought-tolerant plants.

History/description: The late Mike Cowell had a 30-year history of horticultural ventures in this area, including a strawberry farm and these four-acre growing grounds. In 2006, he sold the nursery and grounds to Henrique Martinez, his longtime associate, who came to work here as a teenager. Grown in full sun, in large pots, plants here are well conditioned to prosper in water-wise gardens.

Central Coast Wilds

336 Golf Club Drive, Santa Cruz 95060
125 Walk Circle, Santa Cruz 95060 (mailing address)
(831) 459-0656 (office); (831) 459-0655
www.ecologicalconcerns.com
Email: info@ecologicalconcerns.com
Joshua Fodor
Retail, wholesale, and custom growing
Open Monday through Friday, 10 a.m.–3 p.m., or by appointment.

Plant specialties: California native plants suited to Monterey and the San Francisco Bay Area, featuring grasses, coastal prairie wildflowers, and shrubs; native wildflower and native grass seeds.

History/description: Josh Fodor studied botany and environmental studies at the Center for Agroecology at UC Santa Cruz, which led to a job managing an organic farm. Increasingly, his focus went wild—literally—and his attention shifted to a fascination with native vegetation. When asked to propagate grasses for a restoration project, he saw an opportunity to start a new pursuit. What started as a backyard nursery in 1992 is today part of Ecological Concerns, Inc., a complete ecological restoration services company comprising a design/grow/build landscaping endeavor, an ecological landscape restoration and management company, and a native plant nursery. Site-specific consultations for restoration projects remain an important part of the business.

Corralitos Gardens

296 Browns Valley Road, Corralitos 95076
295 Alitos Drive, Corralitos 95076 (mailing address)
(831) 596-0323
www.cgdahlias.com
Email: kevin@cgdahlias.com
Kevin Larkin, Karen Zydner
Retail and mail/online order
Open by appointment only.

Plant specialties: Dahlias, all grown on site.

History/description: Kevin Larkin and Karen Zydner started collecting and growing dahlias in 1985—first as a hobby and then for the cut-flower business. In 2000, they started producing plants for sale. Their collection today includes about 250 varieties, encompassing all sizes, from giant to miniature, and shapes, including stellar, tree, ball, pompom, open-centered, and more. Each year they add and subtract varieties from their collection as they develop new hybrids or as new plants come to their attention. The two-acre nursery has a display garden of labeled mother plants. The nursery custom produces cuttings for shipping, believing that cuttings have more reliable results than shipped tubers. Very active in the passionate world of dahlia collectors, Kevin is first vice president of the American Dahlia Society and Karen is the classification chair for the Pacific Southwest Dahlia Conference. They regularly judge and participate in Bay Area Dahlia Society shows, and several times, including in 2010, they have won the Derrill Hart Award for the top-scoring dahlia variety, as tested in American Dahlia Society–sanctioned trial gardens throughout the United States. The best time to visit to see the display gardens in full bloom is July through October.

Drought Resistant Nursery

850 Park Avenue, Monterey 93940 (retail)
(831) 375-2120
7421 Cypress Lane, Carmel Valley 93923 (wholesale)
(831) 624-6226
10 Scarlett Road, Carmel Valley 93924 (wholesale)
www.droughtresistant.com
Email: tcrow@droughtresistant.com
Thom Crow
Retail, wholesale, and contract growing
Retail open Monday through Saturday, 8 a.m.–4:30 p.m.
    Wholesale open Monday through Friday, 8 a.m.–4 p.m.

Plant specialties: Plants for coastal gardens, especially drought-tolerant, Mediterranean (special collections of *Lavandula, Cistus*), Australian, South African, and California native plants, including *Ceanothus* (16 varieties) and *Arctostaphylos* (8 varieties)—as well as vines, succulents, and trees in sizes up to 24-inch box.

History/description: Thom Crow had five acres of family property with water on flatland in the Carmel Valley—conditions ripe for a nursery, which he opened as a wholesale business in 1987. He bought the Monterey location in 1996 and continued to run it as a retail nursery. He propagates and grows nursery stock in Carmel Valley, both on the old family property and at a newer location on Scarlett Road. The nursery has good connections with local botanical gardens, plant lovers, and hobbyists, who provide a steady stream of unusual plants to propagate. Thom is currently expanding his collection of succulents, realizing the need to adapt to California's water realities.

Ecoscape

424 National Street, Santa Cruz 95060
(831) 566-0185
www.ecotree.net

Email: spiralaloe@yahoo.com
Alan and Joan Beverly
Retail, wholesale, and mail order
Open by appointment only.

Plant specialties: The succulent *Aloe polyphylla* and other aloes for landscapes of Northern California.

History/description: When Alan Beverly was a Peace Corps volunteer in Lesotho, South Africa, from 1974 to 1977, he discovered a wild population of the spectacularly sculptural *Aloe polyphylla* and gathered some seed. This plant proved exceptionally slow to flower and hence to propagate. He had to wait 18 years before he was able to introduce it at a Cactus and Succulent Society gathering in Pasadena. Since then, he has perfected his propagation technique to keep up with the demand for this unusual plant. Now a landscape contractor, Alan operates this backyard nursery with his wife, Joan.

Elkhorn Native Plant Nursery

1957B Highway 1, north of Moss Landing
P. O. Box 270, Moss Landing 95039
(831) 763-1207
Robert Stephens; Rob de Bree, manager
www.elkhornnursery.com
Email: enpn@elkhornnursery.com
Retail and wholesale
Wholesale open Monday through Friday by appointment.
    Retail open Fridays, 8 a.m.–4 p.m., or by appointment.

Plant specialties: California native plants suited to the Central Coast and coastal ranges, including native grasses, riparian plants, and succulents.

History/description: The Packard family had been growing native grasses for use on their 1,100-acre Elkhorn Ranch on the edge of Elkhorn Slough for several years when they realized that there was a commercial demand for the seeds. In 1989, Mr. Packard started a native-seed business, which diversified in the early 1990s to include a five-acre nursery of plants for habitat restoration and landscape use. From Elkhorn's demonstration garden of bunchgrasses and native flowering plants, there are great views of oak woodlands and the nearby wetlands area of Elkhorn Slough National Estuarine Research Reserve, an important bird-watching site in the Pacific Flyway.

Four Winds Growers

887 Casserly Road, Watsonville 95076
(877) 449-4637
www.fourwindsgrowers.com
Email: cs@fourwindsgrowers.com
Don Dillon, Jr., and family
Wholesale only at site, mail/online order for retail customers
Wholesale open Monday through Friday, 8 a.m.–3 p.m.

Plant specialties: Edible ornamentals, specializing in dwarf and standard citrus; avocado, blueberry, caneberry, fig, grape, jujube, olive, persimmon, pomegranate, and multi-grafted deciduous fruit trees.

History/description: A true pioneer in the citrus business, Floyd Dillon realized the possibilities of grafting citrus scions on cultivar-specific dwarf rootstocks, thus creating a smaller tree with full-size fruit, much better suited for landscape use. Starting a nursery for this purpose in 1949 in Ventura County, he moved it to Fremont in 1954 to escape the citrus tristeza virus quarantine down south. The business has grown, as has the family, expanding into new growing grounds and new crops. Don Sr. started working with his father in 1952, taking over after Floyd's death in 1963. Don Jr. is in charge now. His sister, Mary Ellen Seeger, and her husband run the 15-acre grounds in Winters, and his son, Aaron, is developing a new facility in Watsonville. The Watsonville location, an old nursery site with many greenhouses, was recently acquired as a strategy to combat the northward-moving Asian citrus psyllid. First discovered in Florida in 2000, this insect has now spread to Mexico and Southern California, from San Diego to the Los Angeles Basin and now farther north. It is the bacteria transmitted by the psyllid that kill citrus trees. The fight against this disease is well under way. The survival solution for citrus growers may be to grow plants exclusively in greenhouses.

The Garden Company

2218 Mission Street, Santa Cruz 95060
(831) 429-8424
www.thegardenco.com
Email: thegardenco@aol.com
Charles and Maria Keutmann
Retail, with discounts for wholesale customers
Open Monday through Friday, 8:30 a.m.–6 p.m.;
   Saturday, 8:30 a.m.–5 p.m.; and Sunday, 9 a.m.–5 p.m.

Plant specialties: Plants with variegated or colored foliage; organic vegetables, fruit trees, unusual perennials, Japanese maples, succulents, grasses, palms, bamboo, South African and Australian natives, and California natives.

History/description: Despite having degrees in horticulture and landscape architecture, Charlie Keutmann started his professional life in the corporate business world. His wife, Maria, had been a hands-on gardener since childhood. In 1986, they moved to Santa Cruz, pursued their primary interest, and bought a neglected retail garden center. With their focus on exceptional plants, the nursery has grown and has been identified as a destination in a *Sunset* magazine article. The Garden Company is always on the lookout for new introductions. This effort is supported by the talents of longtime staff member Lance Reiners, respected plantsmith and propagator. Lance has been able to pursue his fascination with variegated and colored foliage by going on collecting excursions throughout California, the Pacific Northwest, the eastern United States, and Japan. He believes that variegation in plants, so respected by the samurai, is still underappreciated in this country.

Gold Rush Nursery

3625 North Main Street, Soquel 95073

(831) 359-9191
www.goldrushnursery.com
Email: info@goldrushnursery.com
Nicky Hughes
Retail and wholesale
Open by appointment only, Monday through Saturday, 8 a.m.–5 p.m.

Plant specialties: Mostly California native plants suited to the San Francisco and Monterey Bay areas, as well as Australian and South African perennials, succulents, ornamental grasses, and shrubs, emphasizing plants that are water wise and that attract butterflies, birds, and beneficial insects.

History/description: A reformed banker, Nicky Hughes opted out of finance during the recession of 1993. She rekindled her love of plants, sparked initially by her grandfather's gift of gardening tools for her third birthday. She returned to the University of London in her native England to obtain a degree in horticulture. While at school, she spent two summers as an intern with the National Park Service in the Golden Gate National Recreation Area, which strengthened her commitment to good land stewardship and her love of California. After teaching horticulture in England for a few years, she moved to Santa Cruz in 1998 and worked for several nurseries before starting her own in 2009. She focuses on plants that enhance local ecologies and grows them without chemical pesticides or fertilizers, even pulling her weeds by hand. Her plants are almost all propagated on her half-acre grounds and also can be found at the Glenn and Blossom Hill farmers' markets in San Jose.

Greenlee Nursery

Wholesale production grounds in Watsonville
(415) 468-1961
Website: greenleenursery.com
Email: sales@greenleenursery.com
John Greenlee
Wholesale

Though John Greenlee has moved north (see Greenlee and Associates entry in chapter 5), his wholesale growing grounds in Watsonville may be visited by appointment.

Meadowlark Nursery

824 Las Viboras Road, Hollister 95023
(831) 636-5912
www.meadowlarknsy.com
Email: meadowlark1@razzolink.com
Claire Steede-Butler
Wholesale
Open by appointment only.

Plant specialties: California native perennials, *Heuchera, Iris, Salvia,* cut-flower plants, and meadow/prairie grasses; drought-, heat-, and deer-tolerant and hardy perennials, especially those that attract beneficial insects and pollinators.

History/description: As a landscape contractor, Claire Steede-Butler was frustrated by the short supply of perennials for her drought-resistant gardens. She opened the Meadowlark Nursery in 1986 and moved it in 1989 to this beautiful valley in the southern extension of the Diablo Range because the climate there was relatively cooler than in surrounding areas. This picturesque five-acre property is home to her family, the nursery, her garden filled with old-fashioned roses and perennials, and her six Peruvian paso horses. Claire will custom grow for special projects and continues to build gardens in San Mateo, Santa Clara, San Benito, Santa Cruz, and Monterey counties.

Monterey Bay Nursery

748 San Miguel Canyon Road, Royal Oaks 95076
P. O. Box 1296, Watsonville 95077
(831) 724-6361
www.montereybaynursery.com
Email: sales@montereybaynursery.com
Luen Miller, Manuel Morales

Wholesale only
Open Monday through Friday, 8 a.m.–5 p.m.

Plant specialties: Perennials, Mediterranean-climate plants, California native plants, Australian plants, ferns, palms, and succulents. Approximately 1,500 varieties of plants are offered at any given time.

History/description: Monterey Bay was founded in 1986 by the late Joe Solomone near Aromas, California, on the site of his former S&S Nursery. Purchased in 1988 by Luen Miller and Manuel Morales, the operation was rapidly expanded and diversified. Luen and Manuel now produce their plants on three closely located facilities on about 60 acres in the Central Coast scrub. Monterey Bay Nursery continues to play a key role in expanding California's horticultural possibilities through its program of breeding, selecting, testing, and introducing new varieties. Though the operation is strictly wholesale, the plant descriptions in Monterey Bay's website catalog should be required reading for every gardener.

Native Revival Nursery

2600 Mar Vista Drive, Aptos 95003
(831) 684-1811
www.nativerevival.com
Email: nativerevival@sbcglobal.net
Erin O'Doherty
Retail, wholesale, and contract growing
Open Tuesday through Friday, 9 a.m.–5 p.m.,
    and Saturday, 10 a.m.–4 p.m.

Plant specialties: California native plants; deer-resistant and drought-, heat-, and salt-tolerant plants; ferns, perennials, and native grasses.

History/description: Trained in ornamental horticulture at Foothill College and by Yerba Buena Nursery, the O'Dohertys started the nursery in 1992 to help customers create landscapes that provide a seamless integration from the garden to the natural beauty of California. They collect much of their seed from the Santa Cruz Mountains and Mount Hamilton Range, believing that well-acclimatized plants are good garden choices both for their ease of maintenance and for the habitat they provide for wildlife.

Plant Horizons

37 McGinnis Street, Watsonville 95076
P. O. Box 57, Aromas 95004
(831) 726-2957
Barbara Solomone
Wholesale
Open by appointment only.

Plant specialties: *Clivia*.

History/description: Californians should know about and be thankful for longtime plant breeder Joe Solomone. He opened Prunedale Nursery in 1960, moving it in 1986 to Watsonville under the name S&S Nursery. Over time, he has introduced many plants into the trade, such as *Ceanothus* 'Snow Flurry' and *Grevillea* 'Aromas', which were propagated from imported plants and his own hybrids. In 1968, he discovered a *Clivia* seedling with a small, pale-yellow flower instead of the usual orange and spent several decades achieving a true yellow. Since *Clivia* seeds take about four years to flower from seed, *Clivia* hybridization is a sport only for the patient. Distribution rights for Joe Solomone's clivias were given to Monterey Bay Nursery when he sold the nursery to them in 1988.

Rana Creek Nursery

7480 Williams Ranch Road, Carmel 93923
(831) 659-2830
www.ranacreeknursery.com
Email: nursery@ranacreeknursery.com
Marta Kephart, nursery manager;
    Ivy Hunt, assistant nursery manager

Retail (limited), wholesale, and contract growing
Open Monday through Friday, 8 a.m.–3 p.m.

Plant specialties: California native plants; specially ordered drought-tolerant nonnative plants; organically grown grasses, grass alternatives, and site-specific restoration plants; succulents for living roofs; fruit trees; and hummingbird and butterfly plants.

History/description: Esteemed ecologist Paul Kephart, who was instrumental in setting up Elkhorn Native Plant Nursery, applied his years of accumulated knowledge here. Plants are grown on this beautiful five-acre property in the Carmel Valley from wild-collected seed and from cuttings, seeds, and plants from botanical gardens. The nursery is part of a full-service habitat restoration company. Paul's "green roof" design expertise is best viewed atop the California Academy of Sciences building in San Francisco.

Redwood Nursery

2800 El Rancho Drive, Santa Cruz 95060
(831) 438-2844
www.redwoodnursery.biz
Email: flora@redwoodnursery.biz
Flora Schweizer
Retail and wholesale
Open every day, 9 a.m.–7 p.m. (winter close at dusk).

Plant specialties: Plants suited to inland coastal mountain areas; California native plants, including *Vaccinium ovatum, Sambucus,* and *Torreya californica;* trees, especially conifers; and shrubs, perennials, and bonsai starters.

History/description: Flora Schweizer's parents moved to this pretty hillside property in the coastal forest in 1959. Enamored with the native vegetation and wanting to be able to stay at home with her children, Flora's mother began propagating from her woodland and creekside backyard. The one-acre nursery now occupies about one-third of their homesite, where mother and daughter still live and collect cuttings and seed and grow their plants.

Roses of Yesterday and Today

803 Browns Valley Road, Watsonville 95076
(831) 728-1901
www.rosesofyesterday.com
Email: postmaster@rosesofyesterday.com
Andy, Jack, and Guinivere Wiley
Retail and mail/online order
Open every day, 9 a.m.–4 p.m.,
    with plants sold on the "honor system."

Plant specialties: Old roses and selected unusual, rare, and modern rose varieties.

History/description: Frances E. Lester left the orange-shipping business in Riverside and moved north in the 1930s. An esteemed authority on old roses, he began his collection here with cuttings from old Mission gardens. Eventually he opened Lester Rose Gardens. Needing some help, he called on a Riverside friend and colleague, Will Tillotson, who continued and expanded Lester's collection of old roses, now known as Tillotson's Roses, from 1948 to 1957. When Will needed assistance, he summoned an old friend, also from Riverside, named Dorothy Stemler, whom he dubbed his "honorable secretary." Dorothy stewarded the business from 1958 to 1976. Dorothy's daughter and her husband, Patricia and Newton Wiley, introduced the name Roses of Yesterday and Today and ran things until their retirement in 1997. The next generation is in charge now, each working several jobs to keep the family business on track. Recently, the Wileys have contracted with a grower to start propagating old-root roses directly from their garden specimens, thus perpetuating the collections of old rose pioneers Lester, Tillotson, and Stemler. The two-level garden in a coastal mountain canyon surrounded by redwoods and ferns includes a "walk though rose history." There is an annual open house on Mother's Day.

Santa Cruz Olive Tree Nursery

P. O. Box 311, Watsonville 95077
(831) 728-4269
www.santacruzolive.com
Email: mail@santacruzolive.com
Bruce Golino
Wholesale
Open by appointment only.

Plant specialties: Olive trees, specializing in Arbosana, Arbequina, and Koroneiki varieties for high-density cultivation, in 3-inch pots, as well as olive varieties from Italy, Spain, France, Greece, the United States, and North Africa (up to 2-gallon sizes).

History/description: Bruce Golino started importing and testing European olive varieties to determine the optimal selection for California soils and climates in 1994, one of the first people to do so in the state. He opened the nursery in 1999 to supply growers for the state's rapidly increasing olive oil production. The nursery includes an expanse of mother stock plants and 16 greenhouses for cuttings. Check the website for minimum orders.

Sierra Azul Nursery (retail)
Rosendale Nursery (wholesale)

2660 East Lake Avenue, Watsonville 95076
(831) 728-2532
www.sierraazul.com
Email: sierraazulnursery@yahoo.com
Jeff and Lisa Rosendale
Retail and wholesale
Retail open every day, 9 a.m.–5:30 p.m. (winter close at 4:30 p.m.).
    Wholesale open Tuesday through Friday, 8:30 a.m.–4:30 p.m.

Plant specialties: Plants for California's Mediterranean climate—California native, Australian, and South African plants; perennials; and drought-tolerant plants, including large collections of *Protea* and *Grevillea*.

History/description: In 1989, the Rosendales had the opportunity to buy an existing nursery business after having been involved professionally with plants for 15 years. Their six-acre site, located at the base of the coastal foothills east of Pajaro Valley near Hecker Pass, has a temperate, coastal climate conducive to growing a great variety of plant material. The two-acre gardens at Sierra Azul demonstrate the myriad possibilities of year-round gardening in California and include a sculpture garden. Generous of spirit and knowledge, Jeff and Lisa have been helpful to many horticultural organizations. Their wholesale business, Rosendale Nursery, operates on four neighboring acres.

Soquel Nursery Growers

3645 North Main Street, Soquel 95073
(800) 552-0802, (831) 475-3533
www.soquelnursery.com
Email: info@soquelnursery.com
Curtis Ferris, manager
Wholesale only; landscapers welcome
Open Monday through Friday, 8 a.m.–4:30 p.m.

Plant specialties: Perennials, California native plants for the coastal area, and ornamental grasses; heat-, shade-, and drought-tolerant plants; shrubs; ferns and rock garden plants.

History/description: Soquel Nursery Growers started life as a bedding-plant nursery in Mountain View called the Flower Garden. A group of five businessmen bought it and moved it to Soquel in the late 1960s, changing its name and some of the partners in the early 1980s. It has grown into a sizable (14-acre) institution noted for its interesting plant selection propagated from a wide variety of sources, including botanical gardens and home gardeners. The nursery occupies a beautiful site along Soquel Creek near Santa Cruz.

Succulent Gardens

2133 Elkhorn Road, Castroville 95012

(831) 632-0482
www.sgplants.com
Email: info@sgplants.com
Megan and John Rodkin
Retail, wholesale, and mail/online order
Open Monday through Saturday, 8 a.m.–4 p.m.,
    and Sunday, 9 a.m.–4 p.m.

Plant specialties: Succulents (700 varieties), especially *Aeonium* and *Echeveria*, and some cactus.

History/description: Succulent Gardens was founded by Robin Stockwell, who has been working with succulent plants since 1972. Active in the nursery industry as a grower and retailer, Robin has collaborated with other retailers, growers, and landscape professionals for over 40 years. In 2014, Robin sold the nursery to John and Megan Rodkin, and together with Robin, they are working to grow the nursery and further expand the appeal of these beautiful and amazing plants. Succulent Gardens covers over three acres, with plants displayed in greenhouses and outside in intricately designed gardens and container plantings. Sizes range from small 2-inch containers to large specimens. In addition to landscape/garden-sized materials, the nursery also offers succulent wreaths, living pictures, and templates for vertical gardening.

Suncrest Nurseries, Inc.

400 Casserly Road, Watsonville 95076
(800) 949-5064, (831) 728-2595
www.suncrestnurseries.com
Email: postmaster@suncrestnurseries.com
Christine Jennifer, executive director;
    Delmar McComb, director of horticulture
Wholesale only
Open Monday through Friday, 8 a.m.–4:30 p.m.

Plant specialties: Plants from all five Mediterranean-climate zones, California native plants (including a large *Arctostaphylos* collection), perennials, bamboo (80 varieties), vines, ferns, ornamental grasses, shrubs, and some trees. About 3,000 plant varieties in stock.

History/description: Although Suncrest started in 1989, it is a synthesis of revered California horticultural enterprises. Located on the site of the former Leonard Coates Nursery (established in 1878), Suncrest combines the historical expertise of this institution with the enviable stock of the former Wintergreen Nursery, established by Nevin Smith, which Suncrest bought in 1991. The nursery continues to experiment and introduce exciting plants from a wide variety of sources. Located on prime agricultural land with views of the Santa Cruz Mountains, it is one of the biggest concerns in this area, with a solid 60 acres covered with landscape plants.

Sunset Coast Nursery

2745 Tierra Way, Aromas 95004
(831) 726-1672
Email: sunsetcoast@razzolink.com
Patti Kreiberg
Retail, wholesale, and contract growing
Open by appointment only.

Plant specialties: California native plants suited to the coastal dunes and five other coastal habitats and salt-marsh revegetation plants. Sunset's collections are growing to include species suited to bluff, prairie, and oak woodland areas. Good collections of *Abronia, Arctostaphylos, Eriogonum, Eriophyllum, Lupinus,* and many others. Limited quantities of *Castilleja latifolia* (Monterey paintbrush).

History/description: Trained as a biologist, Patti Kreiberg was a home gardener with an enviable crop of winter flowers and vegetables. Her hobby got serious when she learned from a friend about the lack of native plant material available for revegetation projects under way to repair the coastline damaged by winter storms in 1983. Now Mother Nature's best friend, Patti also does habitat restoration for vertebrate and invertebrate animals' use. Note: after 32 years in the business, Patti is thinking of retiring, so email may be a better way to contact her than phone.

Terra Sole Nurseries

240 Pioneer View Road, Corralitos 95076
(831) 240-5737
www.terrasolenurseries.com
Email: terrasole@charter.net
Sherry and John Hall
Retail
Open by appointment only.

Plant specialties: Drought-tolerant ornamentals, California native plants, succulents, and other interesting perennials and shrubs.

History/description: Sherry Hall is a plantaholic—or, as she describes it, a plant-a-*Hall*-ic. She had been propagating and growing plants for many years as a hobby. Then, when John retired and they found this perfect piece of land in 2003, the hobby became a business. Sherry and John propagate over 90 percent of their plants and are always on the lookout for what is new. They preach and practice low-impact gardening, handpicking snails and encouraging birdlife to deter predator insects. On-site test gardens experiment with just how little water certain plants need.

Tiedemann Nursery

4707 Cherryvale Avenue, Soquel 95073
(831) 475-5163
www.tiedemannllc.com
Email: info@tiedemannllc.com
Jon Beard
Wholesale
Open Monday through Friday, 7:30 a.m.–4 p.m.

Plant specialties: Perennials (1,000 varieties), California native plants (50 varieties, including large *Ceanothus* and

Romneya collections); tree fuchsias, cyclamens (grown outdoors), poinsettias, pelargoniums, and hellebores.

History/description: Jon Beard, manager of Tiedemann Nursery since 1980, bought the nursery in 1999. Previously, Tiedemann Nursery had taken over the lease of the old Nix Nursery, and it continues to propagate Nix's varieties of *Fuchsia, Poinsettia,* and *Pelargonium,* especially *P. domesticum,* the 'Martha Washington' geranium. The nursery also focuses on water-wise perennials and natives.

Notable Garden Centers

Dig Gardens

420 Water Street, Santa Cruz 95060
(831) 466-3444
www.diggardensnursery.com

Opened in 2009 by Will and Cara Meyers (also the owners of Hidden Garden Nursery, below), Dig Gardens specializes in succulents, exotic bromeliads (many of which are artistically displayed in pots or mounted), and show-worthy orchids. It also sells drought-tolerant plants, large specimen trees, and living wall systems. Open Monday through Saturday, 10 a.m.– 6 p.m., and Sunday, 10 a.m.–5 p.m.

Far West Nursery

2669 Mattison Lane, Santa Cruz 95062
(831) 476-8866
www.farwestnursery.com

Two acres of plants contain a huge variety of garden favorites and specialty finds, offered by Harry Petrekus since 1973.

Hidden Gardens Nursery

7765 Soquel Drive, Aptos 95003
(831) 688-7011

www.aptoshiddengardens.com

Cabrillo College horticulture graduates Will and Cara Meyers jumped at the chance to start their own nursery when Hidden Gardens came up for sale in 2005. A full-service nursery, Hidden Gardens has a good selection of fruit trees, shade plants, edible starts, and shrubs. A promoter of backyard chicken keeping, the nursery also sells baby chicks.

El Paraiso Nursery

215 Hecker Pass Road, Watsonville 95076
(831) 840-0885
www.theemonosonico.wixsite.com

Five acres of a wide variety of water-conserving landscape plants, including vegetables, herbs, ornamental grasses, trees, and shrubs, are for sale at El Paraiso Nursery, cared for by the family of Margarito Silva since 2010.

San Lorenzo Garden Center

235 River Street, Santa Cruz 95060
(831) 423-0223
www.sanlorenzogardencenter.com

Part of Santa Cruz Lumber and Home Centers, which itself is part of the large ProBuild, the San Lorenzo Garden Center was started in 1973. The proprietors buy in rare and unusual plants from California growers, especially California native plants, Japanese maples, rhododendrons, succulents, and tropical plants.

Horticultural Attractions

Cabrillo College Environmental Horticulture Center and Botanic Gardens

6500 Soquel Drive, Aptos 95003

(831) 479-6241
www.cabrillo.edu/academics/horticulture/

Cabrillo College's exceptional Environmental Horticulture Department built an Environmental Horticulture Center in 2003 to complement its research and instruction. Botanic gardens surrounding the center and the nursery include a native garden, riparian pond, and salvia garden. Cabrillo has introduced several *Salvia* cultivars, including S. 'Cabrillo Sunrise', S. 'Cabrillo Sunset', and S. 'Katheena'. A huge annual Mother's Day weekend sale features perennials, especially salvias, California native plants, succulents, and vegetables, all suited to the coastal climate. There is a student-run organic farm on the premises. Gardens are open Monday through Saturday, 7 a.m.–dark, during the school year.

Lester Rowntree Native Plant Garden

25800 Hatton Road, Carmel 93921
(831) 624-3543
www.flandersfoundation.org

This one-acre hillside native plant garden honors naturalist, botanist, and writer Lester Rowntree. Born in England and raised in the United States, Mrs. Rowntree arrived in 1920 in Carmel, which served as her home base for 50+ years of native plant exploration and cultivation. She was an inspiration to many through her prolific writings. The garden is next door to Flander's Mansion, part of Mission Trail Park.

UC Santa Cruz Arboretum

1156 High Street, Santa Cruz 95064
(831) 427-2998
www.arboretum.ucsc.edu

UC Santa Cruz Arboretum specializes in drought-tolerant plants from the Southern Hemisphere and has extensive collections of Australian, New Zealand, and South African proteas. The 50-acre arboretum also has special collections of California native plants, conifers, primitive flowering plants, and rare fruit, as well as a eucalyptus grove and an aroma garden. A research and teaching facility, the arboretum is a poster child for the important role arboretums and botanic gardens play in plant introductions. The arboretum, in partnership with several wholesale growers, launched Koala Blooms, a program that imports, tests, and distributes Australian natives into the retail nursery trade. The arboretum also hybridizes certain plants from its collection to create new plant introductions, such as *Correa* 'Ray's Tangerine', *C.* 'Dawn in Santa Cruz', and *C.* 'Sister Dawn'. Major plant sales occur in April and October. The nonprofit Arboretum Associates (831/423-4977) operates Norrie's Plant and Gift Shop (open every day, 10 a.m.–4 p.m.), organizes lectures and classes, and raises money to support the arboretum. The arboretum is open every day, 9 a.m.–5 p.m., and there is an admission fee. The Jean and Bill Lane Horticultural Library is open Wednesday through Sunday, 12 p.m.–3 p.m.

UC Santa Cruz Center for Agroecology and Sustainable Food Systems

1156 High Street, Santa Cruz 95064
(831) 459-3240
www.casfs.ucsc.edu

This research and education center, dedicated to increasing ecological sustainability and social justice in agriculture, manages a 25-acre farm and the 2-acre Alan Chadwick Garden. It also offers a six-month apprenticeship program in ecological horticulture and bio-intensive gardening methods. Organically grown plants are available at the spring and fall plant sales. A membership group, Friends of the Farm and Garden, hosts events and tours, puts on a harvest festival, and publishes the biannual *Cultivar*.

Mediterranean Climate

Mediterranean climates occur on only 2 percent of the earth's landmass, in five regions: southwestern Australia, California, central Chile, the Mediterranean Basin, and the southwestern tip of Africa. All lie on the western or southwestern coasts of their continents, where ocean currents temper climate.

Summers in Mediterranean-climate regions are hot and dry, with bright sunlight and rainfall occurring primarily during mild winters. Temperatures and rainfall vary depending on the region; some have longer summers, or cooler winters, or more or less rainfall. From 10 to 40 inches of rain falls annually, with 80 percent falling during the cooler winter months; while frost can form, snow rarely falls except at high elevations. Mean summer temperatures range from 72°F to 81°F; winter means are 41°F to 50°F.

The gardener faces both opportunities and challenges in a Mediterranean climate. The garden year starts in fall, as early rains and cooler temperatures wake plants from their summer dormancy. Winter rains can be enough to succor plants through the rest of the year if the plants are adapted to the summer dry–winter wet cycle. Days of rain alternate with clear skies in winter, but winter storms can be torrential. As the rains cease in spring, warm temperatures come and native plants finish flowering, set seed, and complete their growth cycle; they rest through the dry summer.

Climate-adapted plants ease the need for summer irrigation, lessening and even offsetting the pressures of drought. But strong summer heat, bright sunlight, and lack of rain can stress plants that are from regions of the world receiving plenty of summer rain; this means more water for the garden and more work for the gardener. Strong winter winds, erosion from torrential rains, and fire during the dry season are other challenges of the Mediterranean climate, though coastal regions benefit from cooling summer fog and moist air, thus reducing the impact of the annual summer dry season.

For year-round interest in this climate, plant evergreen trees and shrubs to frame the garden, provide shade, and buffer winds. Use plants with low water needs and surround them with mulch to retain moisture.

Calochortus venustus

Chapter 6

Central Coast

Counties: San Luis Obispo, Santa Barbara, Ventura
Elevational range: Sea level to 6,820 feet in the Big Pine Mountain
(Santa Barbara County); 8,831 feet at Mount Pinos (Ventura County)
Sunset climate zones: 2A, 3A, 7, 14, 15, 16, 17, 18, 20, 21
22, 23, 24
Annual rainfall: San Luis Obispo, 15.35 inches; Santa Barbara,
18.56 inches; and Ventura, 15.35 inches
Winter temperatures: Lows average 48°F to 43°F; extreme lows
34°F to 27°F. Gray pine belt temperatures dip to 16°F; snowy cold
mountain and intermountain area lows drop to between −20°F
and −30°F.
Summer temperatures: Average highs range from 72°F to 77°F.

South of Monterey and San Benito counties down to Oxnard stretch three remaining Central Coast counties. They boast warmer coastal temperatures than their northern counterparts, but rugged coastline, mountain ranges, foothills, and interior valleys likewise make up the terrain. Moist air and fertile soil give farmers and nursery people favorable conditions for crops.

As elsewhere along the coast, regional climate varies with proximity to the ocean. Hot, dry Santa Ana winds blow in summer and fall. San Luis Obispo—the northernmost of these counties, lying midway on the coast between San Francisco and Los Angeles—has pockets of chilly winters in interior valleys. Thermal belts in western Santa Barbara and Ventura counties and along south-facing coastal foothills give subtropical plants stretches to grow free of summer heat or winter cold. Avocados thrive where there is little frost, although cold winters can at times descend. Pears and other fruit trees with higher chill needs are hard to grow here.

Inland lie gray pine zone belts with mild, albeit more pronounced sharp winters and hot summers. Plants craving good winter chill, such as bulbs, deciduous fruit trees, and ornamental flowering cherries, thrive here.

While small beach towns like Cambria, Morro Bay, Avila Beach, and Pismo Beach stud the coast, San Luis Obispo County remains predominantly rural, with an emphasis on wine grapes. Displacing Chumash Indians, early Spanish settlers venerated the rich farmland of Santa Barbara county, calling it *la tierra adorada,* meaning "chosen land." Farmers raise Chardonnay and Pinot noir grapes, as well newer Syrah and Viognier varietals. Around Santa Barbara, pockets of mild mountain climates offer long summers, with five to six months of frost-free growing. Vegetables needing long periods of heat grow heartily, as do fruit trees needing winter chill. This region offers 100 to 150 growing days annually.

In contrast to moist, fertile coastal areas, Cuyama Valley, known for its dry, sparsely populated land, covers the county's eastern edge. Despite harsher natural conditions, farming and cattle ranching prosper, as does oil production.

The Central Coast region offers ideal climates not only for cultivated plants that numerous nurseries stock but also for native flora. Included among natives are bigleaf maple (*Acer macrophyllum*), madrone (*Arbutus menziesii*), chamise (*Adenostoma fasciculatum*), crimson columbine (*Aquilegia formosa*), and Parry's larkspur (*Delphinium parryi* ssp. *parryi*) in forested foothills and mountains. White globe lily (*Calochortus albus* var. *albus*) grows in canyons and wooded slopes and mariposa

lily (*Calochortus venustus*) in sandy soil in grassland and moist valley areas, near the coast. Its botanical name comes from the Greek words *kalos,* for "beautiful," and *chortus,* for "grass," which this wildflower resembles, with its spare, narrow leaf blades. The chalice-shaped blooms of mariposa lily, named after the Spanish word for "butterfly," emerge in late spring to early summer, and the colors of this variable species range from white to purple, red, brown, or yellow. Often reddish blotches mark its silky, evanescent petals, as eyespots do a butterfly.

Specialty Nurseries and Growers

Robert Abe Nursery

5649 Cassitas Pass Road, Carpinteria 93013
(805) 705-4061
Robert Abe
Email: rd.abe@verizon.net
Wholesale and contract growing
Wholesale open Monday through Friday, 8 a.m.–4 p.m.
    Best to call first.

Plant specialties: Ornamental grasses and grass-like material, such as *Carex, Lomandras,* and *Dianella,* with a focus on California native grasses, in plugs and 4-inch and 1-gallon sizes.

History/description: Robert Abe's lifelong involvement with nurseries has made him an irrepressible collector of plants. After graduating with a degree in horticulture from Cal Poly San Luis Obispo, he worked at his father's nursery for 10 years. In 1992, he bought a neighboring nursery from Daryll Combs, which he renamed Chia Nursery, and expanded its collection of plant exotica. Over time and in a new location, Robert has downsized and simplified, now specializing in smaller grasses, well suited for water-wise gardens, and lawn substitutes.

Aloes in Wonderland

114 Conejo Road, Santa Barbara 93103
(805) 965-0895
www.aloesinwonderland.com
Email: jeff@aloesinwonderland.com
Jeff Chemnick
Retail and wholesale
Open by appointment only.

Plant specialties: Cycads (150 taxa and hybrids); aloes (over 100); and other xerophitic plants, such as agaves, bromeliads, crassulas, palms, cacti, and yuccas, including rare species of *Dioon* and *Encephalartos,* as well as some remarkable hybrids.

History/description: During his collegiate studies in botany, Jeff Chemnick became fascinated with cycads, the prehistoric, cone-bearing gymnosperms that were a favorite food of the dinosaurs. Starting out as a research associate at Lotusland, Jeff began growing and selling cycads in 1976 and is now a recognized authority on Mexican cycads and a stalwart of the Santa Barbara horticultural community. He has traveled all over the world to observe cycads and other botanical wonders in habitat and is a staunch supporter of CITES (the Convention on International Trade in Endangered Species of Wild Fauna and Flora), the law protecting wild plant habitat. Located at the top of a five-acre residential site, the nursery looks out over the ocean and a hillside garden of cycads, aloes, and other plants, brilliant in late-winter bloom. Jeff also leads botanical ecotours to Mexico (www.mexiconaturetours.com).

Australian Native Plants Nursery

Nye Road, Casitas Springs (between Ventura and Ojai)
9040 North Ventura Avenue, Ventura 93001 (mailing address)
(805) 649-3362, (800) 701-6517
www.australianplants.com
Email: jo@australianplants.com
Jo O'Connell, Byron Cox
Retail, wholesale, and online order

Open most weekdays and Saturdays, by appointment only.
Call first, as owners are not always there.

Plant specialties: Australian and South African plants, including *Banksia* (70 species), *Leucadendron* (30 species), *Grevillea* (65 species), *Acacia* (50 species), *Hakea* (46 species), and a variety of other plants.

History/description: Jo O'Connell is an Australian horticulturist who came to Ojai in 1989 to design the Australian garden at the Center for Earth Concerns (see Taft Gardens entry in this chapter). She returned to Australia but came back to California on holiday in 1992. As one would expect in this land of milk and honey, she soon found both a landscape design business and a husband. Realizing that there was an inadequate supply of plants to specify for her clients, she opened this nursery in 1994 in a lovely, small rural town a few miles north of Ventura.

Berylwood Tree Farm

1048 East La Loma Avenue, Somis 93066
(805) 485-7601
www.berylwoodtreefarm.com
Email: sales@berylwoodtreefarm.com
Victoria Culver, general manager
Wholesale
Wholesale open Monday through Friday, 8 a.m.–4 p.m.,
    by appointment only.

Plant specialties: Trees, especially large, field-grown specimens, including many species of *Quercus* (oak), *Camellia,* and *Magnolia;* bonsai for landscape use; and espaliered vines.

History/description: Founded in 1969 by the late Rolla J. White, horticulturist and the 836th registered landscape architect in California, Berylwood Tree Farm endures as his legacy, along with his signature design projects, such as the Annenberg Estate and Levi Plaza in San Francisco. This amazing 25-acre arboretum-like nursery originated from the need to supply his designed landscapes with quality large trees. Several of Berylwood's towering specimens are included on the California Registry of Big Trees (www.californiabigtrees.calpoly .edu), such as the current champion, *Beaucarnea recurvata.*

California Bonsai Studio

4015 North Moorpark Road, Thousand Oaks 91362
(805) 832-7114
www.californiabonsai.com
Email: contact@californiabonsai.com
Travis Goldstein
Retail and mail/online order
Open Saturday, 10 a.m.–4 p.m., or by appointment.

Plant specialties: Developed bonsai trees, pre-bonsai stock, bonsai gardens, and bonsai pots, soil, and tools.

History description: Travis Goldstein has been enamored with bonsai ever since he persuaded his parents to buy him a bonsai tree at K-Mart in 1989. A collector since then, his studies began in earnest in 2000 following a trip to Japan. He has taken lessons from Japanese bonsai master Masura Ishii and his son Gary in California, has visited bonsai masters such as Kunio Kobayashi and Takahito Hanazawa in Japan, and continues to pursue his study of the Japanese style of bonsai. The nursery opened on this two-acre site in 2008.

Cal-Orchid, Inc.

1251 Orchid Drive, Santa Barbara 93111
(805) 967-1312
www.calorchid.com
Email: calorchid@cox.net
James and Lauris Rose
Retail, wholesale, and mail/online order
Open Monday through Saturday, 9 a.m.–4 p.m.

Plant specialties: Orchids (150 genera), particularly those suitable for outdoor West Coast gardens (cold-hardy to 27 °F), including a new line of reed-stem *Epidendrum* and *Cymbidium* hybrids.

History/description: James and Lauris Rose began their orchid careers as coworkers at a local Santa Barbara nursery in the early 1970s. In 1987, they purchased the nursery across the street from where they had been employed and started Cal-Orchid, Inc. They offer decades of experience in orchid hybridizing, having had particular success with *Lycastes*, their "Pacific line" of reed-stem *Epidendrums*, *Neofinetia falcata*, African species, and a wide variety of *Cattleyas*. This two-acre nursery reflects the personal interests they have developed from years of extensive, international travel.

Daylily West

2420 Green Place, Arroyo Grande 93420
(805) 481-5344
www.daylilywest.com
Email: daylily@daylilywest.com
Penny and Phil Ben
Retail and mail/online order
Open during bloom season, about mid-May to Labor Day.
    Email for an appointment.

Plant specialties: 250 varieties of *Hemerocallis* (daylilies).

History/description: In 1995, when Penny and Phil Ben bought this 10-acre property in the coastal dunes near Pismo Beach and built their house, a friend gave them a couple of daylilies, which Penny flung on a dirt pile out back. Very busy as a mother, she occasionally sprinkled water on them but never got around to planting them. Her awe at their eventual blooming led her to look into this tough little plant that seemed to take care of itself. Today, her half-acre field of daylilies is an official American Hemerocallis Society display garden. Husband Phil joined in after his retirement from working in county government in 2003. The Bens are always on the lookout for varieties that thrive in California and are evergreen and repeat bloomers. Once established, daylilies are wonderfully drought tolerant.

Foxtail Farms

Nipomo (growing grounds)
(619) 669-7242 (wholesale); (619) 807-5242 (retail inquiries)
www.foxtailfarms.com
Email: russmcmillan@mac.com
Russ McMillan
Wholesale
Open by appointment only.
    Address given when appointment is made.

Plant specialties: *Phormium* (25 varieties).

History/description: About 15 years ago, retired fire captain Russ McMillan decided to start a second career growing foxtail palms, having always enjoyed "getting his hands dirty." The switch to phormiums came about when a landscaper friend mentioned the high demand for them in his business. Acquiring mother stock of this New Zealand plant took time, since the mortality rate of shipped plants was high and tissue culture produced varieties that would often revert. But he was clearly successful, and he now has 20,000 plants on hand. Since his move from Ventura to Nipomo in 2014, his business model has changed, and now Foxtail Farms mostly sells large quantities to outlets in the Northwest and Vancouver.

Gallup & Stribling Orchids

3450 Via Real, Carpinteria 93013
(805) 684-1998
www.gallup-stribling.com
Email: sales@gallup-stribling.com
The Stribling family
Retail and wholesale
Open every day, 8:30 a.m.–5 p.m.

Plant specialties: *Cymbidium* and other varieties of orchids.

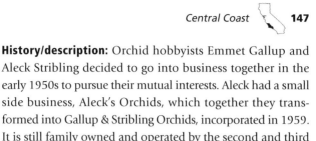

History/description: Orchid hobbyists Emmet Gallup and Aleck Stribling decided to go into business together in the early 1950s to pursue their mutual interests. Aleck had a small side business, Aleck's Orchids, which together they transformed into Gallup & Stribling Orchids, incorporated in 1959. It is still family owned and operated by the second and third generation of Striblings, and the fourth generation is well in production; six Striblings currently work here, a testimonial to family solidarity. Today, Gallup & Stribling is the largest cymbidium grower in North America, with 1.5 million square feet of greenhouse space on 45 acres in production. Bloom time (October to May) is a sight worth seeing. Their laboratories develop new varieties each year and clone the very best.

Greenwood Daylily Gardens, Inc.

8000 Balcom Canyon Road, Somis 93066
(562) 494-8944
www.greenwoodgarden.com
Email: info@greenwoodgarden.com
Cynthia and John Schoustra
Retail, wholesale, and mail order
Open to the public April through June, Saturdays, 9:30 a.m.–4 p.m.; wholesale only at all other times.

Plant specialties: Daylilies (thousands of varieties), irises (tall bearded and heritage), clivias, cannas, roses, pelargoniums (500 varieties), and agapanthus. New varieties introduced include *Rosa* 'Incendio', *Pelargonium* 'Florence Bixby', *Agapanthus* 'Deja Sky Blue', and *Syringa* 'Snowy Beach Party'.

History/description: Landscape architect and contractor John Schoustra started a soil business and then this nursery when he discovered that no one was selling quality, named daylilies well suited to Southern California. The Schoustras bought their initial stock of daylilies from the Greenwood Nursery in Goleta when it switched its specialty to palms. Irises were added, with the purchase of several collections, as were pelargoniums more recently. The nursery now has widened its scope and is focused on "plants that perform like daylilies"— in other words, those that are showy, reliable, durable, and well adapted to the region. In 1998, the nursery moved to a 40-acre site on the old Rancho de las Flores, which includes a 1.5-acre display garden that is also used for weddings and filming. All plants are propagated on site.

Island View Nursery

3376 Foothill Road, Carpinteria 93013
(805) 684-1296, (805) 684-0324
www.islandviewnursery.com
Email: nacho@islandviewnursery.com
Win Overbach; Nacho Mendez, garden manager
Retail and wholesale
Retail open Monday through Saturday, 9 a.m.–5 p.m.,
    and Sunday, 10 a.m.–4 p.m.
    Wholesale open Monday through Friday, 7:30 a.m.–4 p.m.

Plant specialties: Succulents, bromeliads, tillandsias, and epiphytic orchids; some Mediterranean plants and palm trees; indoor plants.

History/description: In the 1970s, Win Overbach opened a wholesale nursery business in Los Angeles that he operated for 20 years. Moving north in 1992, he bought the existent Island View Nursery, named for its view of Anacapa Island, then moved it in 2002 to this 10-acre location, the site of the old Stewart's Orchids. The nursery, located a half mile from the coast, has a huge greenhouse area and artful displays.

Las Pilitas Nursery

3232 Las Pilitas Road, Santa Margarita 93453
(805) 438-5992
www.laspilitas.com
Email: penny@laspilitas.com
Celeste Wilson, Penny Nyunt
Retail, wholesale, and mail/online order

Open Friday and Saturday, 9 a.m.–4 p.m.;
   wholesale by appointment only.

Plant specialties: California native plants (500–1,000 species on hand at any one time). *Penstemon* 'Margarita BOP', *Salvia* 'Pozo Blue', and *Arctostaphylos* 'Mama Bear' were introduced by Bert Wilson at Las Pilitas.

History/description: Las Pilitas Nursery was founded in 1975 by the late Bert Wilson and his wife, Celeste. Bert was working his way through college at Cal Poly doing landscaping and couldn't find the native plants he needed for his projects. Celeste was getting a degree in biology, and starting a native plant nursery seemed like a good idea. Their daughter Penny Nyunt is now well involved. The once-solitary old farmhouse is now surrounded by three acres of shade houses, greenhouses, and open stock. Vintage oaks protect large demonstration plantings of dryland oak understory species. The nursery includes test gardens where plants are tested for drought tolerance, heat and cold tolerance, deer tolerance, and general usefulness. Son Ian designed Las Pilitas's highly informative website with plant photos and descriptions, enabling online plant sales. In 2000, the family opened another facility in Escondido (see chapter 8). In 2003, Bert developed an interactive software program that provides users with an appropriate plant palette based on their zip code, much used by landscapers today (mynativeplants.com).

Manzanita Nursery

880 Chalk Hill Road, Solvang 93463
(805) 688-9692
www.manzanitanursery.com
Email: manzanitanursery@earthlink.net
Diane and Ron Griffin
Retail and wholesale
Open Friday and Saturday, 9 a.m.–4 p.m.;
   otherwise by appointment.

Plant specialties: California native plants from the Central Coast area; some other Mediterranean-climate plants.

History/description: Always interested in nature, and with 13 acres of their own land in the coastal hills, Diane and Ron Griffin slowly and carefully developed this nursery. They took classes at the Santa Barbara Botanic Garden, started collecting and growing, and gradually gave up their day jobs. Now, 10 years later, most of their plants are sold wholesale for site renovations and mitigation work. The nursery occupies three of their acres and includes a small demonstration garden. All sales by cash or check only.

Matilija Nursery

8225 Waters Road, Moorpark 93021
P. O. Box 429, Moorpark 93021
(805) 523-8604
www.matilijanursery.com
Email: matilijanurseryweb@gmail.com
Robert Sussman
Retail, wholesale, and contract growing
Retail open Monday through Thursday, 8:30 a.m.–noon;
    Friday and Saturday, 8:30 a.m.–2 p.m.; or by appointment.

Plant specialties: California native plants, especially those suited to coastal, chaparral, and montane regions; large collections of *Arctostaphylos, Ceanothus* (40 varieties), *Rhamnus,* and *Rhus;* Pacific Coast iris, Louisiana iris, and reblooming tall-bearded iris.

History/description: Wanting to shed his coat and tie, former banker Robert Sussman decided that the nursery business offered the greatest opportunity for the least amount of capital, and the most rewards for personal initiative—to say nothing of the fact that he had been successfully growing natives for some time in Santa Monica. The Santa Barbara Botanic Garden and the California Native Plant Society encouraged his interest and supplied much of his early stock. In business since 1992, the nursery has developed a reputation for fine plant selection. Matilija bought the iris collection of the Iris Gallery in Fort Bragg and is a worldwide seed-bank connection for Pacific Coast native irises. Matilija is named for the Matilija poppy, *Romneya coulteri*.

Mesa Grande Wholesale Nursery

809 Guadalupe Road, Arroyo Grande 93420
(805) 863-3392
Enrique Martinez
Wholesale

Plant specialties: Proteas; landscape plants including phormiums, kangaroo paws, and grasses; and California natives.

History/description: Having worked in nursery growing fields, Enrique Martinez started this nursery in 2009, which he now operates with the help of his brother Gabriel. Almost two acres are covered with potted stock propagated by the brothers.

Native Sons Wholesale Nursery, Inc.

379 West El Campo Road, Arroyo Grande 93420
(805) 481-5996
www.nativeson.com
sales@nativeson.com
Dave Fross, Robert Keeffe
Wholesale
Open Monday through Friday, 7:30 a.m.–4:30 p.m.,
    and Saturday by appointment.

Plant specialties: California native plants especially suited to coastal areas, including *Arctostaphylos* 'Austin Griffiths' and *Ceanothus maritimus* 'Point Sierra', both introduced here; Australian plants, Mediterranean plants, drought-tolerant plants, perennials, ornamental grasses, herbs, ground covers, and rock-garden plants.

History/description: With a Master of Science in agriculture, Dave Fross and partner Bob Keeffe decided to open a wholesale nursery in 1979. Since Fross and Keeffe are both fourth-generation Californians, they were bound to have an inborn fascination with California native plants. Inspiration for the nursery's name came from their favorite Loggins and Messina song, "Native Sons." Today, the nursery covers nine acres of greenhouse and field production. The public may visit during the nursery's annual open house (usually held on a Saturday in April).

Rose Story Farm

Carpinteria 93013
(805) 566-4885
www.rosestoryfarm.com
Email: info@rosestoryfarm.com
Bill and Danielle Hahn
Retail (plants and cut flowers) and wholesale (cut flowers)
Retail open Monday through Saturday by appointment.

Plant specialties: 120 varieties of European and American modern roses, cut flowers, and potted plants.

History/description: Bill and Danielle Hahn's initial success in growing 1,000 varieties of roses on their lemon and avocado farm in 1998 evolved into this full-time family business. Now, 25,000 rose bushes carpet these flats and hillsides of the Carpinteria Valley. During the season, mid-April to the end of November, tours with luncheons are offered Thursday and Saturday by appointment. Both florists and growers, the Hahns provide floral arrangements as well as garden design services.

San Marcos Growers

125 South San Marcos Road, Santa Barbara 93111
P. O. Box 6827, Santa Barbara 93160
(805) 683-1561
www.smgrowers.com
Email: sales@smgrowers.com

Randy Baldwin, manager
Wholesale only
Open Monday through Friday, 7:30 a.m.–4:30 p.m.
   (winter close at 4 p.m.).

Plant specialties: More than 1,500 varieties of drought-tolerant plants, perennials, California native plants, Mediterranean plants, Australian plants, South African plants, bulbs, ferns, ornamental grasses, ground covers, succulents, vines, and trees.

History/description: Since 1979, San Marcos has been actively introducing water-conserving plants from Mediterranean areas around the world. The nursery seeks out plants that have horticultural merit and ornamental value and are appropriate to the microclimates of California. Much of the credit for the lush look now possible in drought-tolerant gardens belongs here. The nursery's 23 acres include two acres of cutting and demonstration gardens using grasses and Mediterranean-climate plants and 20 acres devoted to nursery production.

Santa Barbara Natives, Inc.

700 Venadito Canyon Road, Gaviota 93112
14900 Calle Real, Gaviota 93117 (mailing address)
(805) 698-4994 (Jeff); (805) 729-3855 (John)
www.sbnatives.com
Email: jeff@sbnatives.com
Jeff Nighman, John Warner
Retail, wholesale, and contract growing
Open Tuesday, Thursday, or Friday by appointment only.

Plant specialties: California native trees, shrubs, herbaceous plants, grasses, and grass-like plants, especially those genetically local to the Santa Barbara coast.

History/description: Jeff and John became reacquainted through their love of horticulture 30 years after they were in preschool together. During the intervening years, both acquired multiple degrees and pursued professional careers before landing in the Environmental Horticulture Department at Santa Barbara City College. John founded this all-organic nursery in 2003, joined by Jeff in 2006. Located 20 miles west of Santa Barbara in a coastal canyon, the nursery covers one acre but is surrounded by a 1,000-acre private ranch. Adjacent to the ranch is the Arroyo Hondo Preserve, where John and his wife are preserve managers. Jeff has a landscape business, Sustainable Landscapes of Santa Barbara. Most of the nursery's plants are grown for Santa Barbara County habitat restorations or revegetation projects. Both Jeff and John are community oriented and involved with several local organizations, through which they hope to spread their zeal about site-specific, indigenous native plants.

Santa Barbara Orchid Estate

1250 Orchid Drive, Santa Barbara 93111
(805) 967-1284
www.sborchid.com
Email: sboe@sborchid.com
Alice and Parry Gripp
Retail and mail order
Open Monday through Saturday, 8 a.m.–4:30 p.m.,
    and Sunday, 11 a.m.–4 p.m.

Plant specialties: A large collection of orchid species and hybrids, including cymbidiums and other outdoor orchids suited to the coastal California climate.

History/description: Santa Barbara Orchid Estate, founded in 1957, was bought in 1967 by the Gripp family from the original owner, for whom they worked. The nursery caters to the whole spectrum of orchid fanciers, from beginning growers to the most discriminating hobbyists to landscapers. Visitors enjoy walking around almost one acre of growing grounds with a small demonstration garden. The Gripps alert readers to the Santa Barbara International Orchid Show, the West Coast's oldest orchid show, held every spring at Earl Warren Showgrounds (www.sborchidshow.com).

Notable Garden Centers

Sage Ecological Landscapes and Nursery

1188 Los Osos Valley Road, Los Osos 93402
(805) 574-0777
www.sagelandscapes.net

In 2008, Todd Davidson bought an established (from 1961) nursery here to combine with his landscape, design, and maintenance business. Offering "California-friendly" plants, the one-acre site is divided into display gardens featuring the five Mediterranean-climate areas of the world, with each garden having a sales area of those plants nearby. There is also an edible garden and greenhouses full of succulents and indoor plants. Open Monday through Saturday, 9 a.m.–5 p.m., and Sunday, 9 a.m.–4 p.m.

Seaside Gardens

3700 Via Real, Carpinteria 93013
(805) 684-6001
www.seaside-gardens.com

Linda Wudl invested her pension in her passion for plants, buying this property in 2001 so that she could develop a botanical garden on three acres of the land. Each of the 11 themed gardens, designed by a different designer, highlights design and planting ideas. Visitors may stroll though tropical, cottage, California native, succulent, grassland, Mediterranean, South African, Central/South American, Asian, Australian, and native wetland bioswale gardens. This nursery is a horticultural attraction in its own right. Open Monday through Saturday, 9 a.m.–5 p.m., and Sunday, 10 a.m.–4 p.m.

La Sumida Nursery

165 South Patterson Avenue, Santa Barbara 93111
(805) 964-9944
www.lasumida.com

Founded by Harold and Ethel Sumida in 1958, and still run by the family, La Sumida offers a wide selection of landscape plants, including edibles, California natives, and drought-tolerant and habitat plants. La Sumida is especially known for its colorful hanging baskets, fruit trees, and full acre of roses. Open Monday through Saturday, 8:30 a.m.–5:30 p.m., and Sunday, 10 a.m.–5 p.m.

Terra Sol Garden Center

5320 Overpass Road, Santa Barbara 93111
(805) 964-7811
www.terrasol-gardencenter.com

Mike Tully and Margaret Peavey spent several years working in the horticultural world before they decided to open up their own shop. Offering a full range of interesting and well-displayed plant material, their succulent collection is a standout. Terra Sol also sells bedding plants, trees, organic vegetables, bonsai, and exotic flowering plants. Open every day, 8:30 a.m.–6 p.m. (winter close at 5 p.m.).

Horticultural Attractions

Dallidet Adobe and Gardens

1185 Pacific Street, San Luis Obispo 93401
(805) 544-2303; (805) 543-0638 (tour information)
www.dallidet.org

The Dallidet Adobe, built in 1856, was home to Pierre Hypo-lite Dallidet and Ascencion Concepcion Salazar and their seven children. It was the site of the first licensed vineyard and brandy distillery in this area of the state. This one-acre garden oasis contains many historic trees and numerous plants that have their roots in its Victorian past. Self-guided botanical walking tours are available. The adobe and gardens are open Fridays, 10 a.m.–4 p.m., and Sundays, 1 p.m.–4 p.m., March through October.

Firescape Garden

2411 Stanwood Drive at Mission Ridge Road, Santa Barbara 93103
(805) 564-5744
www.santabarbara.gov

Firescape is a 1.7-acre demonstration garden showing how to use fire-resistant plants in the four basic fire zones surrounding your home to reduce a continuous fuel system. It was created by a local committee of civic-minded garden experts and is maintained by the City of Santa Barbara.

Franceschi Park

1510 Mission Ridge Road (at Franceschi), Santa Barbara 93103
(805) 564-5433
www.santabarbaraparks.gov/parks

This is the former grounds of Montarioso, the homesite of turn-of-the-century Italian botanist and nurseryman Francesco di Franceschi, whose Southern California Acclimatizing Association let it be known worldwide that almost anything could be grown in Santa Barbara. Franceschi's lifetime celebration of native plants, such as Catalina ironwood (*Lyonothamnus floribundus*) and plant introductions from other countries with similar climates, proved that this was true. New species and varieties that he introduced into the trade include Montezuma cypress (*Taxodium mucronatum*), palms, acacias, and the Brazilian flame bush (*Calliandra tweedii*). In this park, 18 acres of his botanical collections on Mission Ridge combine with great ocean views.

Alice Keck Park Memorial Gardens

1500 Santa Barbara Street, Santa Barbara 93101
(805) 564-5433
www.santabarbaraparks.gov/parks

The site of the old El Mirasol Hotel was relandscaped in 1980 to include a wide variety of plants in a natural setting along streams and ponds, courtesy of philanthropist Alice Keck.

Leaning Pine Arboretum

California Polytechnic State University
San Luis Obispo 93407
(805) 756-2888; (805) 756-1106 (Plant Poly Shop)
www.leaningpinearboretum.calpoly.edu

Part of the Horticulture and Crop Science Department at Cal Poly, the five-acre Leaning Pine Arboretum, located at the northern end of campus with views of the nearby Santa Lucia Mountains, serves as a laboratory for students, showcasing plants from the world's five Mediterranean-climate regions. Plants are arranged to show their relationships within specific plant communities. There are also special collections of palms, aloes, dwarf and unusual conifers, and primitive plants, a formal topiary garden, and an All-American Selections

display garden that gives the public a chance to view new cultivars being tested around the country for their performance under different growing conditions. An organic farm on campus is open to the public Monday through Thursday, 3 p.m.–6 p.m. (org.farm@calpoly.edu). The Poly Plant Shop sells student-propagated plants and is located near the arboretum in Building 48 (Horiculture Unit), Via Carta Road.

Lompoc Flower Fields

West of downtown Lompoc, map on website
www.explorelompoc.com

From June to early September, these roadside fields are striped with color.

Lotusland

695 Ashley Road, Santa Barbara 93108 (administrative office)
(805) 969-9990 (reservations); (805) 969-3767 (office)
www.lotusland.org
Email: reservation@lotusland.org (reservations)

In the twilight of her erratic career as an operatic diva, Madame Ganna Walska turned her full energies and attention to her garden. Living here since 1941, for a brief while with husband number six, she focused on the gardens until her death at age 97 in 1984. Her flair for theatricality is evident everywhere. Over 2,000 species of tropical and subtropical Mediterranean-climate plants fill the garden's 37 acres with spines, whorls, hairy tufts, and fanciful forms. The Lotusland Foundation was created by Mme. Walska to preserve the garden and opened it to the public in 1993. Reservations are required (admission fee): tours are given Wednesday through Saturday at 10 a.m. and 1:30 p.m., mid-February to mid-November. Plants are for sale in the garden shop, and Lotusland holds an Exceptional Plant Auction in early fall.

San Luis Obispo Botanical Garden

El Chorro Regional Park on Highway 1
(805) 541-1400
www.slobg.org

In 1996, a preview garden opened on a 150-acre site in El Chorro Regional Park, followed by an education center in 2004. Future gardens will feature Mediterranean plant communities from around the world and will demonstrate sustainable gardening practices. The gardens are open 8 a.m. to sunset all days. The nonprofit Friends of SLO Botanical Garden organizes lectures, docent tours, and children's activities and can use your support (3450 Dairy Creek Road, San Luis Obispo 93405). Eve's Garden shop sells volunteer-grown plants Tuesday through Friday, 9 a.m.–5 p.m.

Santa Barbara Botanic Garden

1212 Mission Canyon Road, Santa Barbara 93105
(805) 682-4726
www.sbbg.org

The 78-acre grounds of the Santa Barbara Botanic Garden are dedicated to the display, propagation, and conservation of California's native flora. Featured areas include a demonstration garden showing landscape use of native plants, and meadow, redwood forest, desert, chaparral, oak woodland, and Channel Island sections. Nestled in Mission Canyon between a backdrop of the chaparral-clad Santa Ynez Mountains and ocean views, it is a natural wonder itself. The Garden Growers Nursery is open 10 a.m.–5:30 p.m. (winter close at 4:30 p.m.).The garden also has spring and fall native plant sales. Admission fee.

Taft Gardens / Conservation Endowment Fund

2162 Baldwin Road, Ojai 93023
(805) 649-2333
Email: taftstarr@gmail.com

John Taft created these gardens in the early 1980s on his 265-acre ranch surrounded by the Los Padres National Forest. Today, the gardens cover about 18 acres and are filled with Australian, South African, and California native plants. The gardens are deeded to a nonprofit to advance the cause of conservation and to keep this tranquil area free from development. Please call for further information and to obtain a map before your visit. From time to time the gardens host spiritual retreats and yoga classes.

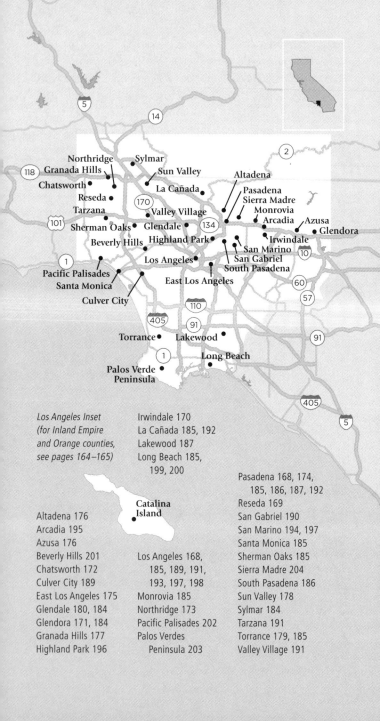

Chapter 7

Los Angeles Basin, Inland Empire, and Orange County

Eschscholzia californica

Counties: Los Angeles; Riverside, Santa Cruz; Orange; Inyo

Elevational range: Sea level to 11,499 feet in the San Bernardino Mountains (San Bernardino County); 14,505 feet at Mount Whitney (Inyo and Tulare counties), the highest US peak; 279 feet below sea level in Badwater Basin, Death Valley National Park (Inyo County)

Sunset climate zones: Los Angeles Basin, Inland Empire, 2A, 7, 18, 19, 22, 23, 24; Orange County, 7, 11, 13, 21, 22, 23

Annual rainfall: Los Angeles, 13 to 15 inches (Los Angeles County); San Bernardino, 16 inches, and Barstow, 4 inches (San Bernardino County); Riverside, 10 inches, and Coachella, 4 inches (Riverside County); Orange County, 10 to 14 inches

Winter temperatures: Average lows 55°F (Los Angeles County); 51°F (San Bernardino); 53°F to 46°F degrees (Laguna Beach). In the mountains, lows dip to 20°F to 10°F.

Summer temperatures: Average highs range from 88°F in Whittier to 80°F in San Bernardino to 85°F in Orange County.

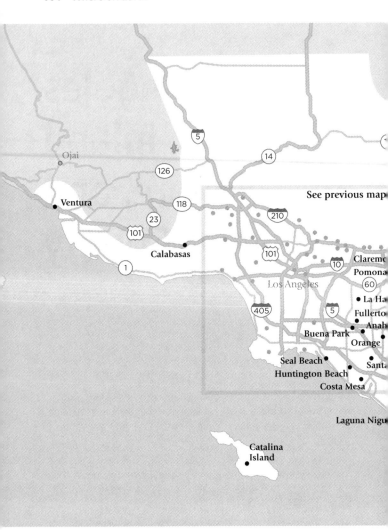

Los Angeles Basin

Los Angeles Basin is a plain between the San Gabriel, Santa Monica, and Santa Ana mountains and the Palos Verdes Peninsula. Its geology includes sedimentary basin, valleys, mountains, deserts, and fault lines.

A variety of climate zones converge in this broad region, but generally dry, warm, sunny summers with mild winters typify it. At 34° north latitude, Los Angeles roughly equals Adelaide, Australia, and Cape Town, South Africa, cities that also enjoy distinct Mediterranean climates. Ocean tempers climate, and though frosts are rare, winter temperatures can drop to freezing in colder pockets.

A milder thermal belt where subtropical plants such as avocados thrive encompasses the Pacific Palisades, Beverly Hills, and Hollywood. As in its neighboring coastal zone, the ocean influences climate, but so do inland air masses, often bringing hot, dry Santa Ana winds.

The Inland Empire

East of Greater Los Angeles sprawls the Inland Empire, an interior region made up of San Bernardino and Riverside counties. The Colorado River flows along its eastern border, separating it from Arizona.

Development pushed farming farther east into the Coachella Valley of the Colorado Desert, where, with mass irrigation, dates, table grapes, citrus, artichokes, and avocados grow year round.

The San Gabriel, San Bernardino, and Santa Ana mountains separate coastal regions and the Los Angeles Basin from the Inland Empire's high and low deserts, the Mojave and Colorado, respectively.

Various thermal belts swirl through interior valleys. A gray pine belt in high foothills separates coast from interior deserts, with shorter growing seasons. Cold, snowy winters in the highest mountains have the shortest growing seasons.

Orange County

Orange County, named for the abundance of citrus grown here, is Southern California's smallest county geographically, with a total area of 948 square miles. It was segregated from Los Angeles County in 1889. The Santa Ana Mountains mark a natural divide between Orange and Riverside counties along this county's eastern boundary. The Santa Ana River flows through the county's middle.

Orange County straddles three climate zones: an extension of the mild Los Angeles Basin, with hilltops or basins experiencing colder winters; a coastal marine influence; and colder canyon winters.

A wide plant palette thrives in this region's year-round growing season. Angelenos have adopted the South African perennial bird of paradise (*Strelitzia reginae*) as their official flower. The state flower, the California poppy (*Eschscholzia californica*), grows throughout interior valleys and foothills. This free-branching perennial bears soft yellow to deep orange satiny flowers from June to September. The Joshua tree (*Yucca brevifolia*) grows in the Mojave high desert.

In Inyo County, on the Nevada border, the oldest non-clonal plant on earth, the Great Bristlecone pine (*Pinus longaeva*), thrives. Methuselah, as it is known, has grown in the Forest of Ancients for some 4,847 years.

Nurseries offer succulents, cacti, subtropicals, and Mediterranean-climate plants. California natives, Matilija poppy (*Romneya coulteri*), farewell-to-spring (*Clarkia amoena*), baby blue eyes (*Nemophila menziesii*), and cream cup (*Platystemon californicus*) fueled the imagination of nurseryman Theodore Payne.

Specialty Nurseries and Growers

C and S Nursery, Inc.

3615 Hauser Boulevard, Los Angeles 90016
(323) 296-6657
www.csnursery.com
Email: csnursery@gmail.com
Cristian and Santiago Rosales
Wholesale, open to the public
Open Monday through Friday, 7 a.m.–4 p.m.,
    and Saturday, 7 a.m.–noon.

Plant specialties: A wide variety of ornamental plants, including trees, shrubs, drought-tolerant plants, California natives, Australian plants, vegetables, annuals, and perennials.

History/description: The best graduation present ever: the father and grandfather of brothers Cristian and Santiago Rosales bought this two-acre nursery on the west side of Los Angeles for them in 1991 while they were at community college, with the proviso that they had two years to make a go of it. Clearly successful, the brothers were able to add 30 acres in Fallbrook as growing grounds sometime later and they now propagate about 60 to 80 percent of what they sell. This nursery is a bit of a hybrid model—not a specialty nursery because they carry a general collection of plants, not a garden center because they just sell plants and soil. C and S mostly caters to landscape professionals, offering large quantities of each well-grown selection. Visitors are escorted in golf carts to collect their purchases, the experience being described by the owners as "sort of an adult Disneyland."

California Cactus Center

216 South Rosemead Boulevard, Pasadena 91107
(626) 795-2788

www.cactuscenter.com
Email: california.cactuscenter@gmail.com
Airee, Molly, Sue, Sammy, Rahpee, and Tuk Tuk Thongthiraj
Retail, wholesale, and (limited) phone order
Open every day but Monday, 10 a.m.–4:30 p.m.

Plant specialties: Large selection of cacti and succulents (20,000 species), some very rare, such as a 100-year-old "Elephant's Foot" *Diascorea.*

History/description: Dr. Rahpee Thongthiraj, a radiologist, came to California in the late 1950s and became awestruck by the wonders of cacti—especially *Euphorbia obesa,* the "baseball plant." A hobbyist and collector, he started this nursery in the 1970s as a sideline to his medical practice and as a future resource for his family, which at that time included six daughters. The girls were recruited early on. At five years old, Molly was promised a trip to Disneyland if she and her sisters watered or planted 1,000 plants. Three sisters work here full-time and the other three work part-time while managing their own families. Their golden barrel cactus now graces the Getty Museum. This half-acre site is supplemented by 20 acres of growing and propagation grounds located elsewhere.

California Nursery Specialties

19420 Saticoy, Reseda 91335
(818) 894-5694
www.california-cactus-succulents.com
Dave Eric
Retail and wholesale
Retail open weekends only, 11 a.m.–6 p.m. (winter close at 5 p.m.); wholesale open Monday through Friday (call first).

Plant specialties: Thousands of varieties of succulents and hundreds of varieties of cacti.

History/description: Dave Bernstein started propagating succulents as part of a high school science project in the mid-1970s and has been collecting ever since. As he sells mostly to landscapers and retail nurseries, his primary interest is in plants that look good in the ground—the pretty and the practical. But his interests are encyclopedic, and the nursery includes hundreds of varieties of low-growing cacti, tall columnar varieties, globular varieties, and succulents of every wild color and shape, including some with wonderful names like Hairy Old Man (*Cephalocereus senilis*), Baby Toes (*Fenestraria rhopalophylla*), and Brain Cactus (*Mammillaria elongata cristata*). The 1.5-acre nursery has ideal growing conditions, located in that part of the San Fernando Valley where the cooling coastal climate meets inland heat.

Garden View Nursery

12901 Lower Azusa Road, Irwindale 91706
(626) 337-4818 (nursery)
www.garden-view.com
Mark and Julie Meahl
Retail and wholesale
Open Monday, 8 a.m.–3:30 p.m.; Tuesday through Saturday,
    8 a.m.–5 p.m.; and Sunday, 10 a.m.–4 p.m.

Plant specialties: Ornamental trees, fruit trees, and shrubs for Southern California climates; reliable hedging plants, such as *Ligustrum, Pittosporum* spp., *Ficus nitida, Prunus caroliniana, Podocarpus gracilior,* and *Dodonea purpurea;* California native plants; drought-tolerant plants; succulents; roses; and ground covers.

History/description: Landscape contractor and outdoor construction specialist Mark Meahl started growing plants to supply his projects, which led him to open a nursery that wife Julie has been managing since 1989. Mark continues to focus on the design, construction, and landscape maintenance part of their business. Several years and several moves later, the nursery is now located at this 13-acre site on the Southern California Edison Power right-of-way.

Glendora Gardens

1132 South Grand Avenue, Glendora 91740
(626) 914-6718
www.glendoragardens.com
Email: info@glendoragardens.com
Melina Ferrandino
Retail and wholesale
Open Monday through Friday, 8:30 a.m.–5 p.m.;
    Saturday, 7:30 a.m.–5 p.m.; and Sunday, 9 a.m. to 3 p.m.

Plant specialties: Drought-tolerant trees, shrubs, perennials, and bedding plants for Mediterranean climates, including California native plants.

History/description: Mike and Carol Downard launched Rainbow Garden Nursery here in 1978 and credited its success to the constancy and hard work of their employees. Recently, those same employees bought the nursery and renamed it under the leadership of former manager Melina Ferrandino. With their retail operation on one side of the street and their growing grounds on the other, the nursery occupies 12 acres on an easement of Southern California Edison Power. The nursery is attractively laid out, with koi and turtle ponds and an aviary providing interest for the whole family.

Greenlee Nursery Garden Gallery

Pomona
www.greenleeandassociates.com
Email: greenleeandassociates@gmail.com
(415) 468-1961
greenleenursery.com
John Greenlee
Open by appointment only.

Though John Greenlee has moved north (see Greenlee and Associates entry in chapter 4), his Garden Gallery in Pomona —one acre of gardens filled with grasses and grass-like specimen plants, including a three-story tree house—may still be visited by appointment.

Instant Jungle

14835 San Bernardino Avenue, Fontana 92335, (714) 267-0154
1 Magazine Street, Irvine 92630, (714) 850-9227
2560 South Birch Street, Santa Ana 92707
Open by appointment only
www.instantjungle.com
Greg Wallace, Andy Blanton
Retail and wholesale
Santa Ana location open Monday through Friday, 8 a.m.–4:30p.m.,
    and Saturday, 8 a.m.–1:30 p.m. Irvine location open Monday
    through Friday, 7 a.m.–3:30 p.m., and Saturday, 7:30 a.m.–3 p.m.
    Fontana location open by appointment only.

Plant specialties: Bamboo, palms, and specimen tropical plants.

History/description: What started in 1980 as an interior plant sales and maintenance business, founded by two friends who played on the same baseball team, grew to include special event installations. Seeing how well large bamboo and palms worked in the landscape, they added a nursery of specimen tropical plants, which now has three locations in Southern California and one up north, Jungle Bamboo and Palm Nursery (see chapter 2), in Cotati. This is the go-to location for landscape designers who spec signature plants for hotel and resort projects. Size matters here, and plants are sold in 15-gallon to 72-inch boxes.

Jurassic Garden—A&A Cycads

11225 Canoga Avenue, Chatsworth 91311
(818) 655-0230
www.cycadpalm.com
Email: info@cycads.com
Maurice Levin

Retail, wholesale, and online order
Open by appointment only, Monday through Friday, 9 a.m.–5 p.m.,
 and Saturday, 9 a.m.–3:30 p.m.

Plant specialties: Cycads (*Cycas, Dioon, Encephalartos, Lepido-zamia, Macrozamia, Zamia*) and other drought-tolerant living fossil plants, such as *Dyckia, Araucaria,* and *Agathis,* as well as other drought-tolerant plants, such as those that grow in habitat with cycads, like aloes and *Strelitzia* 'Mandela's Gold'.

History/description: In 1989, while on vacation with his wife in the Virgin Islands, Maurice Levin took a horticultural tour and became fascinated by cycads. An ardent history buff, he was intrigued by the concept of living fossil plants, especially cycads—primeval, fernlike, cone-bearing survivors of the pre-flowering world. Further research showed that these tough survivor plants were facing real challenges, many endangered in the wild. The philosophy at Jurassic Garden is that "preservation through propagation" can ensure the survival of endangered species. Maurice's mission is to propagate as many of these plants as possible, thereby making them more affordable in order to reduce the incentive for wild plant pilfering. Plants grown on site include ones Maurice and his colleagues have grown from seeds, reestablished from offsets and imports, and rescued from gardens and wild predation. The nursery started in 2000 as A&A Cycads and has moved a few times.

Kimura Bonsai Nursery

17230 Roscoe Boulevard, Northridge 91325
(818) 343-4090
www.kimurabonsainursery.com
Email: bonsaibp@earthlink.net
Robert Pressler
Retail and mail/online order
Open Monday, Wednesday, Friday, and Saturday, 10 a.m.–5 p.m.,
 or by appointment.

Plant specialties: Bonsai specimens and pre-bonsai material and supplies.

History/description: Robert Pressler started Robert Pressler Landscape Design in 1995, offering a full range of design and construction services and specializing in traditional Japanese-style gardens. His aesthetic was influenced by his love of bonsai, a hobby of his since age 10. He bought this established bonsai nursery in the San Fernando Valley in 1996 and has greatly expanded its collection.

Magic Growers

2800 Eaton Canyon Drive, Pasadena 91107
(626) 797-6511
www.magicgrowers.com
Email: info@magicgrowers.com
Lance Tibbet, Joe Brosius
Wholesale
Open Monday through Friday, 7:30 a.m.–4:30 p.m.;
    Saturday, 7:30 a.m.–noon.

Plant specialties: Herbaceous perennials, succulents, herbs, Mediterranean-climate plants, California native plants, ferns, grasses, and vines. Over 200 genera, including special collections of *Cistus, Geranium, Pelargonium, Iris* and native *Iris, Lavandula, Penstemon, Salvia,* and *Thymus.* The dwarf *Penstemon* 'Eaton Canyon' was introduced here.

History/description: Occupying nine acres at the base of Eaton Canyon along the San Gabriel Mountains, Magic Growers produces container-grown plants (from 4-inch to 5-gallon) for retail nurseries and the landscape trade. Started in 1980 to take advantage of the owners' growing interest in perennials, the nursery soon expanded to offer flowering Mediterranean shrubs and herbs. Close relationships with local botanic gardens and garden designers help create an inventory of useful and desirable plants. Visitors may wander through the nursery's display garden.

Mimosa LA Nursery

6270 Allston Street, East Los Angeles 90022
(323) 722-4543
www.vuoncayla.com
Gilbert Guyenne (Nguyen Dung Tien)
Retail, wholesale, and contract grafting
Open every day, 8 a.m.–4:30 p.m.

Plant specialties: Tropical fruit trees and other tropical trees in 5- to 15-gallon pots.

History/description: Arriving in this country via New Caledonia, Gilbert Guyenne opened Mimosa LA Nursery in 1982 as a backyard venture to satisfy his love of plants and to remind himself of bygone times in Vietnam. It was the first such nursery in the growing Vietnamese community here, and its very presence was healing. Soon discovered by other immigrant people for whom tropical fruit was a soothing reminder of home, the nursery grew to include 20 acres in four locations. Now concentrated on these three acres and humming with birds and chickens, it is a tropical oasis in East LA.

Mockingbird Nursery

1670 Jackson Street, Riverside 92504
(951) 780-3571
www.mockingbirdnursery.com
Email: joni@mockingbirdnursery.com
Donn and Keith Eikoff
Retail, wholesale, and contract growing
Open Monday through Friday, 7 a.m.–3:30 p.m.

Plant specialties: Mostly California native plants; some drought-tolerant plants from Australia and Mediterranean-climate areas.

History/description: Brothers Donn and Keith Eikoff set about to determine the best use for their hot, dry, inland-climate property. Following advice to grow native plants primarily for mitigation and revegetation projects throughout the state, they opened a nursery in 1984 on this 10-acre site. The nursery is "dedicated to the promise to make sure California has a sustainable future" and is named for the Mockingbird Reservoir near Arroyo—indeed a magnet for mockingbirds.

El Nativo Growers, Inc.

200 South Peckham Road, Azusa 91702 (mailing address)
(626) 969-8449
www.elnativogrowers.com
Email: sales@elnativogrowers.com
James Campbell and Rebecca Nash, managers
Wholesale only
Wholesale yard open Monday through Friday, 7:30 a.m.–4 p.m.;
    growing grounds open by appointment only.

Plant specialties: California native plants (600 species and varieties) and low-water-use plants from Australia (especially *Grevillea*) and other Mediterranean-climate regions; ornamental grasses.

History/description: Plant pathologist James Campbell helped set up this nursery in 1996 and was soon joined by Rebecca Nash, now in charge of sales and marketing. Both are growers and native plant aficionados by training and instinct. They manage various growing grounds in Azusa and Somis on agriculturally protected, leased land, thus being able to grow plants suited to the hot, dry San Gabriel Valley and the milder Ventura County. About 22 acres of their more extensive holdings are in active production. Virtually all of their plants are propagated on site from mother plants or those collected with agency permission; all propagation is done outdoors.

Nuccio's Nurseries, Inc.

3555 Chaney Trail, Altadena 91001
(626) 794-3383
www.nucciosnurseries.com
Julius, Tom, and Jim Nuccio
Retail, wholesale, and mail order

Open Friday through Tuesday, 8 p.m.–4:30 p.m.
(June through December, closed on Sundays).

Plant specialties: Camellias (600 species and special hybrids), including *C.* 'Guilio Nuccio', *C.* 'Nuccio's Cameo', *C.* 'Nuccio's Carousel', and *C.* 'Nuccio's Gem'; azaleas (more than 500 varieties), including more than 100 varieties of Satsuki azaleas.

History/description: Brothers Joe and Julius Nuccio started this nursery in 1935. Their sons now run the business, just as fascinated by the scientific possibilities of hybridizing and as thirsty for new introductions as were their fathers. They strive to remain small enough to keep focused on being knowledgeable and exceptional. Plants displayed during blooming season offer a major springtime spectacle.

Papaya Tree Nursery

12422 El Oro Way, Granada Hills 91344
(818) 363-3680
www.papayatreenursery.com
Email: alex@papayatreenursery.com
Alex Silber
Retail
Open every day, 8 a.m.–6 p.m., by same-day appointment only,
so call before you come.

Plant specialties: Tropical, subtropical, temperate, and exotic fruit trees and spice plants specifically adapted to various Southern California growing conditions. Many improved varieties of lychee, sapote, mango, starfruit, cherimoya, jujube, and, of course, papaya. Mostly grafted (clonal) plants.

History/description: Since the early 1980s, while still an electrical engineer, David Silber began tracking down, propagating, and collecting rare tropical fruit trees. He and his wife, Tina, started experimenting with the adaptability limits of a variety of tropical fruiting species. By the mid-1980s their backyard was bursting with excess trees and they opened this nursery and demonstration orchard. Son Alex Silber grew up at the nursery and has been working there since 1997. He continues to seek out new varieties, such as *Synsepalum dulcificum*, commonly known as miracle fruit, from West Africa, which, for a period of time after consumption, confuses the sweet and sour sensations of your taste buds. Papaya Tree's website includes YouTube videos on topics such as "How to Prune a Guava Tree" and "Natural Pest Control."

Theodore Payne Foundation

10459 Tuxford Street, Sun Valley 91352
(818) 768-1802
(818) 768-3533 (wildflower hotline)
www.theodorepayne.org
Email: info@theodorepayne.org
Retail and mail/online order
Open Tuesday through Saturday, 8:30 a.m.–4:30 p.m.

Plant specialties: California native plants (900 species and cultivars, 100 of which are endangered) and native seeds. Large collections of *Arctostaphylos* and *Ceanothus*. The flowering shrub *Mahonia nevinii* was saved from extinction by the foundation.

History/description: Named in honor of Englishman Theodore Payne (1872–1963), who arrived in Southern California in 1893, this nonprofit foundation was established in 1961 to preserve California's native flora through propagation and public education about its value. Theodore Payne's impact on the California landscape was immense, occurring at a critical time when underappreciated native vegetation was being lost to farming and progress. As a nurseryman and designer, Payne's hand helped shape Rancho Santa Ana Botanic Garden, the Los Angeles County Arboretum and Botanic Garden and Torrey Pines State Park. He popularized California natives in his native England even before they caught on at home. He is credited with introducing 400 to 500 wildflowers and native plants into the trade. In addition to the nursery and mail-order seed business, the foundation offers classes, field trips, a library, and horticultural consultations. The 21-acre site includes a 5-acre wildflower hill, trails, and picnic facilities.

Rainforest Flora, Inc.

19121 Hawthorne Boulevard, Torrance 90503
(310) 370-8044
www.rainforestflora.com
Email: sales@rainforestflora.com
Jerry Robinson, Paul Isley; Kacey Isley, manager
Retail, wholesale, and mail order
Open Monday through Saturday, 9 a.m.–5 p.m.,
    and Sunday by appointment.

Plant specialties: Bromeliads, including *Tillandsia, Neoregelia, Vriesea, Cryptanthus; Platycerium* (staghorn ferns), palms, and cycads.

History/description: That little tillandsia plant glued on wood that you picked up at Home Depot probably got its start here. Although their business is now big and mostly wholesale, it started as a hobby. Paul Islay's fascination with tillandsias started in college and blossomed during a collecting trip to Mexico and Guatemala in 1974. After two years gluing air plants on wood, he went into partnership with Jerry Robinson. Today the nursery occupies five acres. There are additional growing grounds in San Diego, and the focus has expanded to feature other bromeliads and related plants. The nursery's complex of greenhouses re-creates a sense of the tropics with specimen plants 30 to 40 years old and a massive stump festooned with epiphytes. Since 1993, the nursery has been completely self-sufficient in the production of tillandsias, no mean feat since they take 6 to 20 years to mature from seed and the nursery sells about 10,000 plants most weeks.

Seaside Growers

33773 Camino Capistrano, San Juan Capistrano 92675
(949) 493-7854
www.seasidegrowers.com
Email: seasidegrowers@earthlink.net
Jim and Ken Cassady
Retail and wholesale
Open Monday through Friday, 8 a.m.–4:30 p.m.,
    and Saturday, 9 a.m.–4 p.m.

Plant specialties: Palms, cycads, tropical plants, bamboo, succulents, ornamental grasses, and water-wise ornamentals.

History/description: The Cassady brothers grew plants initially for their landscaping business, which they started in 1980. During the 1991 recession, they began selling excess plants to make ends meet, and they have been at it ever since. Their two-acre property is packed with plants, from gallon-size to towering specimen plants, artfully arranged to give a sense of their landscape effect. Getting to Seaside Growers is "quite an adventure," so consult their website for directions.

Tarweed Native Plants

1307 Graynold Avenue, Glendale 91202
(626) 705-8993
www.tarweednativeplants.com
Email: tarweed@tarweednativeplants.com
Joanne Burger, Paul Jacobson
Retail, some wholesale
Open by appointment, Wednesday through Sunday most likely.

Plant specialties: California native plants, especially those well suited for lawn replacement, such as salvias, eriogonums, grasses, and perennials.

History/description: In 1990, Paul Jacobson bought a small property in Chatsworth that included a native plant nursery. Suddenly in the business, he quickly learned about natives and started to specialize in plants that would produce climate-friendly beds and borders for lawn substitutes. Paul and his wife, garden enthusiast Joanne Burger, mastered propagation (cuttings and seed culture) and moved to this location in 2009. The backyard nursery is small and growing. Online plant profiles provide photographs and information about available plants.

Tree of Life Nursery (wholesale)
Casa "La Paz" Plant and Book Store (retail)

33201 Ortega Highway, San Juan Capistrano
P. O. Box 635, San Juan Capistrano 92675
(949) 728-0685
www.californianativeplants.com
Email: inquiries@californianativeplants.com
Mike Evans, Jeff Bohn
Retail, wholesale, and contract growing
Wholesale open Monday through Friday, 8 a.m.–4:30 pm.
    Retail open Monday through Friday (and Saturdays,
    fall through spring), 9 a.m.–4 p.m.

Plant specialties: Over 400 species and varieties of California native plants for all regions of the state, especially plants of the coastal mountains.

History/description: Mike Evans and Jeff Bohn, native plant enthusiasts and former landscape contractors, knew from their garden installation experience that California natives made first-rate garden plants. Though Tree of Life is now a major native supplier in California, Mike and Jeff took a gamble in 1978 by starting a nursery devoted exclusively to California natives. Presently, 20 of the nursery's 36 acres in Rancho Mission Viejo next to the Cleveland National Forest are under cultivation; the nursery includes a display garden and propagation and sales buildings made out of plastered straw bale. Tree of Life brings longtime experience to ecological restoration, habitat enhancement, and authentic landscaping.

Tuition Growers

Buena Park 90620
(714) 828-5368
www.tuitiongrowers.net
Al Garofalow
Wholesale
Open by appointment only.

Plant specialties: "Cottage garden" plants—flowering annuals, biennials, and perennials, particularly old-fashioned, heirloom varieties.

History/description: Al Garofalow grew up with vegetable gardens and cannot remember a time when he did not have something growing in his backyard. Today his backyard is a raised carpet of flower seedlings grown for various retail outlets. The business started quite by accident. Al's plants, adorning the booth of the Organic Vegetable Garden Club at a local Green Scene plant sale, were noticed by Mary Lou Heard of Heard's Country Garden. She persuaded him to grow specialty plants for her, and this civilian employee of the Los Angeles Police Department suddenly had a sideline business. Its success paid for the tuitions of his children, hence the nursery's name.

Upland Nursery

1518 North Tustin Street, Orange 92867
(714) 538-4500
www.uplandnursery.com
Email: uplandnursery@yahoo.com
Malee Hsu
Retail and online order
Open every day, 9 a.m.–5 p.m.

Plant specialties: Plumerias (400-plus kinds), bonsai, cacti and succulents, tropical fruit trees, Japanese maples, water plants, native and drought-tolerant perennials, and rare plants.

History/description: As a child growing up on her family's ranch in Thailand, Malee loved to take melon seeds from the table, plant them, and watch them grow in her moist and tropical world. Her fingers have really never left the soil. Moving to California in the early 1970s, she devoted herself to bonsai. Always on the lookout for plants that remind her of home, her interests evolved into a quest for tropical plants and others suited to the area. A visit to Hawaii brought back childhood memories and a fascination with hybridizing plumeria, now a primary focus. Her travels and connections with other growers have resulted in the rescue of many plants that otherwise would have been lost due to changing tastes or natural extinction. Her growing grounds are in Upland, surrounding the family home. This 3.5-acre sales location, acquired in 1993, includes a perennial area, a water plant garden, pot arrangements of cacti and succulents, and a large maple garden. Four members of her family help her out here.

Van Ness Water Gardens, Inc.

2460 North Euclid Avenue, Upland 91784
(800) 205-2425
www.vnwg.com
William C. Uber, president
Retail and mail/online order
Open Tuesday through Saturday, 9 a.m.–4 p.m.

Plant specialties: Aquatic plants, aquatic ecosystem components, bog plants, small flowering aquatics, and tropical water lilies. The newest introductions are a hardy water lily that changes color from pale pink to fiery crimson, which president William Uber named *Nymphaea* 'Amanda Uber' after his daughter, and the peach-colored *N.* 'Makenna Uber'.

History/description: There have been a lot of changes in Upland since this family business was launched in 1922. The lemon grove that surrounded the nursery at that time is today a residential area. Three generations have run the business;

the original Mr. Van Ness was a cousin of Bill Uber's father, who took over the business in 1952. It was Bill's turn in 1976. The one-acre-plus growing area makes a noteworthy display.

Worldwide Exotics

11157 Orcas Avenue, Sylmar 91342
(818) 890-1915
www.worldwideexoticsnursery.com
Email: shelly.jennings5824@hotmail.com
Ken and Shelley Jennings
Retail and wholesale
Retail open Saturdays, 9:30 a.m.–4 p.m.

Plant specialties: Drought-tolerant perennials from all over the world, tropical and subtropical plants, cacti and succulents, and a "Dr. Seuss collection" of exotica.

History/description: The Jennings have been collecting drought-tolerant perennials since the early 1990s and initially sold their plants through Gary Hammer's Desert to Jungle Nursery in Montebello. Shelley then worked with Hammer and joined him on plant collection trips, eventually taking over his former growing grounds, a six-acre site along Freeway 210. The Jennings moved their nursery here in 1995. Gary Hammer was a prime mover in the new horticulture of California, and his legacy is honored here. The Jennings also sell their plants at local farmers' markets. The website describes 800 plants.

Notable Garden Centers

Armstrong Garden Centers

5780 East La Palma, Anaheim 92807, (714) 779-209
2123 Newport Boulevard, Costa Mesa 92627, (949) 646-3925
5816 San Fernando Road, Glendale 91202, (818) 243-4227
1350 East Route 66, Glendora 91740, (626) 963-0328

17552 Goldenwest Street, Huntington Beach 92647, (714) 843-6347
15285 Cluver Drive, Irvine 92604, (949) 857-9278
1515 Foothill Boulevard, La Cañada/Flintridge 91011,
    (818) 790-2555
28992 Golden Lantern, Laguna Niguel 92677, (949) 495-7205
1340 South Harbor Boulevard, La Habra 90631, (714) 626-0129
3842 East 10th Street, Long Beach 90804, (562) 433-7413
7540 South Sepulveda Boulevard, Los Angeles 90045, (310) 670-1277
(626) 914-1091 (main office)
635 West Huntington Drive, Monrovia 91016, (626) 358-4516
1500 East Coast Highway, Newport Beach 92660, (929) 644-9510
352 East Glenarm Street, Pasadena 91106, (626) 799-7139
32382 Del Obispo Street, San Juan Capistrano, (949) 661-6666
3226 Wilshire Boulevard, Santa Monica 90403, (310) 829-6766
12920 Magnolia Boulevard, Sherman Oaks 91423, (818) 761-1522
25225 Crenshaw Boulevard, Torrance 90505, (310) 326-1892
505 El Camino Real, Torrance 92780, (714) 542-4145
www.armstronggarden.com

Armstrong has deep roots in California's horticulture. The founder of this garden empire, John S. Armstrong, was an earnest plantsman and grower who made many plant introductions from the beginning of his career in 1889 until the 1950s. Keenly focused on roses and fruit trees, he either bred or introduced the boysenberry, the Babcock peach, the seedless Valencia orange, and *Rosa* 'Charlotte Armstrong', among many others. The first Armstrong nursery opened in Ontario around 1910, run by John, followed by his son and then his grandson. In the 1980s, ownership was transferred to the employees. Armstrong's expansion to its present 29 locations in Southern California and 3 in Northern California got a boost when the company bought the Nurseryland chain based in San Diego in the 1990s. Three large growing grounds—one in the desert, one near the coast, and one inland—enable Armstrong to supply plants for its stores that are locally grown and weather tested. Each store manager "curates" that store's particular plant offerings so that they are appropriate and "friendly" to the neighborhood.

Barristers Nursery

915 Meridian Avenue, South Pasadena 91030
(626) 441-1323
www.barristersnursery.com

This small gem of a nursery on a former parking lot is the brainchild of Stella Binns. Growing up in England, she was introduced to the pleasures of gardening by her father and embarked on a career as a landscaper. She moved to California in 1982 and opened this nursery in 2006. The nursery sells a good selection of water-wise perennials, unusual trees, shrubs, and roses. Open Tuesday through Saturday, 9 a.m.–5:30 p.m., and Sunday, 10 a.m.–5 p.m.

Bellefontaine Nursery

838 South Fair Oaks Avenue, Pasadena 91105
(626) 796-0747
www.bellefontainenursery.com

Alan and Dale Uchida, the grandsons of Bellefontaine Nursery's founder, took the reins of the family business in 2006. This 1.3-acre nursery in the southwest section of Pasadena features California native and drought-tolerant shrubs, roses, citrus, stone fruit and tropical fruit trees, bedding plants, and vegetables. Open Monday through Saturday (except for Wednesdays), 8 a.m.–4:30 p.m., and Sunday, 8 a.m.–1 p.m.

Brita's Old Town Gardens

225 Main Street, Seal Beach 90740
(562) 430-5019
www.britasgardens.com

Brita Lemmon understands plants. As a former grower who worked various farmers' markets, she was glad to settle down here when this location became available in 1998. She specializes in unusual perennials and herbs for the collector's garden, especially those that are drought tolerant and that attract butterflies and hummingbirds (the gardens have been discovered by a local flock of monarchs). Seal Beach is just south of the Los Angeles River. The nursery is open Monday through Saturday, 9 a.m.–5 p.m., and Sunday, 10 a.m.–5 p.m.

Burkard Nurseries, Inc.

690 North Orange Grove Boulevard, Pasadena 91103
(626) 796-4355
www.burkardnurseries.com

Started by Hans and Rosa Burkard in 1937, this nursery is in its third generation of stewardship, currently led by Frank and Penny Burkard. Burkard offers unusual perennials and uncommon nursery stock, including citrus (80 varieties), vegetables (300 varieties of tomatoes, 20 types of melon, 60 types of peppers), herbs (80 varieties), salvias (80 varieties), Japanese maples (60 varieties), South African bulbs, and roses (over 500 varieties, including antique and David Austins). Open Monday through Saturday, 8:30 a.m.–4:30 p.m., and Sunday, 9 a.m.–4 p.m.

H & H Nursery

6220 Lakewood Boulevard, Lakewood 90712
(562) 804-2513
www.hhnursery

Landscaper Jeff Shibata and his wife, Jane, bought H&H Nursery in Downey in 1976, moving it to this 5.5-acre location in 1986. Jeff credits his wife with doing most of the nursery work in the early days while he was out on jobs. Now both of their daughters also work here. Known especially for its extensive rose, fruit tree, and bedding-plant collections, the nursery offers everything from vegetable starts to 24-inch boxed specimen trees.

Lincoln Avenue Nursery

804 Lincoln Avenue, Pasadena 91103
(626) 792-2138
www.lincolnavenuenursery.com

Longtime landscaper Ramon Franco bought this venerable business in 2003, having been a customer for years. He is just the third owner of the nursery, which was founded by a German couple in 1904 and owned and operated by the Matsuzawa and Takemura families from 1930 to 2003. The nursery offers a full range of plants, with an emphasis on drought-tolerant plants. Plants in containers are attractively arranged and accented by colorful sculpture and pots. Open Monday through Friday, 7 a.m.–5 p.m.; Saturday, 7 a.m.–4 p.m.; and Sunday, 8:30 a.m.–3 p.m.

M & M Nursery

380 North Tustin Street, Orange 92867
(714) 538-8042
Facebook: M & M Nursery

Family owned and operated since 1956, M & M was taken over by Ted Mayeda from his father and uncle in 1980. Though the nursery carries a wide selection of plants, the emphasis is on hard-to-find, water-wise perennials that they buy in from a cadre of mom-and-pop growers who grow exclusively for M & M. The nursery is also known for its hanging baskets and "fairy gardens"—dish gardens each containing a tableau of miniature plants and accessories, which can also be ordered online at www.fairygardenexpert.net. Several specialty display areas highlight this well-appointed emporium. Open Monday through Saturday, 9 a.m.–5:30 p.m., and Sunday, 9 a.m.–4:30 p.m.

Plant Depot

32413 San Juan Creek Road, San Juan Capistrano 92675
(949) 240-2107
www.plantdepot.com

Brent Kittle has worked with plants since high school—starting with maintenance jobs, then working for large plant wholesalers, then launching his own wholesale growing operation and starting this retail nursery. This choice remainder of all his efforts is now run by his daughters, Kristina and Jennifer Kittle. The four-acre nursery located in a residential valley in the coastal hills five miles from the ocean is packed with plants, mostly in containers. It also includes a large koi and turtle pond, several display areas, and a 60-foot succulent wall to inspire planting ideas. The nursery offers a large selection of perennials, annuals, herbs, vegetables, succulents, and cacti, as well as shrubs, trees, water plants, bamboo, houseplants, and orchids. Open Monday through Saturday, 8 a.m.–6 p.m., and Sunday, 9 a.m.–5 p.m.

Rogers Gardens

2301 San Joaquin Hills Road, Corona del Mar 92625
(949) 640-5800
www.rogersgardens.com

Seven acres of plants are artfully arranged along pathways and anchored with hedges, statuary, and stately trees. The gardens' large Christmas display has become a family tradition, and other seasonal events occur throughout the year. Classes are offered every weekend in an outdoor amphitheater. Started by Roger McKinnon in 1965, the nursery was bought in 1970 by Gavin Herbert, Sr., who kept the original name and moved the nursery to its current location in 1975. Very water conscious, the nursery has a large selection of succulents, California natives, and other drought-tolerant plants. It also sells roses (200 varieties), orchids, indoor plants, and color bowls. Design/build/maintenance services are offered, and there is an online boutique. Open every day, 9 a.m.–6 p.m.

Rolling Greens Nursery

9528 Jefferson Boulevard, Culver City 90232, (310) 559-8656
7505 Beverly Boulevard, Los Angeles 90036, (323) 934-4500
www.rollinggreensnursery.com

Having long admired the Culver City wholesale nursery, designer and gardener Greg Salmeri leapt at the chance to buy it when it became available in 2001. He added the Los Angeles store in 2008, making them both retail emporiums with a distinctive artistic flair. Specializing in drought-tolerant and California native landscapes, Greg designs gardens throughout Southern California. Rolling Greens's signature Arrangement Bar encourages customers to pot up their own creations or learn from an expert in a DIY class. The nursery sells a lifestyle along with a remarkable assortment of plants. The Culver City location is open Monday through Saturday, 7:30 a.m.–4 p.m., and the Los Angeles location is open Monday through Saturday, 10 a.m.–6 p.m., and Sunday, 11 a.m.–6 p.m.

San Gabriel Nursery and Florist

632 South San Gabriel Boulevard, San Gabriel 91776
(626) 286-3782
www.sgnursery.com
Retail and wholesale

Founded in 1923 by Fred and Mitoko Yoshimura as Mission Nursery, the nursery started from cuttings made during Fred's work installing irrigation systems in old estate gardens. After internment during World War II, the Yoshimuras began again across the street from their old nursery and incorporated the new nursery under its present name in 1955. The nursery has been family owned and operated for three generations. This long history accounts for the family's extensive knowledge about plant sources and plant production and is why San Gabriel is everyone's recommendation for an all-around nursery in the Los Angeles area. Though its growing grounds have been sold, San Gabriel is responsible for many plant introductions, including *Azalea* 'Mission Bell', *Michelia champaca* 'Alba', and *Pachira aquatica* (known as "the good luck money tree"). This two-acre retail location, with its large bonsai display, offers bonsai, bulbs, citrus, fruit trees, herbs, houseplants, perennials, subtropical plants, aquatic plants, over 300 varieties of bare-root roses, Asiatic shrubs and trees, azaleas, camellias, hydrangeas, and gardenias. Open every day, 8 a.m.–5 p.m.

Sego Nursery, Inc.

12126 Burbank Boulevard, Valley Village 91607
(818) 763-5711

The Sego family opened their first nursery in the San Fernando Valley in 1919, moving to this location in 1947. Now in the fourth generation of ownership, the nursery has a nice selection of roses, fruit trees, and vegetables, as well as general nursery plants. After so many years in the business, the Segos really know what they are selling. Open every day but Thursday and Sunday, 9 a.m.–4 p.m.

Sunset Nursery

4365 Sunset Boulevard, Los Angeles 90029
(323) 661-1642
www.sunsetblvdnursery.com

This small nursery has been owned and operated by the Kuga family since 1960. Now run by the third generation, it has a wide variety of plants and will custom order anything you want. With water restrictions on in Los Angeles County, the nursery is expanding its collections of cacti, succulents, California natives, and other drought-tolerant plants.

West Valley Nursery

19035 Ventura Boulevard, Tarzana 91356
(818) 342-2623

Jon Tsuchiyama now runs this mom-and-pop garden center started by his father, Shig, in 1951. A full-service center, it offers all kinds of plants, including succulents, California natives, orchids, roses, color plants, and houseplants. Open every day but Thursday, 8 a.m.–4:30 p.m.; Sunday, close at 4 p.m.

Horticultural Attractions

La Casita del Arroyo

177 South Arroyo Boulevard, Pasadena 91105
(626) 744-7275

A charming old casita with the original garden from the 1930s, redesigned in 1988 by Isabelle Greene to illustrate water-wise and low-maintenance plantings. The clubhouse is managed by the Pasadena Department of Human Services and Recreation. Reservations are required.

Descanso Gardens

1418 Descanso Drive, La Cañada / Flintridge 91011
(818) 949-4200 (automated); (818) 949-4290
www.descansogardens.org

Descanso Gardens is a botanic garden with 160 acres of natural and cultivated beauty just minutes from downtown Los Angeles. Living collections here include a five-acre rose garden, with more than 3,000 specimens, the largest collection of camellias in North America, an ancient forest of cycads, a native garden designed by Theodore Payne, an oak woodland, and a tranquil Japanese garden. This was the former Rancho del Descanso of newspaper publisher Manchester Boddy, who built a 22-room house on the property in 1939 and planted the first of Descanso's famed camellias. He sold the property to Los Angeles County in 1953. The property is now managed by the Descanso Gardens Guild, a nonprofit organization that offers classes, tours, and events. Plants are sold at the gift shop and at sales in April and October. Gardens are open every day, 9 a.m.–5 p.m. Admission fee.

The Fullerton Arboretum

California State University, 1900 Associated Road
   (corner of Yorba Linda Boulevard), Fullerton 92831
(657) 278-3407
www.fullertonarboretum.org

This 26-acre arboretum was opened in 1979 through the joint efforts of the California State University at Fullerton, the City of Fullerton, and community resources. The arboretum includes over 4,000 plants from all parts of the world that grow well in Southern California, organized according to cultural requirements. Hence, moisture-loving plants grow alongside a stream and ponds, and dryland plants are found in the chaparral section. Other areas include a palm garden, subtropical fruit grove, conifer area, cactus and succulent garden, and "historic area"—a re-creation of an 1890s garden surrounding a Victorian house (the Heritage House Museum). There are also community gardens, a children's garden, an organic "vegetable farm," and a state-of-the-art visitor's center that includes the Orange County Agricultural and Nikkei Heritage Museum. The Friends of Fullerton Arboretum, a membership support group, organizes events, coordinates volunteer activities, and raises funds to support the arboretum. A retail nursery (the Potting Shed) offers unusual, drought-tolerant plants propagated on site. The arboretum is open every day, 8 a.m.–4:40 p.m., closed in August and January.

J. Paul Getty Center Gardens

1200 Getty Center Drive, Los Angeles 90049
(310) 440-7300
www.getty.edu

Central gardens designed by American artist Robert Irwin provide a stylized series of parterres, paths, and plazas that complement the large Getty Center and offer a serene setting overlooking the city of Los Angeles. Reservations are required.

The gardens and museum at the Getty Villa in Pacific Palisades (17985 Pacific Coast Highway, Pacific Palisades 90272) were restored in 2006.

King Gillette Ranch

26800 West Mulholland Highway, Calabasas 91302
(818) 880-6400
www.lamountains.com

The estate of King Camp Gillette (who brought us the disposable razor) includes his late 1920s Spanish Colonial Revival home, designed by architect Wallace Neff, and 588 acres of scenic land in the Santa Monica Mountains. Remnants of the original landscape plan include a eucalyptus allée, man-made pond, courtyard, terrace, and sweeping lawn. It was bought by a consortium of agencies (California State Parks, National Park Service, Mountains Recreation and Conservation Authority, and Santa Monica Mountains Conservancy) and opened in 2007 as a park.

Huntington Library, Art Collections, and Botanical Gardens

1151 Oxford Road, San Marino 91108
(626) 405-2100 (main)
www.huntington.org

Moving his railroad and real estate empire south, Henry Huntington bought the San Marino Ranch in 1903. He spent the rest of his life creating this estate to house his art and book collections. Though it was primarily a working ranch, many rare and unusual plants were brought in by Mr. Huntington to beautify the property and establish the first of many botanical collections (such as palms and desert plants). In 1919, Henry and his wife, Arabella, signed a trust indenture that transferred the property to a nonprofit trust to ensure its care in perpetuity. His pleasure garden is today's 120-acre botanical garden, containing more than 14,000 plants. Specialized gardens include the world-renowned desert garden, Japanese garden, rose garden, camellia collection, and Chinese garden. The Huntington also mounts plant expeditions, publishes books on the botanical collections, and provides school tours, docent-led group tours, garden talks, horticultural workshops, botanical art classes, and children's gardening programs. Plants are sold on the second Thursday of each month during the garden talk and at plant sales in May and November. Open Monday, Wednesday, Thursday, and Friday, noon–4:30 p.m., and Saturday and Sunday, 10:30 a.m.–4:30 p.m. Admission fee.

The Living Desert

47900 Portola Avenue, Palm Desert 92260
(760) 346-5694
www.livingdesert.org

This combination zoo, playland, and botanical garden is dedicated to desert habitat and wildlife appreciation and conservation. The 200-acre site includes over 1,600 species of desert plants from around the world, including North America, Africa, and Madagascar. There are hiking trails throughout the park's natural areas. The Palo Verde Garden Center is a retail nursery specializing in hard-to-find desert-specific flora. Plant sales are held in the spring and fall. Open every day but Monday, 9 a.m.–1:30 p.m. in the spring and summer, 9 a.m.–5 p.m. in other seasons. Admission fee.

Los Angeles County Arboretum and Botanic Garden

301 North Baldwin Avenue, Arcadia 91007-2697
(626) 821-3222
www.arboretum.org

The Los Angeles County Arboretum's 127 acres include more than 4,000 species of plants from around the world. Founded in 1947, the arboretum has introduced more than 100 plants to Southern California landscapes, including *Tabebuia impetiginosa* (pink trumpet tree). The grounds, which were part of the old Rancho Santa Anita, contain several historical winery buildings and vestiges of the former estate of mining magnate Lucky Baldwin. Sights include special sections highlighting plants from Australia, Africa, Asia, and the Americas; collections of perennials, palms, cycads, bamboo, herbs, magnolias, and ficus; and a 3.5-acre lake. The faint-footed can get around by shuttle for a fee. The arboretum is jointly administered by the Los Angeles County Department of Parks and Recreation and the Los Angeles Arboretum Foundation, which organizes tours and events and provides funding. A giant plant sale takes place in late May, and some plants are sold in the gift shop.

Charles F. Lummis Home and Garden

200 East Avenue 43, Highland Park 90031
(323) 222-0546
www.socalhistory.org

This two-acre garden, also known as El Alisal, on the west bank of the Arroyo Seco was redesigned in 1986 by Robert Perry using water-wise plantings and gardening techniques. The Lummis home now houses the Historical Society of Southern California.

Maloof Foundation Discovery Garden

Sam and Alfreda Maloof Foundation for Arts and Crafts
5131 Carnelian Street, Alta Loma 91701
www.malooffoundation.org

This garden of Mediterranean-climate and California native plants was designed to complement the hand-built residence of master woodworker Sam Maloof. The house is now a center for the perpetuation of arts and crafts. The site covers six acres, with specimen coast live oak trees, a relic lemon grove, an alluvial terrace, and a eucalyptus windrow. Open Thursday and Saturday, 12 p.m.–4 p.m.

Mildred E. Mathias Botanical Garden

University of California, Los Angeles 90024
(310) 825-1260; (310) 206-6707 (tours)
www.botgard.ucla.edu

Established in 1929 on a seven-acre arroyo on the southeastern corner of the UCLA campus, this frost-free botanical garden is a showplace for tropical and subtropical plants and includes many rare and mature trees. Special collections include Vireya rhododendrons, Hawaiian native plants, bromeliads, cycads, and ferns.

"El Molino Viejo" (The Old Mill)

1120 Old Mill Road, San Marino 91108
(626) 449-5450
www.old-mill.org

This walled mission garden is attached to a Spanish grist mill built in 1816 to service the Mission San Gabriel. The garden, now tended by the Old Mill Foundation, contains old citrus and fruit trees, plants used by the padres, and a pomegranate patio. Tours are offered Tuesday through Sunday, 1 p.m. –4 p.m.

Franklin D. Murphy Sculpture Garden

University of California, Los Angeles 90024
Charles E. Young Drive East near Wyton Drive, Los Angeles 90095
(310) 443-7020; (310) 443-7055 (tours)
www.hammer.ucla.edu

This sculpture garden with trees and earthwork was designed by landscape architect Ralph D. Cornell. Founded in 1967, the five-acre garden on the UCLA campus contains works by more than 70 internationally acclaimed sculptors and is operated by the Hammer Museum.

Natural History Museum of LA County Nature Gardens

900 Exposition Boulevard, Los Angeles 90007
(213) 763-3466
www.nhm.org

A full-on habitat garden surrounding the museum includes a pollinator garden, a family edible garden, and a "Get Dirty Zone," to acquaint little ones with the splendor of soil.

Newport Library and City Offices

100 Civic Center Drive, Newport Beach 92660

This stunning and informative drought-tolerant landscape surrounds city buildings designed by PWP Landscape Architecture.

Noguchi Garden in South Coast Plaza

San Diego Freeway at Bristol Street, Costa Mesa 92626
www.southcoastplaza.com
(714) 435-8571

Sculptor Isamu Noguchi has created the "California Scenario," a 1.6-acre reflective environment portraying elements of the California landscape. Noguchi's sculptures evoke a forest walk, desert land, water use, a water source, and the "spirit of the lima bean," a reference to the agricultural use of land in Southern California.

Orange County Great Park

7000 Trabuco Road, Building #13825, Irvine 92618 (office)
P. O. Box 19575, Irvine 92623
(949) 724-7425
www.ocgp.org

When the Lennar Corporation bought the decommissioned El Toro Marine Corps Air Station in 2005, it transferred 1,316 acres to public ownership. Today the Orange County Great

Park Corporation, a public benefit corporation and agency of the City of Irvine, oversees the development of this work in progress. The parks' guiding landscape principles are to showcase a California-friendly landscape and to celebrate and promote agriculture in this once-rich agricultural land. To this end, all plantings will be water and resource conserving, locally sourced using repurposed and recycled materials, and visually inspiring. The Balloon Park is complete and includes a farm and food lab and a demonstration landscape featuring a sensory garden, an ornamental edible garden, and container gardens for the "patio farmer." The Western Sector is under development and will include a lawn surrounded by native landscapes, a palm court, a 100-plus-acre community farm, and olive and citrus orchards that hark back to this area's agricultural past. Open Thursday through Sunday.

Pomona College

333 North College Way, Claremont 91711
(909) 621-8146
www.pomona.edu

Collegiate landscape and small gardens designed by Ralph D. Cornell.

Rancho Los Alamitos

6400 Bixby Hill Road, Long Beach 90815
(562) 431-3541
www.rancholosalamitos.com

Part of the Spanish land grant to the Manuel Nieto family, bought sequentially by Governor Jose Figueroa (for 500 dollars!), by Don Abel Stearns, by Michael Reese, and then by John Bixby (in partnership with I. W. Hellman) in 1898. Bixby's daughter-in-law Florence developed four acres of gardens in the 1920s and 1930s, calling on the talents of Florence Yoch, the Olmsted brothers, and others. She lived there until her death in 1961, when the complex was given to the City of Long Beach. Admired then and now for its restraint in an era of opulence, this garden today is considered an extraordinary example of historic garden restoration. Open Wednesday through Sunday, 1 p.m.–5 p.m.

Rancho Los Cerritos

4600 Virginia Road, Long Beach 90807
(562) 570-1755
www.rancholoscerritos.org

Another part of the enormous land grant given to Manuel Nieto (see above), this parcel (27,000 acres) was sold in 1843 to John Temple, who built the adobe still here. He created formal gardens on his cattle ranch, and several large old trees date from this time. Following years of hardship in the cattle business, the rancho was sold to sheep ranchers Flint, Bixby & Co. and ultimately bought by partner Jotham Bixby in 1869. Bit by bit, the property was sold off during tough times. In 1931, the Bixby family commissioned landscape architect Ralph D. Cornell to create a private estate garden surrounding the old adobe house. Restored to their 1930s design, the gardens boast many interesting, historical varieties of plants. Now a 4.7-acre state and national landmark owned by the City of Long Beach, Rancho Los Cerritos is the only private estate garden designed by Cornell that is open to the public.

Rancho Santa Ana Botanic Garden

1500 North College Avenue, Claremont 91711
(909) 625-8767; (909) 625-8767, ext. 404 (Grow Native Nursery)
www.rsabg.org

Rancho Santa Ana was the first botanical garden in California devoted to scientific study of its native flora. Founded in the 1920s on the Orange County ranch of its benefactor, Susanna Bixby Bryant, the garden served as a catalyst for the efforts of native plant pioneers. In its present location since 1951 and affiliated with the Claremont Colleges, the garden offers wildflower walks in season and public classes. A leading research center, it has an herbarium and a library. Half of the 86-acre garden is devoted to research projects, and half is public, organized by plant communities—desert, coastal, woodland, and riparian—with special manzanita, ceanothus, conifer, and wildflower display areas. The California Cultivar Garden highlights cultivated forms of native flora. Grow Native Nursery offers native plants for sale, 10 a.m.–5 p.m., Thursday through Sunday, from October through May. Open every day, 8 a.m.–5 p.m. The Friends of Rancho Santa Ana Botanic Garden, a membership support group, offers guided tours. Admission fee.

Virginia Robinson Gardens

1008 Elden Way, Beverly Hills 90210
(310) 550-2087 (tours);
    (310) 550-2068 (Friends of Robinson Gardens)
www.robinsongardens.org
Email: visit@robinsongardens.org

Plucky Virginia Robinson married the heir to the Robinson department stores and then ran the company for 30 years following her husband's death in 1932. Upon her own death at the age of 99 in 1976, her gardens and mansion were given to the County of Los Angeles. Hollywood's first grand estate, built in 1911, includes a six-acre Italianate garden on a terraced hillside with an Australian king palm forest, a citrus garden, a rose garden, an Italian terrace garden, and exotic trees. Tours are given by appointment.

San Juan Capistrano Mission Gardens

26801 Ortega Highway, San Juan Capistrano 92675
(949) 234-1300
www.missionsjc.com

San Juan Capistrano Mission was founded in 1776 as the seventh of California's 21 missions, icons of California history and part of Catholic Spain's effort to colonize Alta California and convert native populations. The 10-acre site includes restored mission gardens and orchards and is owned by the Diocese of Orange and entirely supported by the Mission San Juan Capistrano's preservation fund. The Mission grape was first planted here, producing California's first wine. Garden tours are given Wednesdays at 10:15 a.m. and 10:45 a.m.

Self-Realization Fellowship Center Lake Shrine Temple

17190 West Sunset Boulevard, Pacific Palisades 90272
(310) 454-4114
www.lakeshrine.org

Ten acres of gardens surround a lake on a stunning oceanside site. Started in 1950 by spiritual leader Paramahansa Yogananda as a yoga retreat, the vibrant gardens with plants from around the world "living in harmony" are designed to encourage tranquility. Inspired by the gardens of Kashmir and influenced by his friend Luther Burbank, Yogananda designed these gardens and planted many of its trees. Open to the public Tuesday through Saturday, 9 a.m.–4:30 p.m., and Sunday, noon–4:30 p.m.

Sherman Library and Gardens

2647 East Pacific Coast Highway, Corona del Mar 92625
(949) 673-0920
www.slgardens.org

Over two acres of botanical gardens surround the Sherman Library, a horticultural retreat and research center devoted to the study of the history of the Pacific Southwest. Special gardens include a rose garden, a cactus and succulent garden, a Japanese garden, an herb garden, a fern grotto, and a tropical conservatory. Several large annual flower beds provide seasonal displays. Tours are offered by the Docent Guild. Open 10:30 a.m.–4 p.m. every day. Admission fee.

South Coast Botanic Garden

26300 Crenshaw Boulevard, Palos Verdes Peninsula 90274
(310) 544-1948
www.southcoastbotanicgarden.org

The South Coast Botanic Garden is California's first major successful reclamation project, begun in 1961. Formerly a mine site and then a landfill, its present natural setting gives no clue to its past. Specialized gardens on its 87 acres on the Palos Verdes Peninsula include the Japanese Garden, Children's Garden, Rose Garden, Garden for the Senses, Mediterranean Garden, and Cactus Garden. There are also palm, pine, ficus, and ginkgo groves and a Volunteer Flower Garden. Everything from weddings and concerts to flower shows takes place here. The South Coast Botanic Garden Foundation, a membership support group, operates a gift shop, which also sells plants and food for the resident ducks. Big plant sales take place in fall and spring, on the first weekend in October and the third weekend in April. The garden is open every day, 9 a.m.–5 p.m. Admission fee for the garden but not for the gift shop.

UC Riverside Botanic Gardens

University of California, Riverside 92521
(951) 784-6962
www.ucr.edu

The UC Riverside Botanic Gardens were founded in 1963 on 40 acres of rugged terrain in the foothills of the Box Spring Mountains on the east side of campus. Established as a teaching facility, plant collections here include a subtropical fruit orchard and rose, herb, cactus, and iris gardens. The gardens also represent climate-compatible geographical areas, such as South Africa, Australia, the Southwest desert, and temperate deciduous forest.

Ventura Botanical Gardens

Grant Park, Ventura
P. O. Box 3127, Ventura 93006
(805) 232-3113
www.venturabotanicalgardens.com

Armed with city approval of its lease on 15 acres of the under-
utilized Grant Park and approval of a master plan developed
by Mia Lehrer + Associates in 2015, the nonprofit Ventura
Botanical Gardens has completed its first project, the Demonstration Trail. Future plans include a Chilean garden, a South
African garden, and a California native plants area.

Wisteria Vine

Sierra Madre 91021
(626) 355-5111 (Chamber of Commerce)

Bought in 1894 for 75 cents, this Chinese lavender wisteria
vine is said to be the world's largest, now gone rampant over
two private backyards. Call for notification of peak bloom
(usually in March) and information about the Wisteria Festival.

Wrigley Memorial and Botanical Gardens

1400 Avalon Canyon Road, Avalon, Catalina Island 90704
(310) 510-1445 (Catalina Island Conservancy)
www.catalinaconservancy.org

Surrounding a stone memorial honoring chewing gum
baron and local civic hero William Wrigley, Jr., are almost 40
acres of gardens with special emphasis on California native
plants and California island endemic plants. Six plants are
endemic to Catalina Island alone, including *Lyonothamnus floribundus* ssp. *Floribundus* (Catalina ironwood), *Arctostaphylos
catalinae* (Catalina manzanita), and the very rare *Cercocarpus
traskiae* (Catalina mahogany). Admission fee.

Signature Plants from Other Mediterranean-Climate Regions

Distinct plants grow in each of the world's five Mediterranean-climate regions, but though continents separate them, plants from one region can often grow in another: owing to similarities in climate, the plants have evolved similar characteristics to native vegetation. This broadens your options for the summer dry–winter wet garden.

Chile

Key plant communities in this narrow and long country are shrubs, vines, herbaceous annuals and perennials, cacti, palms, and terrestrial bromeliads. From the shrubby vegetation of the matorral comes litre (*Lithraea caustica*), soapbark tree or quillay (*Quillaja saponaria*), and espino (*Acacia caven*). Garden-worthy vines also grow in the matorral: nasturtium relative *Tropaeolum tricolor,* red-flowered salcilla (*Bomarea salcilla*), and *copihue,* or Chilean bellflower.

In moist settings, hummingbird or hardy fuchsia (*Fuchsia magellanica*) and Chilean or giant-rhubarb (*Gunnera tinctoria*) thrive. Bromeliads are widespread, as are *Alstroemeria* bulbs.

Broadleaf evergreen trees, peumo (*Cryptocarya alba*), southern beech (*Nothofagus*), mayten (*Maytenus boaria*), and monkey puzzle (*Araucaria araucana*) grow widely.

Western Cape, South Africa

In the crescent-shaped coastal strip of South Africa's Mediterranean climate, the most extensive native vegetation grows in the *fynbos,* or "fine bush." This includes plants from the genera *Protea* and *Leucospermum;* king protea (*Protea cynaroides*) is the national flower. *Erica* and other heather family members grow here, as does the rush-like *Restio,* or Cape reed.

Bulbs from western Cape communities include iris family members (*Babiana, Freesia, Gladiolus, Ixia, Sparaxis,* and *Watsonia*), lily family members (*Kniphofia*), calla lily or arum (*Zantedeschia aethiopica*), and amaryllis family members (*Agapanthus*).

Trees include silver tree (*Leucadendron argenteum*), Cape chestnut (*Calodendrum capense*), and wild almond (*Brabejum stellatifolium*).

Australia

Two separate Mediterranean-climate areas exist on this continent. The three chief plant families are myrtle (*Myrtaceae*), pea (*Fabaceae*), and protea (*Proteaceae*). Kwongan, or open scrub vegetation, is a key plant community that includes scrub heath and broombush thicket. Scrub vegetation mallee, named for multiple-trunked eucalyptus species, occurs in drier parts.

Widespread myrtle family members include the eucalypts jarrah (*Eucalyptus marginata*) and karri (*E. diversicolor*). The pea family include wattles (*Acacia*), wisteria (*Hardenbergia*), and red coral (*Kennedia coccinea*) vines, all extensive in the area and garden worthy in California. *Protea* family members include *Banksia, Dryandra, Grevillea,* and *Hakea.*

Mediterranean Basin

The Mediterranean Basin stretches around the Mediterranean Sea and across three continents—Europe, Africa, and Asia.

It accounts for a larger area and more complex geography than other Mediterranean climates. Rainfall patterns vary and, among all Mediterranean climates, summers here are the hottest. Plant communities include maquis (high and low), garigue, woodland, and forest.

In the high maquis region, you will find low-growing trees and evergreen shrubs: holm oak (*Quercus ilex*), kermes oak (*Q. coccifera*), strawberry tree (*Arbutus unedo*), and myrtle (*Myrtus communis*). Evergreen shrub rock rose (*Cistus* spp.) pervades low maquis habitats.

In the driest and hottest parts you will find garigue, including low shrubs and spiny plants such as Greek spiny spurge (*Euphorbia acanthothamnos*), and aromatic plants of the mint family (*Lamiaceae*): rosemary (*Rosmarinus officinalis*), lavender (*Lavandula stoechas* and *L. dentata*), oregano, marjoram, and Jerusalem sage (*Phlomis fruticosa*).

Oaks dominate forests and woodlands; species include holm (*Quercus ilex*), kermes (*Q. coccifera*), cork (*Q. suber*), and downy (*Q. pubescens*). To a lesser degree you will find conifers, including stone (*Pinus pinea*) and Aleppo (*Pinus halepensis*) pines and cypress (*Cupressus*).

Olive trees (*Olea europaea*), palms, and tree heather (*Erica arborea*) are common sights, and bulbs such as tulip, iris, crocus, cyclamen, orchid, and narcissus abound.

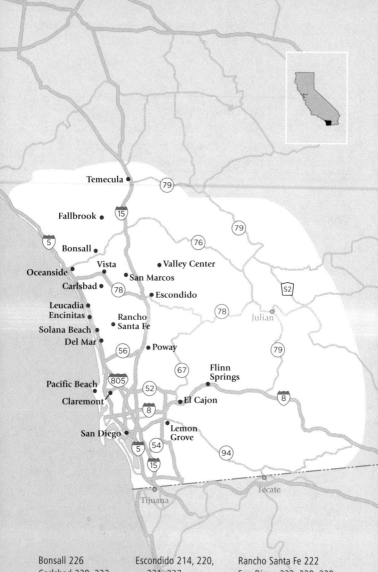

Chapter 8

San Diego County

Washingtonia filifera

Counties: San Diego
Elevational range: Sea level to 823 feet
Sunset climate zones: 7, 11, 13, 21, 22, 23
Annual rainfall: San Diego, 10 inches; Borrego Valley, 7 inches
Winter temperatures: Lows average 55°F,
with Julian an anomaly at 23°F to 9°F.
Summer temperatures: Average high temperature in San Diego
74°F. Borrego Valley and Borrego Badlands, within Anza-Borrego
Desert State Park, average 107°F and can vault as high as 125°F.

As the southernmost part of the state, San Diego County stretches south from Orange County to the Mexican border. Its terrain ranges from coastal bluff and sandy shoreline to mountains, canyons, fertile valleys, forested hills, and desert. The Anza-Borrego Desert spans its eastern side.

A warm, Mediterranean climate ideal for tender plant life graces this county. Ocean currents push warm waters up from Mexico, making this area hotter than maritime San Francisco. The air stays moist through mild winters and cool summers. A high overcast sky in spring and early summer often lingers until sun finally burns it off in the afternoon. For the most part, gardeners can grow papayas, macadamias, palms, and orchids outdoors.

Temperature zones vary as one travels inland from coastal climate thermal belts around La Mesa and Vista, to interior valley thermal belts such as Rancho Santa Fe, down to Lakeside. Valley floors form pockets farther inland, where air can be hot and dry, as at Escondido and Ramona. A general lack of winter chill makes fruit trees risky, but a stretch of high foothills from Warner Springs to Julian offer sufficient winter chill for good apple production. An annual October Apple Festival features pies, cider, or fresh fruit. Growing seasons shorten in the desert, lasting from April to early November in the high desert and from mid-February through November in the low desert.

Many plants grow wild in this region. San Diego sunflower (*Viguiera laciniata*) brightens natural landscapes, as does canyon sunflower (*Venegasia carpesioides*). Sages flourish, including Munz's sage (*Salvia munzii*), rose sage (*Salvia pachyphylla*), and Point Sal purple sage (*Salvia leucophylla* 'Point Sal'). The California fan palm (*Washingtonia filifera*), the country's largest native palm, grows here in moist areas from sea level to 3,500 feet, primarily around desert springs. This is a strapping, columnar tree between 20 to 75 feet tall with waxy, fan-shaped leaves; when its fronds die, they stay attached and drop down, skirting the trunk. Under the skirt, small birds and invertebrates find shelter. The palm flowers on long stems.

Specialty Nurseries and Growers

Bird Rock Tropicals

221 Princehouse Lane, Encinitas 92024
P. O. Box 231458, Encinitas 92023
(760) 436-3088
www.birdrocktropicals.com
Email: info@birdrocktropicals.com
Pamela Koide Hyatt
Retail, wholesale, and mail/online order

Open by appointment only, Monday through Friday, 9 a.m.–3 p.m., and sometimes on Saturday.

Plant specialties: Bromeliads (2,000 types, including 600 species and 300 hybrids, 225 of which are hybrids of *Tillandsia*); orchids (species and hybrids).

History/description: Visiting Puerto Vallarta in the 1970s, Pamela Koide saw her first bromeliad, the unusual *Tillandsia caput medusae*. Thus started her odyssey of collecting bromeliads and orchids all over Mexico and Central and South America. She is credited with the discovery of more than 20 species and more than 40 natural hybrids of *Tillandsia* in Mexico and Peru. Pamela opened her business in the Bird Rock area of La Jolla in 1981 as a backyard specialty nursery devoted exclusively to bromeliads, especially tillandsias, which at that time were hard to find. In 1986, she moved the successful operation to Carlsbad for more space and began selling orchids, palms, and cycads as well. That year, Pamela also began hybridizing tillandsias, making over 3,000 hybrid crosses, some of which took 15 to 20 years to mature and bloom. In 2013, one of her creations, *Tillandsia* 'Samantha', won the FloraHolland Glass Tulip Award. By 2002, her "little" collection had grown to over a million plants. In 2005, the nursery moved to Encinitas, California, where Pamela continues to grow and propagate the best of the collection and her hybrids. She has been a featured speaker in the United States, Japan, Singapore, Australia, and New Zealand, lecturing on *Tillandsia*, her successful hybrids, and her plant discoveries in Mexico and Peru. In 2015, she developed an iOS application called Tilli-Cards, the first-ever reference app for identification and culture of these unique plants. A plant availability list is on the nursery's website.

Botanical Partners
(home of **Bamboo Headquarters Nursery**)

3763 Silverleaf Lane, Vista 92084
(760) 758-6181
www.botanicalpartners.com

Email: sales@botanicalpartners.com
Ralph Evans
Retail, wholesale, and online order
Bamboo Headquarters (bamboohq.com) is Botanical Partners's
    website primarily for bamboo information and retail Internet sales.
Open Monday through Saturday, 9 a.m.–3 p.m.
    Appointments suggested.

Plant specialties: Bamboo (over 270 species, including clumping, running, dwarf, desert-hardy, and cold-hardy varieties), palms (100 species), and cycads (70 species), as well as exotic plants, flowering trees, grasses, shrubs, succulents, and water-wise plants.

History/description: Ralph Evans has been in the nursery business since 1965 and started Botanical Partners in 1994. Originally the nursery was wholesale only, specializing in uncommon plants—palms, flowering trees, and exotics; over time its focus shifted to concentrate on bamboo, as well as companion and water-efficient plants. The 42-acre site includes large specimens, as well as artful arrangements of plants in display gardens and in containers.

Buena Creek Gardens

418 Buena Creek Road, San Marcos 92069
(760) 744-2810
www.buenacreekgardens.com
Email: info@buenacreekgardens.com
Steve and Shari Matteson
Retail
Open Thursday through Sunday, 9 a.m.–4 p.m
    (winter open at 10 a.m.).

Plant specialties: Uncommon varieties of ornamental plants: perennials, shrubs, vines, subtropicals, drought-tolerant plants, California native plants, succulents, cacti, reblooming daylilies, and reblooming irises.

History/description: The nursery started as an iris farm in the 1970s, with daylilies added in the 1980s, operating then as a mail-order business called Cordon Bleu Farms. With the arrival of horticulturist Steve Brigham, the four-acre site was developed as a nursery and the gardens were started. Steve bought the nursery and property in 1996 from Bob Brooks and, in 2008, sold it to Steve and Shari Matteson. Steve Matteson honed his horticultural skills in his family's cut-flower business, in operation since 1955. This is a true horticultural mecca for plant enthusiasts, containing over 5,000 outstanding varieties of flowering plants from temperate and tropical regions around the world. Featured gardens include a bird and butterfly garden, a sun perennial terrace, a drought-tolerant garden, a shade garden, and a palm canyon, plus nearly two acres of daylily and iris flower fields. Picnic under redwoods or stroll in the shade.

C & J Cactus Nursery

2369 East Vista Way, Vista 92084
(760) 724-6848
Carl Volkers, Jim Kampwirth
Wholesale only
Open to landscape professionals, Monday through Friday, 8 a.m.–3 p.m.

Plant specialties: Cactus (350 varieties) and many unusual succulents.

History/description: Both Carl Volkers and Jim Kampwirth were cactus and succulent collectors back in Illinois. Wanting to transform their hobby into a business, they moved to Southern California for its better climate and greater proximity to native growing areas. This five-acre nursery, which officially opened in 1976, propagates from seeds and cuttings of stock plants acquired during Carl and Jim's many years of collecting. Phone the nursery for an availability list.

California Tropical Fruit Trees

2081 Elevado Road, Vista 92084
(760) 434-5085

www.tropicalfruittrees.com
Email: SITJewelry2000@gmail.com
Perry Coles
Retail and wholesale
Open Monday through Friday by appointment, 9 a.m.–4 p.m.; Saturday open house, 9 a.m.–4 p.m. (no appointment necessary).

Plant specialties: Exotic tropical/subtropical fruit trees well suited to Southern California climates, especially large-size specimens; some *Plumeria* and other tropical flowering trees.

History/description: Unable to find local sources for the tropical fruits he enjoyed on his travels, Perry Coles started to investigate and import tropical fruit trees. He opened the nursery in 1994 with the fruits of his labors. Years of testing just which tropical fruit trees will thrive in subtropical Southern California make him confident that every one of his trees will grow well from Santa Barbara to San Diego. All are container grown; some trees have been in their boxes for 25 years, attesting to the fact that fruit trees grow and fruit well in containers, growing about half as fast as in-ground trees. All plants are propagated on site and there is minimal spraying here—good for the environment and for employees who regularly eat the fruit.

Desert Theater

800 Sunset Drive, Vista 92081
9655 Kiwi Meadow Lane, Escondido 92026
(760) 594-2330
www.deserttheater.com
Brandon Bullard
Retail, wholesale, and mail order
Open by appointment only.
    Please call one day in advance for both locations.

Plant specialties: Cacti and succulents. Many huge specimens, with special collections of *Aloe, Echeveria,* cactus (200 varieties), *Euphorbia* (145 varieties), *Haworthia, Notocactus, Mammillaria, Gymnocalycium,* and *Rebutia.*

History/description: Desert Theater was started by Jay and Kate Jackson in 1984 in Watsonville as an outlet for their large collection of succulents and cacti. They added the Vista location and brought Brandon Bullard in to manage it. Bullard bought Desert Theater in 2006, combining it with other growing grounds he already owned in Escondido for a total of 15 acres of production. Known as "the Cactus Guy," Brandon, along with his team, offers design, transportation, and installation services.

East West Trees

1719 Rainbow Valley Boulevard, Fallbrook 92028 (office)
(760) 728-0040
www.eastwesttrees.com
Peter Doljanin, Saul Nadler
Wholesale only
Open Monday through Friday, 7:30 a.m.–3 p.m.

Plant specialties: 600 varieties of plants including palms, succulents, cacti, protea family plants, grasses, unthirsty subtropicals, cycads, and Australian natives.

History/description: Started in 1998 by Peter Doljanin as a plant brokerage business, East West Trees evolved into a palm-growing nursery when Peter joined forces with Saul Nadler of San Francisco's Palm Broker and Flora Grubb Gardens. Now with 35 acres under cultivation in four locations around Fallbrook, East West is a major grower of a variety of plants suited to summer-dry California. Check in at the office for further directions.

Exotica Rare Fruit Nursery

2508B East Vista Way, Vista 92083
(760) 724-9093
Email: gmleoa@gmail.com
Steven and Genette Spangler
Retail, wholesale, and mail order
Open every day, 8 a.m.–5 p.m.

Plant specialties: Edible landscape plants, especially hard-to-find tropical fruits. Subtropical and Mediterranean shrubs, such as sweet pomegranates (over 50 varieties); Asian and South American fruiting, flowering, and fragrant plants (longan, lychee, jujube); bamboo; and palms (such as date palm, Chilean wine palm, and butia palm), as well as rare mangoes, figs (30 varieties), old guavas, mulberries, tropical cherries, bananas (18 types), and the Buddha's tree of enlightenment (the Bodhi Tree, or *Ficus religiosa*). All plants are organically and biodynamically grown. Seeds for wholesale contract only.

History/description: Steven Spangler supplemented his oceanographic studies in Hawaii picking pineapples. He discovered a unique Tahitian squash and advertised its seeds in *Organic Gardening*. English seed company Thompson and Morgan ordered a huge amount and the Exotica Seed Company was born. Jessica Leaf joined the partnership in 1984 and propagator specialist Leo Garcia joined in 1995, ever expanding the varieties of edible fruits on offer. The nursery is a six-acre jungle-like paradise guarded by wild butterflies and birds, planted with mature fruit trees from all over the world to give you a sense of their ultimate size and the taste of their fruit.

Garden Glories Nursery

1356 Douglas Drive, Vista 92084
(858)449-5342
www.gardengloriesnursery.com
Email: gardengloriesnursery@gmail.com
Liz Youngflesh
Retail and local wholesale
Open most hours, but call for appointment.

Plant specialties: Hard-to-find perennials for water-wise Mediterranean climates, especially evergreen, florist-quality *Alstroemeria* (20 varieties).

History/description: A chat with the late plantsman and designer Bill Teague while both were volunteering at a San

Diego Horticultural Society event proved life-altering for Liz Youngflesh. An avid gardener, Liz wanted to work from home. Bill suggested she start a home nursery and offered to help source plants to get her started. Eleven years later, Liz has an enviable collection of perennials and florist-quality (large-flowered), sterile alstroemeria hybrids, which she tests and divides in her backyard garden. The sterility of her alstroemeria (no runners, no seeds) results in plants that are evergreen, profuse bloomers and require no staking, since none of the plant's energy has been diverted for reproduction.

The Good Earth Nursery

Mission Road at the I-15 freeway exit, Fallbrook (retail location)
(760) 728-8066
www.palms4u.com
Email: jennifer.goodearth@gmail.com
Jennifer Gaggero, Stephanie Boren
Retail and wholesale
Open Monday through Friday, 7 a.m.–4:30 p.m.,
    and Saturday 7 a.m.–3:30 p.m.

Plant specialties: Indoor foliage, succulents, and specimen trees, including palms, ornamentals, and aloes.

History/description: The landscaper father of sisters Jennifer Gaggero and Stephanie Boren found some property in Fallbrook and built a greenhouse there. Back in 1975, during the Jimmy Carter era, his first cash crop, naturally, was peanut plants, which he sold to a variety of supermarkets. Getting to know plant brokers, he began to produce indoor foliage for these same markets. Then, in the early 1980s, he bought more property and started growing palms. Since the sisters took over in 1996, the nursery has diversified to keep up with landscape trends, retaining the old palms and indoor plants but adding water-conserving plants as well. The nursery has three locations, two for wholesale growing and shipping and the 35-acre one listed above for retail.

Grigsby Cactus Gardens

2326–2354 Bella Vista Drive, Vista 92084-7836
(760) 727-1323
www.cactus-mall.com/grigsby/
Madelyn Lee
Retail, wholesale, and mail order
Open Tuesday through Saturday, 9 a.m.–2 p.m.
   Always best to call first. No wholesale on Saturdays.

Plant specialties: Cacti and succulents, including *Euphorbia, Sansevieria,* and large specimen plants for collectors and landscape use.

History/description: Madelyn Lee, Grigsby's longtime manager and an avid collector of cacti and succulents in her own right, bought this business from David Grigsby, who started planting out his "hobby plants" in 1965 as a retirement activity. What began as a hobby run amok is now a three-acre hillside nursery interspersed with special display gardens. Some mature specimens are more than 30 years old. Most plants are propagated on site.

Jungle Music Palms and Cycads

450 Ocean View Avenue, Encinitas 92024 (nursery)
3233 Brant Street, San Diego 92103 (mailing address)
(619) 291-4605
www.junglemusic.net
Email: phil.bergman@junglemusic.net
Phil Bergman
Retail and mail order
Open Monday through Saturday, 9 a.m.–4 p.m.

Plant specialties: Over 1,100 species of palms, cycads, and other tropical plants, including rare species unavailable elsewhere, such as *Encephalartos, Dioons, Cycas, Stangeria, Ceratozamia, Macrozamia, Zamia,* and other genera. Palm availability includes more common to extremely rare species, including new introductions from Madagascar and New

Caledonia. The nursery also has a wide selection of bromeliads, Hawaiian ti plants, *Heliconia, Pandanus, Philodendron, Alocasia,* and other tropical plants.

History/description: This San Diego Hospital emergency-room physician grew up in a gardening family in Southern California and majored in biology at Stanford. He became interested in palms while a medical student in San Francisco and started collecting them during his residency in San Diego in the early 1970s. Pretty soon, Phil Bergman was collecting and trading seed with palm specialists all over the world. He opened Jungle Music in 1977, initially at his home and since 1994 at this location in Encinitas, just minutes off Interstate 5. For almost 20 years his son Jesse has joined him at the nursery. Featuring a vast assortment of large, rare, coning-sized cycads, the nursery has over 200,000 plants for sale on several acres of grounds and many greenhouses, as well as a demonstration garden and an education center for lectures and classes. Plentiful horticultural information is available either at the nursery or on the website.

Kartuz Greenhouses

1408 Sunset Drive, Vista 92083-6531
(760) 941-3613
www.kartuz.com
kartuz@kartuz.com
Michael Kartuz
Retail and (primarily) mail/online order
Open Tuesday through Saturday, 9 a.m.–noon, 1 p.m.–3 p.m.
    Best to call first.

Plant specialties: *Begonia* (cane, rex, rhizomatous, shrubby, and others), *Gesneriad, Hoya,* and *Passiflora* (passionflower); flowering subtropicals; and vines and climbers, especially those suited to small spaces and container gardening.

History/description: In 1979, Michael Kartuz brought his business west from Wilmington, Massachusetts, attracted by the infinitely nicer weather and lower heating costs. Although most plants are still grown in greenhouses, they summer (April to October) outside in shade houses. Michael will custom grow for clients.

Las Pilitas Nursery

8331 Nelson Way, Escondido 92026
(760) 749-5930
www.laspilitas.com
Email: escondido@laspilitas.com
Celeste Wilson; Valerie Phillips, manager
Retail and some wholesale
Open Tuesday through Saturday, 9 a.m.–4 p.m. (subject to change).

Plant specialties: California native plants (200–300 species on hand), perennials, shrubs, trees, and vines.

History/description: In 2000, at the urging of friends, Bert and Celeste Wilson opened a satellite nursery here as an additional outlet for plants propagated at their Santa Margarita location (see chapter 6), as well as those propagated here by Valerie Phillips. The nursery is in a 21-acre park-like setting with towering native sycamore trees growing along a stream. There are also demonstration gardens and an office run entirely on solar power. The excellent website serves as a primer on California's climates and plant communities.

Moosa Creek

27201 Cool Water Ranch Road, Valley Center 92082
11760 Betsworth Road, Valley Center 92082 (office)
(760) 749-3216
www.moosacreeknursery.com
Email: nursery@moosacreeknursery.com
Hank and Su Kraus
Wholesale and contract growing
Open Monday through Friday, 7 a.m.–4 p.m.

Plant specialties: Southern California native plant species, including the endemic *Salvia munzii* and endangered *Agave* *shawii,* in addition to some cultivars and native plants from Central and Northern California.

History/description: Unable to find sources for native plants to landscape around their house, the Krauses began collecting and propagating seed from plants on their property. Living on pristine coastal sage scrub with riparian areas alongside Moosa Creek, they were successful in growing a variety of native plants. This success was noted by others, initiating the "accidental nursery" in 2004. The nursery moved to this new 14-acre growing ground a little farther upstream on Moosa Creek in 2016. Retail customers, take note: Moosa Creek has a special relationship with its retail vendors and you can order plants online for pickup at one of these retail sites near you. Tea drinkers, take note: tea made from woolly blue curls, or *Trichostema lanatum,* can also be bought online under the label Wild Chaparral. Moosa Creek is proud to offer plants grown from cuttings, obtained via Rancho Santa Ana Botanic Garden, from the last *Arctostaphylos hookeri franciscana* found in the wild, long thought to be extinct; this plant from San Francisco's Presidio grows well here, too. The nursery also offers mitigation, habitat restoration, site-specific seed collecting, and landscape services.

Oasis Water-Efficient Gardens

10816 Reidy Canyon Trail, Escondido 92026
(760) 277-0214
www.oasis-plants.com
Email: marketing@altmanplants.com
Carmen Conteras, manager
Retail and wholesale
Open Wednesday through Saturday, 8 a.m.–4 p.m.,
    and Sunday, 10 a.m.–4 p.m.

Plant specialties: Succulents, cacti, and other water-efficient plants, including perennials and grasses.

History/description: The behemoth wholesale business Altman Plants (now in six states) started as a backyard hobby of succulent collectors Ken and Deena Altman in 1975. Oasis Water-Efficient Gardens is their effort to share their plant material with retail customers in their primary community. Their list of plant introductions is large, including *Aeonium* 'Emerald Eyes' and *A.* 'Fiesta', *Crassula* 'Candy Cane', and *Echeveria x imbricata* and *E.* 'Crimson Tide'. Succulents remain the nursery's core business, though other water-conserving plants are offered as well. This half-acre nursery has well-displayed plants, arrayed in pots in front of its succulent-studded hillside growing grounds.

Protea USA

482 Rainbow Crest Road, Fallbrook 92028
(760) 731-6584
www.proteausa.com
Email: dennis@proteausa.com
Dennis Perry, Rua Petty
Wholesale and contract growing
Open by appointment only.

Plant specialties: South African proteas and other members of the protea family.

History/description: Because they "find joy in our horticultural and floricultural activities," protea growers Dennis Perry and Rua Petty started Protea USA as a retirement project. Joining his father in the business, Dennis formed Perry's Panorama in Somis in 1981. Rua and wife Linda bought RJT Ranch in Rainbow in 1996, developing it into a protea flower operation. Their mission is to develop and promote both plants and flowers of the protea family.

Rancho Soledad Nurseries

18539 Aliso Canyon Road, Rancho Santa Fe 92067
(858) 756-3717
www.ranchosoledad.com
Email: sales@ranchosoledad.com

Peggy Hunter; Heather Hunter May, president
Retail and wholesale
Open Monday through Saturday, 8 a.m.–4:30 p.m.

Plant specialties: Large specimen plants, succulents, cycads, palms, bamboo, and tropical plants.

History/description: Founded by the late Jerry Hunter and his wife, Peggy, in 1954 as Mount Soledad Nursery in Pacific Beach, the nursery moved here in 1965 and changed its name to Rancho Soledad. Jerry Hunter brought the first dracena canes and rhapis palm seeds to California and, with Dr. Henry Donselman, developed many new palms and anthuriums. A succulent breeding and collecting program was started in 1998 with propagator Kelly Griffin, resulting in many introductions, including *Agave* 'Blue Glow'. A sea of potted specimens flows over 25 acres of rolling hills, all accessible by golf cart. Truly a botanical garden, 350 species of aloes adorn its "Botanical Hill," and "Palms of Paradise," a misted jungle of palms and cycads, occupies an acre under shade cloth. On-site Rancho Tissue Technologies, a separate company, continues to propagate hard-to-grow and interesting plants.

Recon Native Plants

1755 Saturn Boulevard, San Diego 92154
(619) 423-2284
www.reconnativeplants.com
Email: info@reconnativeplants.com
Ryan West, general manager
Wholesale, with retail sales at four plant sales during winter/spring
Wholesale open by appointment, Monday through Friday, 7 a.m.–4 p.m.

Plant specialties: Native plants from the southwestern United States and the Pacific coast.

History/description: This employee-owned nursery was started in 1999 by Recon Environmental, Inc., to supply plants for its habitat restoration work and was spun off as a separate entity in 2002. It occupies 15 acres in the Tijuana River valley on an old dairy farm, just three miles from the ocean, where the mild climate enables the growing of a wide selection of plants. Mature plants for the nursery's seed collection are grown on 2.5 acres, and the nursery also propagates hybrids and cultivars from cuttings. Retail customers should sign up on the website to receive notice of Recon's plant sales.

Serra Gardens Landscape Succulents

897 Quail Hill Road, Fallbrook 92028
   (entrance on Santa Margarita Road)
(760) 990-4762
www.shop.cacti.com (web nursery)
don@serragardens.com, beth@serragardens.com
Don and Beth Newcomer
Retail, wholesale, and mail/online order
Open Tuesday through Saturday, 8 a.m.–4 p.m.
   Appointment recommended.

Plant specialties: Rare and unusual specimens of cacti and succulents from all parts of the world, including *Pedilanthus bracteatus, Geradanthus macrorhizus,* and *Ruschia lineolata,* and a wide variety of *Aloe, Agave, Sedum,* and *Euphorbia.* Plants are available at the nursery in 4-inch pots to 48-inch boxes, or available via online order in 1-gallon bare-root sizes. All plants are field grown.

History/description: Collecting cacti and succulents is a generational habit in the Newcomer family. Equipped with his father's collection and his own, Don Newcomer opened this nursery in the Serra Retreat area of Malibu in 1986. In 2008, he moved the nursery to Fallbrook in north San Diego County, a prime location for field-grown cacti and succulents.

Solana Succulents

355 North Highway 101, Solana Beach 92075
(858) 259-4568

www.solanasucculents.com
Email: solanasucculents@sbcglobal.net
Jeff Moore
Retail
Open Wednesday through Saturday, 10 a.m.–5 p.m. (winter close at
    4 p.m.); Sunday, 12 p.m.–4 p.m. Best to call first.

Plant specialties: Succulents, especially *Aloe, Aeonium, Echeveria,* and *Agave,* including small collector's bonsai and large landscape specimens; some cactus.

History/description: Jeff Moore found himself riveted by a display of bonsai succulents at the San Diego County Fair in Del Mar and became an instant collector. Soon he was selling bonsai succulents at local street fairs as a "sanity"-preserving sideline business to his regular job as a mortgage broker. In 1992, he succumbed entirely to succulents and found this small site on the Pacific Coast Highway. He does some division but increases and refines his collection mainly by building relationships with the many large wholesale growers in San Diego's North County, ground zero for succulent production in the United States. Also a garden designer, Jeff's award-winning garden Under the Succulent Sea, created for the county fair in 2002, has spawned others at San Diego Botanic Garden and in private gardens. His second book, *Aloes and Agaves in Cultivation,* was published in 2016. This jam-packed small nursery has perfected profusion.

Summers Past Farms

15602 Olde Highway 80, Flinn Springs 92021
(619) 390-1523
www.summerspastfarms.com
Email: summerspastfarms@cox.net
Sheryl and Marshall Lozier
Retail
Open Wednesday through Saturday, 9 a.m.–5 p.m.,
    and Sunday, 10 a.m.–5 p.m.

Plant specialties: Culinary and landscape herbs, perennials, vegetables, succulents, and annuals.

History/description: This nursery is the sanguine result of opportunity and interest. The availability of Marshall Lozier's beautiful family property, his talent as a contractor, and Sheryl's love of cooking and desire for fresh herbs created this five-acre garden. Many Cuyamaca College classes later, the two opened the nursery in 1992. The property is a strolling cottage garden, with two barns—one for soap making, one for gifts—a little pond, picket fences, and a sweet-pea maze, all enjoyed by lots of pets and chickens. The nursery's website includes information about classes and special events, including an annual lavender celebration and "fairy festival."

Waterwise Botanicals (formerly **Daylily Hill**)

32151 Old Highway 395, Bonsall 92003
(760) 728-2641
www.waterwisebotanicals.com
Email: talkplants@waterwisebotanicals.com
Tom and Jackie Jesch
Retail and wholesale
Open Monday through Saturday, 8 a.m.–5 p.m.

Plant specialties: Field-grown cacti and succulents, water-wise perennials, shrubs, ornamental grasses, and roses.

History/description: Tom Jesch has been in the nursery business forever, after having developed a passion for plants in his youth. As a kid growing up in Reno, he had a little business selling his cactus collection. In 1995, he decided to concentrate exclusively on his own nursery, and two years later he found this 21-acre property in the rolling hills of San Diego's North County. His plant interests continue to expand, and today the hillsides are covered in striped swaths of cacti and succulents, roses, shrubs, and perennials that create a "plant lover's paradise." The flatland below is filled with container plants with an emphasis on "water wise without the compromise."

This destination nursery includes picnic tables, gazebos, and ponds. Artistic Jackie creates succulent bowls and keeps the website full of good information and photographs. The nursery puts on two major events each year, Succulent Celebration and Fall Garden Party.

Weidners' Gardens

695 Normandy Road, Encinitas 92024
(760) 436-2194 (retail); (760) 436-5326 (wholesale)
www.weidners.com
Email: contact@weidners.com
Oliver Storm, Kalim Owens
Retail and wholesale
Retail open every day, 9 a.m.–5 p.m. (winter close at 4:30 pm);
    wholesale open Monday through Friday, 6:30 a.m.–4 p.m.

Plant specialties: Subtropical plants, including tuberous *Begonia*, *Fuchsia*, *Mandevilla*, *Scaevola*, *Brunfelsia*, succulents (100 varieties), fruit trees, and perennials.

History/description: Robert Weidner retired from many years in the foliage business, moved to Encinitas, and set up a single greenhouse to grow plants for friends. Never intending to really retire, he bought 25,000 tuberous begonia seedlings and created a garden of raised beds and shade houses. In 1973, with his wife, Evelyn, he opened Weidner's Begonia Gardens. Then, as now, customers dig their own begonias and pansies in season. The nursery no longer confines its offerings to begonias, and over the years it has introduced *Scaevola* 'Blue Wonder', *Dipladenia* 'Fair Lady' and *D.* 'Scarlet Pimpernel', and *Verbena* 'Temari'. In 2012, the nursery was bought by two longtime employees, grower Oliver Storm and Kalim Owens, now in charge of wholesale sales. It is Evelyn Weidner's legacy that this property remains in horticulture. She still writes the newsletter and occasionally can be spotted in the nursery. The greenhouses are ablaze with Ecke poinsettias and cyclamen in November and December.

Notable Garden Centers

Walter Andersen Nursery

12755 Danielson Court, Poway 92064, (858) 513-4900
3642 Enterprise Street, San Diego 92110, (619) 224-8271
www.walterandersen.com

With deep roots as pioneer farmers in Nebraska, the Andersen family has been working with plants for generations. Walter Anderson, Sr., opened this nursery in Old Town in 1928 in conjunction with his landscaping and maintenance business. As plant sales prospered, he gave up his maintenance business to focus full time on the nursery. Son Walter Jr. took over in the mid-1970s and is today joined by son Ken, daughter Karen, and several in-laws; the fourth generation is being groomed for action. The five-acre Poway store was opened in 1998 to serve inland gardeners and includes demonstration gardens and a garden railway. Very community oriented, Andersen's offers Saturday classes, participates in local flower shows, and partners with the Rotary Club and local schools and organizations. The emphasis here is on "collector's plants"—unusual bedding and perennial plants—such as palms, cycads, cacti, vines, bamboo (50 varieties), bougainvillea (20 varieties), and hibiscus (20 varieties). The nursery also has an online store for garden supplies.

Anderson's La Costa Nursery

400 La Costa Avenue, Encinitas 92024
(760) 753-3153
www.andersonslacostanursery.com

Founded by Horace Anderson in 1954, this nursery was bought a couple of years ago by the Smith family, keeping it a family-owned and -operated independent nursery for over

60 years now. Just three blocks from the ocean, the nursery's coastal location offers an ideal climate in which to nurture its 3,000 types of plants, featuring drought-tolerant plants, native plants, and cacti and succulents, as well as annuals, perennials, water plants, and organic, non-GMO vegetables. The nursery also has an online store for garden supplies and offers garden design services and clinics. It is open every day, 8:30 a.m.–5 p.m.

Armstrong Garden Centers

5702 Paseo Del Norte, Carlsbad 92008, (760) 804-7330
735 East Foothill Boulevard, Claremont 91711, (909) 445-0744
2840 Via de la Valle, Del Mar 92014, (858) 755-1574
1755 East Main Street, El Cajon 92021, (619) 442-9281
701 North El Camino Real, Encinitas 92024, (760) 634-2975
10320 Friars Road, San Diego 92120, (619) 563-1433
1350 West Morena Boulevard, San Diego 92110, (619) 276-9970
9939 Carmel Mountain Road, San Diego 92129, (858) 538-6062
27401 Ynez Road, Temecula 92591, (951) 308-9100

(See listing in chapter 7.)

Barrels & Branches

1452 Santa Fe Drive, Encinitas 92024
(760) 753-2852
www.barrelsandbranches.com

Samantha Owens was bred into the nursery business, being the daughter of a nursery owner and a flower farmer. The one-acre hillside nursery is located on the old farm site where Samantha grew up. Set up as a garden with meandering paths, the nursery brims with planting ideas and inspiration. Specialties here include perennials, succulents, drought-tolerant plants, ornamental grasses, trees, and California native plants—unusual plants suited to local climates. Open every day, 8 a.m.–5 p.m. Landscape design and maintenance services are offered. The nursery also serves as an event space for weddings.

Evergreen Nursery

9708 Flinn Springs Road, El Cajon 92021
3231 South Oceanside Boulevard, Oceanside 92054, (760) 754-0340
13650 Carmel Valley Road, San Diego 92130, (858) 481-0622
www.evergreennursery.com

Mark Collins was literally raised in the nursery business, with his father, grandfather, and grandfather's grandfather all preceding him as nurserymen. Today, he oversees 300 acres of growing grounds in Escondido, San Pasqual, and Valley Center and three landscape centers that blanket San Diego County. Each landscape center is about 50 acres, sort of a drive-through nursery where customers use their cars as shopping carts. Laid out for the wholesale trade, the nursery welcomes retail shoppers who "behave like wholesale customers"—in other words, those who do not require a lot of service. The lack of personal attention is more than made up for by the access to such a large inventory of each plant. Open every day, 7:30 a.m.–5 p.m. (winter close at 4:30 p.m.).

Ganter Nursery

3016 Fruitland Drive, Vista 92084
(760) 758-8375
www.ganternursery.com

Wanting to grow plants for his landscape business, Manuel Jimenez bought seven acres from his father-in-law, Emil Ganter, who had a growing ground here for his nursery business, the old Dana Point Nursery. As people started to take note of his plants and want to buy them, a can was put on a post for drive-by "honor sales." The nursery officially opened to the public in 1979. Five more acres were added in this unincorporated area of gently sloping rural agricultural land. A few vestigial avocado trees remain, witnesses to the avocado grove this once was in the 1950s. These and a fine collection of mature flowering specimen trees and old palms preside over a sea of containerized hardy and subtropical fruit trees, flowering trees, palms, roses, ornamental grasses, ferns, vines, and drought-tolerant plants from around the world. Open Monday through Friday, 7:30 a.m.–4:30 p.m.; Saturday, 8 a.m.–4 p.m.

Gardens by the Sea Nursery

1500 North Coast Highway 101, Leucadia 92024
(760) 840-0270
www.gardensbytheseanursery.com

Truly the "hidden treasure of Leucadia," tucked in behind a liquor store, this nursery is a destination garden. Owned and operated by the Hirsch family since 2006, it offers a large selection of cacti, succulents, and drought-tolerant landscape plants, many unique and rare. Open Monday through Saturday, 8 a.m.–6 p.m. (winter close at 4:30 p.m.).

Green Gardens

4910 Cass Street, Pacific Beach 92109
(858) 483-7846
www.sdgreengardens.com

This well-appointed small nursery operates in conjunction with Green Gardens Landscape and Design, making it a one-stop shop for complete garden projects. Family owned and operated since 1979, the nursery has several display areas featuring potted succulents, California native and Australian plants, and orchids and indoor plants. Open Monday through Saturday, 8 a.m.–5 p.m., and Sunday, 9 a.m.–5 p.m.

Hunter's Nursery

3110 Sweetwater Road, Lemon Grove 91945
(619) 463-9341
www.huntersnursery.com

The Hunter family has been offering plants for sale here since 1919. Started by Howard Hunter as a citrus grove, the nursery began offering a wider range of plants in the 1940s. Today the selection includes lots of roses, fruit trees, drought-tolerant plants, vegetables, and bedding plants, as well as a big selection of bamboo and California native plants for the dry, inland San Diego area. Open Monday through Saturday, 7:30 a.m.–5 p.m., and Sunday, 9 a.m.–4 p.m.

Mission Hills Nursery

1525 Fort Stockton Drive, San Diego 92103
(619) 295-2808
www.missionhillsnursery.com

Founded by Kate Sessions, the "Mother of Balboa Park," in 1910, Mission Hills has a proud history. The nursery was sold to the Antonicelli brothers in 1926, and they in turn sold it to Fausto Palafox in 1985. Family owned and operated for 100 years, the nursery still prides itself on its ability to find unique plants. Each month, they go hunting among the large number of wholesale and specialty growers in Bonsall, Fallbrook, and Escondido for plants not usually available. To encourage customers' organic gardening habits, they have on-site compost bins, a "worm café," and online tutorials. Seeds, roses, and tools are also sold online. Fausto Palafox offers garden consultations informed by his 40 years of garden experience. The nursery is open every day, 8 a.m.–5 p.m.

Plantplay Gardens

4915 El Camino Real, Carlsbad 92008
(760) 730-0012
www.plantplaynursery.com

With a passion for plants since childhood and years spent working in other nurseries and doing landscape design, Michael Wirth and Sergio Regalado launched Plantplay in

2004. They specialize in the unusual and their plant collection reflects their personal and far-flung interests. Their design backgrounds and love of plants make this an enterprise "where art and nature meet." Plants offered include bamboo, succulents, ornamental grasses, palms, trees, shrubs (including a large camellia collection), vines, tropical plants, and fruit trees—in other words, plants from all around the world that thrive in Southern California climates. Open every day, 10 a.m.–6 p.m.

Horticultural Attractions

Alta Vista Botanical Gardens

1270 Vale Terrace Drive, Vista 92084
(760) 945-3954
www.altavistagardens.org
Email: info@altavistagardens.org

North San Diego County's fledgling botanical garden will be a museum of plants, a place for art, and a venue for the performing arts and community events. Located on 14 acres of ocean-view land in the heart of Vista, the garden is being developed by the nonprofit Friends of Alta Vista Garden Botanical Gardens, who welcome all support and volunteers. The master plan includes a sensory garden, a Japanese garden, a Mediterranean garden, an Australian garden, a labyrinth, and an arid garden. Kid-friendly.

Balboa Park

1549 El Prado, San Diego 92101 (visitor center)
(619) 239-0512
www.balboapark.org

Enlightened city fathers set aside 1,200 acres of coastal sage scrub on a mesa overlooking the "New Town" for a park in

1868. Little happened until Kate Sessions leased a corner of it for her nursery's growing grounds in 1892, in exchange for planting 100 trees a year and donating many more. Sessions is considered the "Mother of Balboa Park," and her horticultural contributions are evident in the park today. Its layout and landscape character date from 1900–1910. Several structures and gardens were added during the 1915–1916 Panama-California Exposition (the Botanical Building lath house and Japanese Friendship Garden) and the 1935 California Pacific International Exposition (Old Cactus Garden), both held here. This great civic park includes the House of Hospitality—a visitor center run by the nonprofit Balboa Park Conservancy—as well as museums, an outdoor stage, and the San Diego Zoo (see below). In addition to the lushly landscaped whole, the park hosts specialty gardens, including a three-acre rose garden with 2,500 roses, a 2.5-acre desert garden, the Alcazar garden, the Australian gardens, and the Florida Canyon Native Plant Preserve, a reminder of what once grew here. The visitor center is open every day, 9:30 a.m.–4:30 p.m.; the Japanese Friendship Garden is open Tuesday through Sunday, 10 a.m.–4 p.m. (www.niwa.org).

The Flower Fields at Carlsbad Ranch

5704 Paseo Del Norte, Carlsbad 92008
(760) 431-0352
www.theflowerfields.com

Overlooking the Pacific Ocean here are 50 acres of fields of South African bulbs (*Ranunculus, Amaryllis, Watsonia, Babiana, Tirtonia, Anemone*). The former growing fields of Edwin Frazee, who perfected the breeding of the Tecolote ranunculus, the working ranch is a joint venture of the Paul Ecke family and Mellano & Company. Cut flowers and bulbs are sold on site. Themed gardens include a miniature rose garden and sweet-pea maze. Open to the public during bloom season, March through early May. Check website for exact dates and hours.

Point Loma Native Plant Garden

Intersection of Mendocino and Greene Streets,
   San Diego near Ocean Beach
P. O. Box 80126, San Diego 92138 (foundation)
(619) 297-7380
www.sandiegoriver.org

The Point Loma Native Plant Garden is part of the ambitious and much-lauded San Diego River Park Foundation project to connect parks and open space along the 52-mile San Diego River via a system of trails. The two-acre garden, located in the watershed of the San Diego River, educates visitors about native plants. Several habitats are represented here, including oak woodland, upland, and Channel Island, as well as coastal sage scrub. Volunteer opportunities abound.

San Diego Botanic Gardens

230 Quail Gardens Drive, Encinitas 92024
P. O. Box 230005, Encinitas 92023
(760) 436-3036
www.sdbgarden.org

In 1957, Ruth Baird Larabee donated to the county her home and 30-acre garden of plants acquired from her worldwide travels, including cork oaks, palms, cycads, aloes, cacti, hibiscus, and unusual subtropical fruit-bearing shrubs and trees. With an additional four acres given by poinsettia grower Paul Ecke, the site opened as Quail Botanic Gardens in 1971. When the county suffered financially in the early 1990s, some members of the Quail Gardens Foundation formed a nonprofit organization and assumed management of the gardens via a long-term lease. The gardens are known throughout the country for having the most diverse collection of bamboo; they maintain a bamboo-quarantine house for imports. Other special collections are of native plants, pan-tropical plants, hibiscus, palms, and cycads. There is also an Australian garden, an African garden, an Old World desert garden, a palm garden, and the Hamilton Children's Garden, the largest interactive children's garden on the West Coast. Four miles of garden trails. Garden-grown plants are sold at the gift shop, open every day, 10 a.m.–4 p.m. Garden open daily, 9 a.m.–5 p.m. Admission fee. Friends of the Garden offers events and membership opportunities in support of the gardens.

San Diego Chinese Historical Museum Chuang Garden

404 Third Avenue, San Diego 92101
(619) 338-9888
www.sdchm.org

A small Joseph Yamada–designed Asian garden with curving stone paths, a quiet stream, antique statues, and a fish pond spreads out behind the museum, founded in 1996 by the San Diego Chinese Historical Society. Open Tuesday through Saturday, 10:30 a.m.–4 p.m., and Sunday, noon–4 p.m.

San Diego Zoo

2920 Zoo Drive, San Diego 92103
(619) 231-1515
www.sandiegozoo.org

Located in Balboa Park (see above), under the auspices of San Diego Zoo Global, the famed San Diego Zoo includes 100 acres containing more than 7,000 plants, with prized collections of bamboo, ficus, acacia, palms, cycads, and aloe. The

Zoo's Orchid House, open the third Friday of each month from 10 a.m. to 2 p.m., features over 3,000 orchid plants. The zoo holds an annual garden festival on Mother's Day weekend.

San Diego Zoo Safari Park

15500 San Pasqual Valley Road, Escondido 92027
(760) 747-8702
www.sdzsafaripark.org

Under the auspices of San Diego Zoo Global, the Safari Park is a botanical garden containing 4,000 plant species, including 260 endangered species, such as the North African cypress. Plant collections, most maintained by local plant societies, include a conifer forest, an herb garden, a Baja garden, a bonsai house, a California nativescapes garden, an epiphyllum garden, a protea garden, and an Old World succulent garden. Special educational programs, group tours, and events are offered. Plants are available all year at the Plant Trader and at scheduled plant sales.

Self-Realization Fellowship Center
Encinitas Retreat

Meditation Gardens
215 K Street, Encinitas 92024
(760) 753-2888

Seventeen acres of meditation gardens surround the sanctuary established in 1937 by Paramahansa Yogananda, who wrote *Autobiography of a Yogi* here in the Hermitage. The ashram and retreat center are in use today; the gardens are open Tuesday through Saturday, 9 a.m.–5 p.m., and Sunday, 11 a.m.–5 p.m. On a cliffside overlooking the ocean, lush exotic plantings intermingled with koi and lily ponds provide a very serene stroll.

Water Conservation Garden
at Cuyamaca College

12122 Cuyamaca College Drive West, El Cajon 92109
(619) 660-0614
www.thegarden.org
Email: info@thegarden.org

Yes, we can garden and be responsible water stewards. This amazing five-acre garden, managed by the nonprofit Water Conservation Garden Authority, was initiated by the Metropolitan Water District of Southern California and Cuyamaca College. Themed gardens include a meadow garden, a patio garden, a sensory garden, a butterfly pavilion, a native habitat garden, and a succulent and cactus garden, as well as how-to displays (on topics such as irrigation and mulch). The garden hosts extensive educational programs, tours, and training sessions for landscape professionals. Open every day, 9 a.m.–4 p.m.

How Plants Are Produced for Consumption

Gardeners don't realize what goes into a plant stocked at a local nursery. Consider a five-gallon *Fremontodendron* 'California Glory' found in the shrub or native section of a nursery. A complex string of events took place over the course of 150 years to bring this plant here for our consideration.

First, someone collected the plant, either by seed or plant specimen, from the wild. In the case of 'California Glory', amateur botanist Major-General John Charles Frémont, California's first United States senator, discovered the genus in 1846 on an expedition near Sacramento. Intrigued by the broadleaf evergreen shrub, Frémont brought it back for study to the east, where he lived prior to moving to California. He deemed it garden worthy, propagated it (more on this later), and sent it to nurseries and botanic gardens. The genus was named in his honor, initially as *Fremontia,* then later as *Fremontodendron.* It is commonly called "flannel bush" for its thick, fuzzy leaves.

A seedling or accidental hybrid between two parent species in close proximity, *F. californicum* and *F. mexicanum,* appeared at Rancho Santa Ana Botanic Garden. Intrigued by this seedling and its attributes, the botanic garden introduced this new plant, *Fremontodendron* 'California Glory', to commerce in 1962. It proved hardier than its antecedents. Its larger, brighter yellow flowers developed lovely rusted tints with age, blooming over a longer period, from spring to early summer, than any other flannel bush. It tolerates rocky, dry soil with little need for summer irrigation and offers an attractive, practical choice for modern gardens. Its success as a garden plant has won it numerous awards, including the Award of Garden Merit from the California Horticultural Society in 1965.

It was not uncommon for botanic gardens to sponsor the efforts of hunters or collectors to acquire seeds or wild specimens to bring into the nursery trade. Commercial nurseries then carried on the work of propagating plants that were considered worthy for gardeners.

Plants are propagated either sexually or asexually. In sexual propagation, plants start as seeds. Seeds are carried in fruits, which are the result of ovules (eggs) fertilized by pollen grains. Wind, birds, bees, or other insects carry this pollen from a male plant's stamen to a female plant's pistil, which connects to its ovary. Plants grown from seed carry genes pooled from both parents, making genetically diverse offspring. Nurseries get seed from seed companies, botanical gardens, or the wild.

Methods for asexual propagation, in which resulting plants genetically match parent plants, abound. Leaf or stem cuttings rooted in a porous medium grow into new plants, as do divided root systems of herbaceous (non-woody) plants. Some trees are best propagated by grafting, a process in which a bud or short stem, the scion, of a desirable plant is joined to the rootstock of a compatible plant. The practice of tissue culture has also become common: minute pieces of a plant's growing tip are cultured in a sterile medium, ultimately developing into hundreds of new plants.

Cultivars, or "cultivated varieties," are those plants selected for special characteristics and propagated asexually to maintain that characteristic in their offspring. Desirable features might include flowers that are brighter in color or larger in size, a greater number of flowers, a longer flowering season, tastier fruit, a smaller or larger plant size, resistance to pests or diseases, or greater tolerance of environmental conditions. Cultivars originate in various ways. One may stand out and be selected from a population of plants in the wild. A grower may select it from a group of cultivated plants. Or it could be a hybrid, the result of accidental or intentional crossing of genes from two closely related plants.

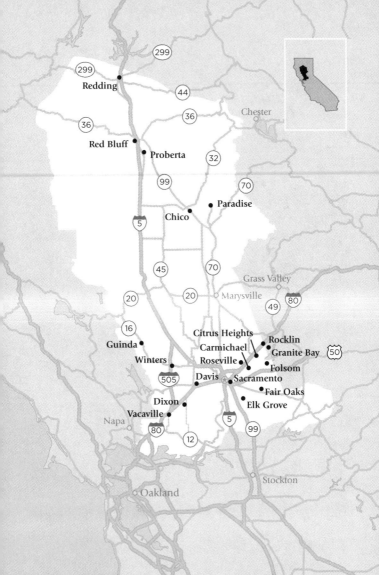

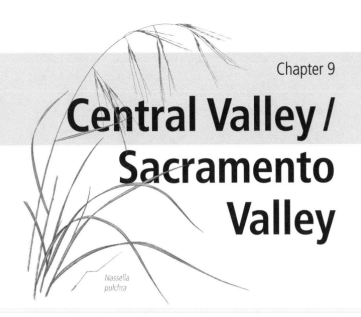

Chapter 9

Central Valley / Sacramento Valley

Nassella pulchra

The great Central Valley is a flat inland trough that covers 42,000 square miles through the heart of the state. Its northern half lies due east of the North Bay region in the Sacramento Valley. And its southern counterpart, the San Joaquin Valley, lies south of Stockton and the Sacramento–San Joaquin Delta. Its climate and water supply are ideal for agriculture, as is its fertile, sediment-filled soil. A large portion of the state's produce is grown here.

In the northern part of the valley, the Klamath, Cascade, and Sierra Nevada mountain ranges frame the Sacramento Valley's north and east sides. Numerous rivers drain melting snow from peaks, filling the Sacramento River, which eventually merges with the San Joaquin River in a broad delta southwest of the city of Sacramento. Once a freshwater marsh covered by peat and alluvium, the delta is now controlled by a network of levees built in the late 1800s to answer the needs of growing farming communities. Subsequently, the land between the levees was changed into rich, productive planted fields. Today pumps drive delta water across miles to central and southern California, where it irrigates farm fields and serves growing urban populations.

The Tehachapi Mountains border the San Joaquin Valley on its southern end, the Sierra Nevada Range on the east, and the inner Coast Range on the west. The San Joaquin River was always a smaller waterway than the Sacramento River, but the damming of most of the rivers in the southern Sierra has significantly reduced the flow of water into the San Joaquin. This puts water at a premium for farmers and valley residents. The delta, filled with snowmelt water from the northern Sierra Nevada, provides the bulk of the water, which travels via a complex system of dams and levees south through the state to bring water to what state historian Kevin Starr calls "the most productive unnatural environment on Earth." Many large-scale farming operations that populate the valley and grow our food rely on this water to irrigate their land.

The Sacramento Valley

Counties: Butte, Colusa, Glenn, Sacramento, Shasta, Solano, Sutter, Tehama, Yolo, Yuba
Elevational range: 25 feet in Sacramento (Sacramento County) to 10,457 feet at Lassen Peak (Shasta County)
Sunset climate zones: 7, 8, 9, 14
Annual rainfall: From 40 inches in Redding and 5 feet of snow to 18 inches in Sacramento with rare snowfall and occasional dusting
Winter temperatures: Lows 29°F to 13°F
Summer temperatures: High 80s°F to 90s°F

In the Sacramento Valley, temperatures vary with the terrain, from higher hill elevations down to the valley floor. A delta breeze that comes in from the Bay Area brings higher humidity and cooler temperatures. The hillside thermal belts of Folsom, Redding, and Rumsey stay warm enough for safe cultivation of citrus. Full sun and high daytime temperatures characterize the growing season on the valley floor. Thick tule fog reduces solar penetration and keeps winter temperatures low, allowing deciduous fruit trees the dormancy needed to set buds.

Wildlings do persist, despite extensive agriculture in the valley. True natives come to life with fall and winter rains, bloom in late winter and early spring, and then go dormant in dry summer. Western redbud (*Cercis occidentalis*), white-leaf manzanita (*Arctostaphylos viscida* ssp. *viscida*), and pine bee flower (*Phacelia imbricata*) are but a few examples. The state grass, purple needlegrass (*Nassella pulchra*), grows widely throughout the valley. This perennial bunchgrass grows in clumps with delicate, featherlike awns or sheaths projecting from its tips.

Specialty Nurseries and Growers

Bushnell Gardens Nursery

5255 Douglas Boulevard, Granite Bay 95746
(916) 791-4199
www.bushnellgardens.com
Email: rich@bushnellgardens.com
David Bushnell; Rich Swanson, general manager
Retail and wholesale
Open Monday through Saturday, 9 a.m.–6 p.m. (winter close
    at 5 p.m.), and Sunday, 9 a.m.–5 p.m. (winter close at 5 p.m.).

Plant specialties: Conifers, Japanese maples, and water-wise plants, including perennials, trees, shrubs, grasses, and heirloom vegetables.

History/description: After graduating from UC Davis with a degree in landscape architecture, David Bushnell formed a small design/build company. This led to Bushnell's Landscape Creations, where he added maintenance services to his portfolio in response to client demand. Then, in order to supply plants for his projects, he started a wholesale nursery. The retail nursery was added in 1993, with the idea of providing a complete landscape company for the Sacramento region. The result is that today David Bushnell is the overseer of Bushnell Landscape Industries, Inc. Most of what the nursery sells is grown on this 20-acre site in the oak woodlands at the base of the foothills. The nursery has perfected the Veggie'Rellis, a potted trellis to enable vining vegetables to be grown in small spaces.

Chamisa Ridge Nursery

16689 Cleveland Street, Guinda 95637
P. O. Box 218, Guinda 95637
(530) 796-0799
www.chamisaridgenursery.com
Email: chamisaridgenursery@gmail.com
Ron and Sandi Lutsko
Wholesale and retail
Open by appointment. Special retail open-house days
    in spring and fall; check website for details.

Plant specialties: California native plants, drought-tolerant plants, trees, shrubs, perennials, bulbs, cacti, succulents, vines, and grasses suited to the arid West, as well as beneficial bird and insect plants.

History/description: Landscape architect Ron Lutsko has an unbridled passion for plants. A frustration with not being able to locate plants for his projects led to the creation of this nursery in 1990. His plant collections started with the propagation of native plants in his backyard in Lafayette and grew to include Mediterranean-climate plants brought back from his travels around the world. Believing that "the use of ecosystem-appropriate (especially drought-tolerant) plants has become recognized as a basic prerequisite to creating meaningful landscapes," he focuses on plants that, once established, need no summer water. Word spread about his stunning and uncommon plants and, in 2005, the Lutskos moved most of the nursery to the Capay Valley (two valleys northeast of Napa Valley), where they also have an organic olive farm and a garden of "mother plants."

Cornflower Farms

9811 Sheldon Road, Elk Grove
P. O. Box 896, Elk Grove 95759
(916) 689-1015
www.cornflowerfarms.com
Email: natives@cornflowerfarms.com
Ann and Jeff Chandler
Wholesale and contract growing primarily;
    retail by mail/phone/email order
Open by appointment only.

Plant specialties: California native plants, water-wise plants, ornamental grasses, and general ornamentals, including perennials; plant material for restoration and revegetation for most of the major plant communities in California; and plants that attract beneficial insects, butterflies, and hummingbirds.

History/description: This business began in 1981 in response to a demand for quality stock of California native and drought-tolerant plant material. Cornflower's philosophy has always been to grow what everyone else will not or cannot grow. Consistently, Cornflower has led the effort to grow plants appropriate to place. The nursery's online "wild gardening" catalog provides information on topics of interest to all those who care about the land: revegetation; drought tolerance; habitat creation for wildlife, beneficial insects, butterflies, and hummingbirds; fire and erosion control; biomass as a renewable fuel source; and biodiversity. The nursery maintains a beneficial insect display border on its five-acre site.

Floral Native Nursery

2511 Floral Avenue, Chico 95973
(530) 892-2511
www.floralnativenursery.com
Email: canative@shocking.com
Germain Boivin, Zeb Puterbaugh
Retail, wholesale, and contract growing
Open Monday through Saturday.

Plant specialties: 150 species of California native plants, especially those suited to the Sacramento Valley and foothills.

History/description: On a visit to California, nurseryman Germain Boivin was deeply affected by California's rich and varied plant life, so different from that of his native Quebec. After moving to California some years later, he started propagating native plants with help from the California Native Plant Society and professors at CSU Chico. Started in 1998, the nursery and its greenhouses sit on these 43 acres, with another propagation site in the foothills. On-site gardens demonstrate the landscape use of native plants. The nursery applauds people's increasing sensitivity to sustainable landscaping and the key role that native plants play in making this happen. The website's plant list is coded by categories such as attractiveness to butterflies and hummingbirds, fire and deer resistance, and drought tolerance.

Four Winds Growers

3373 Sackett Lane, Winters 95694
(877) 449-4637
www.fourwindsgrowers.com
Email: cs@fourwindsgrowers.com
Don Dillon, Jr.
Wholesale only at site, retail by mail/online order
Open Monday through Friday, 8 a.m.–3 p.m.

Plant specialties: Edible ornamentals, specializing in dwarf and standard citrus, along with avocado, blueberry, caneberry, fig, grape, jujube, olive, persimmon, pomegranate, and multi-grafted deciduous fruit trees.

(See listing in chapter 5.)

Geffray's Gardens

741 Carpers Court, Chico 95973
2790 Alamo Avenue, Chico 95973 (mailing address)
(530) 345-2849

www.creativecacti.com
Claude Geffray
Retail and wholesale
Open by appointment only.

Plant specialties: Cacti and succulents, both indoor and hardy outdoor varieties.

History/description: Arriving in the Bay Area from Normandy, France, Claude Geffray was struck by the exoticism of cacti and succulents. Their structure and geometry was especially appealing to this student of ceramic arts. After moving to Chico in 1985 with a truck full of his collections, he started selling at local farmers' markets, then opened the nursery in 1988 as Geffray's Gardens (note: Creative Cacti is the website name only). Claude can help you relandscape your garden or "potscape" your indoors.

Lemuria Nursery

7820 Serpa Lane, Dixon 95620
(707) 678-4481
www.lemurianursery.com
Email: lemuriamen@msn.com
Peter and Eric Fink
Retail and wholesale
Open Monday through Saturday, 8 a.m.–4:30 p.m.,
    and Sunday, 10 a.m.–3 p.m. (winter closed Sundays).

Plant specialties: 1,250 species of fruit trees, shade trees, roses, shrubs, perennials, daylilies, ornamental grasses, vines, and succulents.

History/description: The Fink brothers are third-generation growers and nursery operators. In 1939, their grandparents opened a nursery and feed store in Oakland, propagating everything right on their grounds. As their operation grew too big for a backyard business, they moved to Richmond in the 1940s. Their parents took over in the late 1960s, managing what was then a retail nursery. Seeking more space and wishing to do more growing, the brothers bought what was Sunshine Nursery Growers in 1999 from the Bennett family. They have retained and amplified the Bennetts' specialty collections of ornamental grasses and trees. A display garden surrounding their home is a primary attraction on this 10-acre site.

McConnell Arboretum & Botanical Gardens Nursery

Turtle Bay Exploration Park
1100 Arboretum Drive, Redding 96001
(530) 242-3169 (gardens)
www.turtlebay.org
Email: gardens@turtlebay.org
Retail
Nursery open Friday and Saturday, 9 a.m.–1 p.m.

Plant specialties: Heat-tolerant, drought-tolerant California native and Mediterranean-climate plants.

History/description: The McConnell Arboretum was established in 1990 by the Arboretum Council and the generosity of a local philanthropist who donated 200 acres of land that was slated for development. Today that land flourishes as an arboretum, a botanical garden, a nursery, and a natural riparian area on the Sacramento River that connects to the Sacramento River Trail. In 1997, a private nonprofit, Turtle Bay Exploration Park, was formed to serve as the parent organization for four Redding cultural institutions—an art museum, a science museum, a forestry museum, and the arboretum. The 20-acre botanical gardens, begun in 2002 and opened in 2005, features five Mediterranean-climate-zone gardens (Californian, South African, Australian, Chilean, and Mediterranean Basin), a children's garden, and a medicinal garden. The one-acre nursery propagates all its plants on site with help from a dedicated cadre of volunteers. It hosts large biannual plant sales. The garden is open year round, 7 a.m.–dusk. Admission fee.

Mendon's Nursery

5424 Foster Road, Paradise 95969
(530) 877-7341
www.mendonsnursery.org
Jerry, Joanne, and John Mendon
Retail
Open Monday through Saturday, 8:30 a.m.–5 p.m.
    (winter close at 4:30 p.m.).

Plant specialties: Trees and shrubs, including unique collections of Japanese maples (more than 50 varieties), dwarf conifers, and dogwood; ornamental grasses, bonsai plants, perennials, and roses.

History/description: After studying at Cal Poly Pomona, Jerry Mendon bought a small general nursery in San Gabriel in 1948, where he was soon joined by his bride, Joanne. The nursery begat additional landscaping and professional tree-moving businesses. As a result of property values (and taxes) rising in San Gabriel, the Mendons sold the nursery in 1968. Seeking a calmer, more rural environment, they found Paradise and vowed never to open another nursery. They started selling fruits and nuts harvested on their eight-acre property, got a few more fruit trees, and sold a few to neighbors. Within four years (in 1974), they were back in business. Their son John joined four years later. They alert you to the Paradise Garden Club's spring garden tour in Paradise and the garden tour in Chico put on by Saint John's Episcopal Church. The seasons are not shy in Paradise, and Mendon's is worth a visit for its vibrant spring and fall displays.

Morningsun Herb Farm

6137 Pleasants Valley Road, Vacaville 95688
(707) 451-9406
www.morningsunherbfarm.com
Email: roseloveall@morningsunherbfarm.com

Dan Sale, Rosemary Loveall-Sale
Retail and mail/online order
February, open Thursday through Sunday, 11 a.m.–4 p.m.;
    March through November, open Tuesday through Sunday,
    9 a.m.–5 p.m.; closed December and January.

Plant specialties: Herbs for landscape use, especially salvia (60 varieties) and lavender (25 varieties); unusual medicinal and culinary herbs, such as nettle, clary sage, and capers; and perennials and ornamental grasses. In the spring, Morningsun sells vegetable starts, including 90 varieties of (mostly) heirloom tomatoes.

History/description: With degrees in forestry and horticulture from UC Berkeley and UC Davis, Rosemary (Rose) went to work for the Forest Service, where she propagated the same four plants every year. Thinking there might be more to life, she applied her propagation skills to the herbs in her own garden, back in the days when she loved—and had time—to cook. This led to the idea of a nursery, which she opened in 1984 on two acres of her parents' property in Vacaville. Dan, a mechanical engineer, spent his weekends at the farm "fixing all of the stuff [she] broke during the week," until he started working full time at the nursery in 2004. The nursery site includes a demonstration garden with a small lavender field and greenhouses that show herbs in all their different growing stages. All plants are propagated and grown on site, with preference given to plants that are open pollinated and of heirloom parentage. A menagerie of two large dogs, three mini-donkeys, and a flock of chickens is there to greet you. Morningsun has an open house each year the weekend before Mother's Day that features talks, workshops, and food tastings. In August, in partnership with Slow Food Solano, they host a tasting of all 90 tomato varieties grown at the farm as a benefit for Solano County public school gardens.

Palm Island Nursery Outlet

6263 Pleasants Valley Road, Vacaville 95688
(707) 344-8350
www.palmislandnursery.com
Email: dale@palmislandnursery.com
Dale Motiska
Retail and wholesale
Open Saturday, 10 a.m.–4 p.m., or by appointment.

Plant specialties: Palms, cycads, bamboo, conifers, cacti, succulents, grasses, flowering shrubs, and fruit trees; large specimen boxed trees.

History/description: Another plant enthusiast whose hobby became a habit and then a business, Dale Motiska opened Neon Palm Nursery, a precursor to Palm Island, in 1984. He continues to make important contributions to the diversification of palm species through travel, collecting, and hybridization. His plant knowledge is now encyclopedic, and he grows all categories of plants, always looking for new introductions or forgotten species of hardy subtropicals that can thrive in his area. In 2009, the nursery moved to its present, larger, seven-acre location in a narrow valley surrounded by foothills. Tree relocation is a specialty; their large cranes can move the 20-ton palms that now highlight various wineries and streetscapes throughout Northern California.

The Plant Barn

406 Entler Avenue, Chico 95928
(530) 345-3121
www.theplantbarn.com
Email: flowerfloozie@sbcglobal.net
Denise Kelly
Retail and contract growing
Open Monday through Friday, 9 a.m.–5 p.m.;
    Saturday, 10 a.m.–4 p.m.; and Sunday, noon–4 p.m.

Plant specialties: Unusual perennials, annuals, succulents, trees, shrubs, roses, and vines.

History/description: Former teacher Denise Kelly developed a landscape design and consulting business and for years was a big admirer of the Plant Barn, started in 1980 by Ilona and David Cronan. When an opportunity came up to buy it in 2006, she jumped at the chance. The two-acre nursery, part of the original Entler ranch, houses their gift shop in its 100-year old barn. Recognition for Sally Greenwood, the grower here for the last 36 years, was bestowed by the naming of *Salvia* 'Sally Greenwood'. The nursery includes greenhouses, display beds, and an array of custom, planted containers.

Sousa Dynasty Herbs

20592 Stewart Road, Red Bluff 96080
(530) 528-1001
www.sousadynastyherbs.org
Email: sousadynastyherbs@yahoo.com
Tony and Michele Sousa
Retail, some wholesale
Open mid-February through November,
    Tuesday through Saturday, 9 a.m.–5 p.m.

Plant specialties: Hard-to-find heirloom, organic, non-GMO herbs and vegetables; grapes, berry bushes, and flowers.

History/description: Michele Sousa has been growing herbs with and for friends for 25 years, determining which do well in the harsh climate of Tehama County (which experiences frost to 120°F temperatures). Advice and sometimes seed from Native American healers, holistic practitioners, and grateful neighbors helped her test a huge variety of herbs and vegetables, such as ginseng, wormwood, and peanut plants. With the help of her contractor husband, Tony, she turned her "hobby" into a business in 2013. This 10-acre family farm is tended by all seven of their children. Plants grown here are well acclimatized; seed is harvested from mother plants on site. Community-minded people, the Sousas donate plants to 17 school gardens in Tehama County. Hoping to spread the word that organic does not have to be expensive, they often sell 3.5-inch potted plants for a dollar.

Three Palms Nursery

26990 County Road 95A, Davis 95616
(530) 756-8355
www.3palmsnursery.com
Email: pk3palms@sbcglobal.net
Phil Kitchen
Retail and wholesale
Open seasonal hours on weekends in February,
and Tuesday through Sunday from March through October.
Closed November through January. Best to call first.

Plant specialties: Drought-tolerant perennials, natives, and grasses; fruit and shade trees, roses, and landscape shrubs.

History/description: Phil Kitchen got into the nursery business by way of cofounding the local Farmers and Craftsmen's Market in Davis in 1972. Through this work, he met and was inspired by local farmers and began to grow fruits, vegetables, and flowers to sell at the Davis Farmers' Market, as it was renamed in 1977. In 1988, he opened a nursery at the historic Schmeiser Ranch, with its three huge signature California fan palms in front of the ranch house (hence this nursery's name). What started as a nursery focused on annuals, vegetables, and cut flowers morphed into a full-fledged perennial and landscape plant business, since there were few growers meeting this need locally. At this five-acre location, which the nursery moved to in 1996, Phil has developed extensive growing grounds and an oak woodland arboretum and picnic area on one side of the slough that runs through the property.

Notable Garden Centers

Goodin's Rock Garden Nursery

9869 Highway 99W, Proberta
(530) 527-2411
www.goodinnursery.com

Cathy Goodin never hired a babysitter because her love of plants and her desire to work where she could always have her children on site led to the creation of this nursery in 1988. Named for her husband's rock-hauling business, this nursery focuses exclusively on plants suited to zone 8 in the Sacramento Valley. It specializes in trees (bare root and potted), shrubs, perennials, and roses. Open Monday through Saturday, 9 a.m.–5 p.m.

Green Acres Nursery and Supply

9220 East Stockton Boulevard, Elk Grove 95624, (916) 714-5600
205 Serpa Way, Folsom 95630, (916) 358-9099
5436 Crossings Drive, Rocklin 95650, (916) 824-1310
901 Galleria Boulevard, Roseville 95678, (916) 782-2273
8501 Jackson Road, Sacramento 95826, (916) 381-1625
www.idiggreenacres.com

Mark Gill worked for 25 years for a Las Vegas nursery until he got the opportunity to start his own in 2003 in Roseville, chosen for its hospitable climate and good demographics, which he opened with his son Travis and daughter Ashley. The Sacramento store opened in 2007, followed by Folsom (2012), Elk Grove (2015), and Rocklin (2016). Green Acres puts a major emphasis on buying locally, and all plants sold by the nursery are California or Oregon grown. The nursery's "idea gardens" provide sensible planting suggestions and its website has good information under "Tips and Trends." Open Monday through Saturday, 7 a.m.–7 p.m., and Sunday, 8 a.m.–7 p.m.

Horticultural Attractions

Capitol Park

1300 L Street, Sacramento 95814
(916) 324-0333
www.capitolmuseum.ca.gov

This 40-acre park, which surrounds the capitol buildings, contains perhaps the largest and most extensive collection of mature trees in California. The historic insectary in the park's center provides visitors with self-guiding maps to some of the more than 500 special trees; the website lists and locates them all. Planting began in 1870 and continues in a sporadic fashion. The park's azalea collection in bloom has been described as "socko." Capitol Park also contains several war memorials and an International World Peace Rose Garden (www.world peacerosegardens.org).

Fair Oaks Horticulture Center

Fair Oaks Park, 11549 Fair Oaks Boulevard, Fair Oaks 95628
(916) 875-6913
www.sacmg.ucanr.edu

The Fair Oaks Horticulture Center is one acre of water-efficient landscape gardens and edible gardens (featuring vegetables, berries, an orchard, and a vineyard). Started in 1998, it is a joint project of the UC Cooperative Extension Sacramento Master Gardeners and the Fair Oaks Recreation & Park District. The water-efficient landscape garden is open every day; the edible gardens are open during workshops and open garden days. Check the website for a schedule.

Genetic Resource and Conservation Center

US Forest Center, Chico

(530) 934-3316
www.fs.usda.gov/

A nature trail with many labeled examples of the center's historic plant introductions, such as the pistachio (1917) and kiwi (1934).

Charles Jensen Botanical Garden

8520 Fair Oaks Boulevard, Carmichael 95608
(916) 944-2025
www.carmichaelpark.com/jensen-botanical-garden

The 3.5-acre private garden of Mr. and Mrs. Charles Jensen is managed by the Carmichael Recreation and Park District and supported by Friends of Jensen Botanical Garden. Large redwoods, magnolias, dogwoods, and maples combine with temperate, creekside woodland plants.

William Land Park

Sutterville Road and Land Park Road, Sacramento
(916) 808-5200

Chock full of recreational amenities, this major city park in midtown Sacramento includes sports fields, a playground, an amphitheater, two lakes, a golf course, an amusement park (Funderland), a children's fantasy park (Fairyland), and a zoo. The horticultural highlights here are the lofty trees, old rock garden, and color garden designed by Daisy Mah.

McKinley Park Rose Garden

H and 33rd Streets, Sacramento 95816
(916) 243-8292
www.mckinleyparkcenter.org

More than 1,200 modern roses and companion plants grace this fifth-acre park setting, now managed by Friends of East Sac. The garden is available for event rentals.

Rusch Park

7801 Auburn Boulevard, Citrus Heights 95610
(916) 725-1585
www.sunriseparks.com/

This site of historical interest, with a two-acre botanical garden devoted to California's seven biomes, is part of the Sunrise Recreation and Park District.

Sacramento Historic Rose Garden

at Old City Cemetery
1000 Broadway (at Riverside Boulevard), Sacramento
(916) 448-0811
www.oldcitycemetery.com

A heritage rose garden filled with 500 rose varieties collected from old and often abandoned garden sites throughout Northern California, organized by famous rosarian Fred Boutin and now maintained by the nonprofit Old City Cemetery Committee, Inc. Tours, events, and volunteer opportunities are available. Since 1997, CNPS has maintained a native plant demonstration garden on site.

Shepard Garden and Art Center

3330 McKinley Boulevard, next to McKinley Park, Sacramento 95814
(916) 808-8800
www.sgaac.org

This is the site of about 35 garden and arts groups' meetings, shows, and sales. Shepard Garden holds a big plant sale each year in March.

UC Davis Arboretum

Valley Oak Cottage (TB-32), La Rue Road,
    University of California, Davis 95616 (office)
(530) 752-4880
www.arboretum.ucdavis.edu

Founded in 1936, the UC Davis Arboretum has 100 acres of themed gardens and special collections emphasizing drought-tolerant, low-maintenance plants. Gardens include a native plant garden, a white flower garden, and a home demonstration garden. Special collections feature oaks, acacias, Australian plants, and desert plants. The Arboretum All-Stars program features the 100 best-performing, best-suited plants for Central Valley gardens (and many other places in California as well), selected and tested by the arboretum's horticultural staff. Plant sales occur several times per year on selected Saturdays in spring and fall at the Arboretum Teaching Nursery. See website for dates and information about family programs.

University Arboretum

California State University
6000 J Street, Sacramento 95819
(916) 454-6494
www.csus.edu/

This three-acre collection of trees, shrubs, and flowers (formerly the Charles M. Goethe Arboretum) has sections devoted to conifers, native plants, and primitive plants, and is maintained by the CSUS Foundation.

WEL (Water Efficient Landscape) Garden

9935 Auburn Folsom Road, Granite Bay 95746
(916) 791-2663
www.sjwd.org/welgarden

A project of the San Juan Water District, nine residential gardens make a great sales pitch for good garden results with minimal water. Open Monday through Friday, 8:30 a.m.–5 p.m.

Water-Wise Gardening

The word *xeriscape* comes from the Greek word *xeros,* meaning "dry." We use it to describe attractive landscapes of water-efficient plants. This disciplined approach reduces or eliminates supplemental irrigation—useful in a Mediterranean climate of long, dry summer spells and mild, wet winters.

How can you implement water-wise gardening practices in your own yard?

1. Choose climate-appropriate plants, whose water needs suit water availability. Thick, tough, leathery-leaved plants adapted to reduce water loss and gray- or light-leaved plants that reflect the sun are good bets, be they California natives or natives of another Mediterranean-climate region.

2. Design your garden so that plants are grouped into planting zones based on their water needs. Group thirsty plants together into one zone that gets greater irrigation.

3. Install an efficient watering system to avoid waste and reduce water use. Drip lines deliver water directly and at low pressure to plants via plastic tubing. Separate irrigation lines and zone the system to get more water to those plants with greater needs. Adjust irrigation seasonally.

4. Provide good drainage—with gravel, for example—to those plants favoring drier conditions.

5. Improve your soil. Healthy gardens have soil that stores water and releases it to plants. Water runs off heavy, compacted clay and hardpan soil and right through sandy soil. Add compost, leaf mold, coconut coir, or peat moss to slow and retain water.

Creating a compost pile can take six weeks to one year, depending on your method. Starting with a "brown" layer, alternate with "green" materials to balance compost. Browns are dry materials such as wood chips, twigs, pine cones, small broken-up branches, dried leaves, dried grass, straw, paper bags, cardboard egg cartons, cereal boxes, and paper. (All should be chopped up or shredded.) Greens are fresh vegetable and fruit food scraps (no meat, fat, or grease); fish and fish bones; clam, mussel, or crab shells; rotted manure from herb-eating animals such as horses, rabbits, fowl, cattle, or goats; coffee and coffee beans; tea dregs and tea leaves; and eggshells.

To speed up the process, throw on a bag of manure and occasionally water the pile. Omit diseased plant material from compost.

6. Once it breaks down to dark, rich earth, use it for planting, and spread two to four inches of compost over the top of your soil as a mulch. Mulch minimizes water evaporation, prevents soil from crusting, and protects and cools shallower roots from the sun's heat. It also prevents wind and water erosion. Other organic fiber mulches include wood grindings and bark chips. Spread inorganic mulches, such as gravel and rocks, two to three inches deep. Since rocks heat up an area, keep them away from plants.

7. Eliminate or limit turfgrass areas. Lawns guzzle water and need fertilizer to thrive, straining water resources and polluting the environment. Consider planting lawn alternatives: a meadow filled with ornamental grasses and wildflowers or a "carpet" of low-growing succulents or herbs.

If you must plant a lawn, warm-season turfgrass generally needs less water, fertilizer, and pesticides than cool-season turf. Cool-season turfgrasses, such as tall fescue (*Festuca arundinacea*), ryegrass (*Lolium perenne*), and Kentucky bluegrass (*Poa pratensis*) keep color year round if well irrigated during dry summers. Warm-season turfgrasses, such as buffalograss (*Buchloe dactyloides*), kikuyugrass (*Pennisetum clandestinum*), St. Augustinegrass (*Stenotaphrum secundatum*), zoysiagrass (*Zoysia* spp.), and bermudagrass (*Cynodon dactylon* and *C.* spp.), go dormant in late fall, turning brown until early spring when winter rains revive them. If you do choose a warm-season variety, mow high and leave clippings as mulch to grow an efficient, healthy lawn without the need for pesticides.

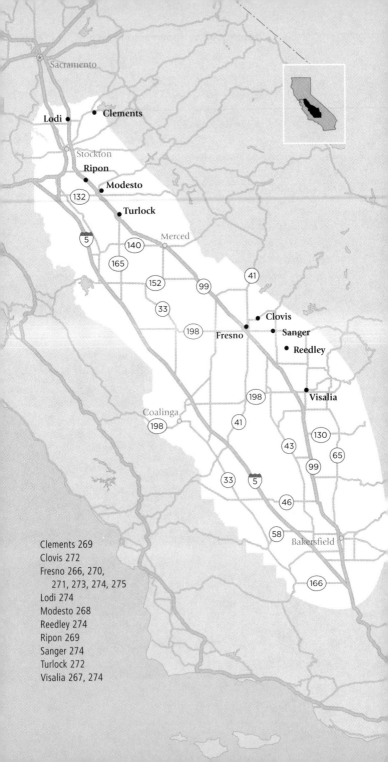

Chapter 10

Central Valley / San Joaquin Valley

Quercus lobata

The San Joaquin Valley

Counties: Fresno, Kern, Kings, Madera, Merced, San Joaquin, Stanislaus, Tulare
Elevational range: Negligible
Sunset climate zones: 8, 9, 14
Annual rainfall: 13.81 inches
Winter temperatures: Average minimum temperature in Stockton, 49°F. Lows can drop to 23°F in the valley.
Summer temperatures: At the region's northernmost tip in Stockton, average annual maximum temperatures hover around 75°F. Summer highs in the Valley can reach 114°F. Bakersfield, at the southern part of this valley in Kern County, has hotter annual average temperatures, reaching 80°F.

The San Joaquin Valley, despite its scarcity of water, grows 25 percent of our country's food supply on some 5 million acres of farmland. The region is known for its food crops: almonds, walnuts, citrus, melons, sugar beets, and other vegetables. As of late, mandarin oranges have become a thriving crop, particularly in the valley's southwestern end. Cotton grows well in the hot, dry summers, provided it is adequately irrigated. Farmers also use land for grazing sheep and cattle.

Hot, dry summers and rainy, cool winters blanketed by tule fog characterize both the northern and southern halves of the Central Valley. Summer temperatures increase significantly toward the southern end of the valley. The San Joaquin Valley rainy season is shorter than its Sacramento Valley counterpart, running from November through April. Much of what falls there evaporates. The flat, open land offers an opportunity to grow plants suited to hot, dry summers: cacti, succulents, drought-tolerant plants such as Australian native acacias, emu bush (*eremophila*), and hakea, and many California natives.

The valley oak (*Quercus lobata*) dots and stands sentinel over the valley landscape. A stately native of interior California, it is found throughout the great Central Valley, both in moist valley bottoms and on wooded hillsides. The largest oak in California, this deciduous tree with deeply lobed, felt-covered leaves can reach heights of 100 feet with a canopy as wide. It prefers deep, fertile soil in which it can send its roots to tap groundwater. Native American Indians used its elongated acorns for food.

Specialty Nurseries and Growers

Belmont Nursery

7730 East Belmont Avenue, Fresno 93737
(559) 255-6645
www.belmontnursery.com
Email: jon@belmontnursery.com
Jon Reelhorn
Retail and wholesale
Open Monday through Saturday, 8:30 a.m.–5:30 p.m.
(winter close at 5 p.m.), and Sunday, 10 a.m.–4 p.m.

Plant specialties: Trees, shrubs, and perennials, especially magnolias, roses, crepe myrtles, and selected varieties that prosper in the warm San Joaquin Valley, such as Don Kleim's introduction, the 'Keith Davey' pistache, a tree that provides great fall color, has no dropping seeds, and is well sized for urban settings.

History/description: City boy Jon Reelhorn attended agriculture school in Fresno, where he discovered that making maples was preferable to milking. After a stint as a professional baseball player, he returned to the agriculture business, eventually (in 2001) buying Belmont, a nursery started by the Palmer family in 1943. In 2005, he bought Henderson Experimental Gardens, renowned for its long history of plant introductions. The gardens were started by William Henderson, who studied under Luther Burbank, created one of the first mail-order catalogs, and developed the seedless Muscat grape. Upon Henderson's death, the gardens were transferred to his longtime protégé Don Kleim, who traveled all over the world collecting horticultural treasures and developed a passion for grafting maples and magnolias. After Kleim's death the venture was sold, then sold again to the Reelhorn family, who have continued to propagate many of the old plant varieties. The 10-acre retail site is a production nursery, featuring large quantities of each offering. Two growing grounds, one the old Henderson Experimental Gardens, are off site.

Burlington Rose Nursery

24865 Road 164, Visalia 93292
(559) 747-3624
www.burlingtonroses.com
Email: burlingtonroses@aol.com
Burling Leong
Retail, wholesale, and mail order
    (at www.helpmefind.com)
Open by appointment only.

Plant specialties: All sorts of roses—old garden, polyanthus, floribundas, hybrid teas, hybrid musks, climbers, and miniatures.

History/description: For 35 years, Burling Leong hybridized and propagated miniature roses for Ralph Moore, a horticultural legend who died in 2009 at the age of 102. What started as a summer job became a lifelong interest. Burling grew up on a walnut farm and eventually bought her own, where she started her personal rose-breeding program, just for the pure pleasure of experimentation. Her two-acre farm is filled with interesting perennials and shrubs, companion plants that attract pollinators. She also grows unusual fruit trees and citrus varieties, such as the new Australian finger lime. Her fascination with the growing world is matched by her desire to educate visitors. An on-site container vegetable garden demonstrates that you can grow vegetables in small spaces. Burling regularly works with rose societies and botanical gardens and is presently restoring the rose garden at Hearst Castle. She opened the nursery for sales of her rose plants in 2009. She remains an ardent fan of Tulare County farmland and suggests a visit to the World Ag Expo in Tulare, the world's largest agricultural fair, held during the second week in February.

Generation Growers

305 North Rosemore Avenue, Modesto 95358
www.generationgrowers.com
Email: info@generationgrowers.com
Roger and Deanna van Klaveren
Wholesale only
Open by appointment.

Plant specialties: Perennials, ornamental shrubs, and trees, especially azaleas and camellias; 26 varieties of grafted citrus.

History/description: A fifth-generation plantsman, Roger van Klaveren is deeply rooted in the nursery business. His forebears were growers and nurserymen in Holland. In the 1950s, his father and uncle—married to sisters—moved to the United

States and gardened in the Bay Area. They started propagating from their garden prunings and soon were in the nursery business, establishing Van's Nursery in 1956 in Campbell and later moving the nursery to Modesto. Roger and his brother Robert, having been raised among rows of plants, entered the trade early. Robert runs Van's Nursery in Oregon, and Roger renamed the nursery here Generation Growers. Generation Growers has 12 acres of containerized grounds and sells primarily to garden centers.

Harlequin Gardens

21450 Clements Road, Clements 95227
(925) 932-7673
Donald Rose and Amanda Meyers
Wholesale only
Open Monday through Friday, 8 a.m.–5 p.m.

Plant specialties: Perennials, especially variegated and unusual foliage varieties; flowering and deciduous shrubs; Mediterranean-climate plants; and California native plants.

History/description: Donald Rose knows his way around plants, having studied horticulture at North Carolina State University with famed horticulturist J. C. Raulston. Moving to California in 1981, he interned at Monrovia Nursery and then was an estate gardener in Lafayette for 10 years. During this time, he amassed a robust collection of hard-to-find plants with unusual foliage. In 1991, with the help of horticulturist Janet Edwards, he began propagating the collection and opened the nursery, the realization of a lifelong dream. Today he runs the nursery with his partner, Amanda Meyers, who has a background in landscape architecture. The nursery has introduced *Verbascum* 'Harlequin Hybrids' and *Aurinia saxatilis* (*Alyssum saxatile*) 'Harlequin'. The name Harlequin reflects the nursery's fascination with all types of variegation.

Poot's Cactus Nursery

17229 East Highway 120, Ripon 95366
(209) 599-7241
www.pootscactusnursery.com
Email: pootscactus@gmail.com
Bill, Roelyn, and Brian Poot
Retail, with discounts for the trade
Open Monday through Saturday, 9 a.m.–5 p.m.

Plant specialties: Cactus, over 300 genera and many species thereof.

History/description: Bill Poot's father was a nurseryman in Holland, so his familiarity with plants started early. In 1975 he saw his first cactus collection and he has not been the same since. What started with ordering a few seeds and getting cuttings from other collectors has resulted in the present collection of 200,000 plants. In 1990, the nursery was launched and, after Bill's retirement as a welder in 1995, it has become a full-time activity. Son Brian, who grew up in the nursery, officially came to work in 2015. The one-acre site in the Central Valley foothills almost explodes with cacti—on benches, in greenhouses, and set out in the landscape on beds of rock. They come in all sizes and shapes; some are wildly weird-looking and several are prize-winning specimens.

Sago Rey Palm Plantation

3535 South Temperance Avenue, Fresno 93725, (559) 268-6650
6706 East Central Avenue, Fresno 93725, (559) 304-2038
Website: sagorey.com
Email: sagorey@gmail.com
Maria Wash
Retail and wholesale
Open Monday through Saturday, 8 a.m.–4 p.m.,
    and Sunday 10 a.m.–4 p.m.

Plant specialties: 50 varieties of palms and cycads, weather hardened for central California landscapes; bamboo, cacti, fruit and shade trees, and flowering plants.

History/description: The son of a farmer, Tom Wash had been growing things for as long as he could remember. Early on, he was a fern spores propagator, amassing a collection of 250 varieties. After high school, he started a nursery, California Ferns, on a three-acre section of his family's 160-acre citrus farm, but high energy costs in the 1980s caused him to change course. In 1986, after a trip to Mexico, he switched crops to palms and cycads, and was joined by his wife, Marie, who has carried on the business since his untimely death in 2011. The collection of 30,000 palms required the recent addition of a second location for more growing space. A mobile "palm doctor" will make house calls for sickly palms and cycads.

Notable Garden Centers

Gazebo Gardens

3204 North Van Ness Blvd, Fresno 93704
(559) 222-7673
www.gazebogardens1922.com

In 2002, Scott Miller bought this venerable nursery that was founded in 1922. Notable for its vast selection of roses, the largest retail offering in the San Joaquin Valley, the nursery offers a wide selection of plants. On Thursday, Friday, and Saturday nights the whole nursery becomes a beer garden, with food trucks and music (Sunday mornings host brunch); these gatherings are a great way to smell the roses. Gazebo Gardens has an arrangement with the Fresno Zoo to compost all of the latter's elephant and hoof-stock manure, which reduces landfill and funds a foundation to increase habitat for wild elephants. Open Monday through Wednesday, 8:30 a.m.–5:30 p.m.; Thursday–Saturday, 8:30 a.m.–9 p.m.; and Sunday, 10 a.m.–4 p.m.

The Greenery Nursery and Garden Shop

742 East Olive Avenue, Turlock 95380
(209) 632-4214
www.greenerynsy.com

This partnership between George and Dee Anna Schumacher and former nursery "cleanup boy" Jay de Graff has business roots extending back to 1969. Located in downtown Turlock, the attractively laid-out nursery, with brick walkways, boxwood topiaries, and plant arrangements imitating garden beds, offers California-friendly trees, shrubs, annuals, and perennials. A special emphasis is on fruit trees, Japanese maples, roses, and shade trees. The website includes the nursery's "eLeaf" news-letter, garden tips, and information about nursery events. Open Monday through Saturday, 8 a.m.–5:30 p.m., and Sunday, 9 a.m.–4 p.m.

Horticultural Attractions

Clovis Botanical Garden

945 North Clovis Avenue, Clovis 93611
(559) 298-3091
www.clovisbotanicalgarden.org

The San Joaquin Valley's only botanical garden is a one-acre water-conserving demonstration garden of plants that are attractive and friendly to the Central Valley climate. An idea since 1993, the garden broke ground in 2002 and now has plans for expansion. It is managed by the nonprofit Clovis Botanical Garden Committee on city land next to Dry Creek

Park. The garden's website includes a listing of the "Sensational 70," plants that dazzle even when they are dry(ish). Open Wednesday through Sunday, 9 a.m.–4 p.m.

Forestiere Underground Gardens

5021 West Shaw, Fresno 93722
(559) 271-0734
www.undergroundgardens.com

This amazing 40-year achievement of Italian immigrant Baldassare Forestiere, begun in 1906, was supposedly patterned on the Roman catacombs and designed to provide an escape from the Fresno heat. At its heyday, underground gardens, courtyards, grottoes, and rooms sprawled over 10 acres. Today it is a California-registered historic landmark, still family owned. The garden includes a variety of plants and trees grown well below grade, with their canopies above ground. Open April though October (weather permitting), Wednesday through Sunday, with regularly scheduled tours. Admission fee.

Garden of the Sun Demonstration Garden

1750 North Winery at the southern end of Reedy Park, Fresno
(559) 456-4151
www.ucanr.edu

This one-acre demonstration garden is a project of the Master Gardener Program of the UC Cooperative Extension in Fresno. Master Gardeners are on hand to answer gardening questions, lead garden discovery programs for children, offer gardening classes on Wednesday and Saturday mornings, and maintain the garden. Specialty garden sections promote food production (orchard, berry patches, and vegetable garden) and ornamental horticulture (such as gardens for small spaces, sun or shade, children, and perennials). Open Monday, Wednesday, Friday, and some Saturdays, 9 a.m.–1 p.m.

Micke Grove Regional Park

11793 Micke Grove Road, Lodi 95240
(209) 331-7400, (209) 953-8800

Micke Grove contains a large oak grove, a three-acre Japanese garden with a distinctive collection of camellias, and a small rose garden—all in a 132-acre park with a zoo, a historical museum, a lake, and Fun Town.

Ralph Moore Rose Garden

Veteran's Memorial Park, Visalia

Dedicated in 2004, this too-small garden honors Ralph S. Moore, "Father of the Modern Miniature Rose," who hybridized 300 miniature roses while operating the Sequoia Nursery in Visalia until his death at the age of 102 in 2009.

Roeding Park

890 West Belmont, Fresno 93728
(559) 498-2124
www.fresno.gov

This 90-acre park is shaded by impressive old, labeled trees and includes Storyland, Playland, and the Chaffee Zoo.

San Joaquin Valley Blossom Trail

Between Routes 99 and 63, start in Sanger or Reedley
(559) 600-4271
www.gofresno.com

A self-guided tour through fruit tree orchards during blossom time, usually late February through mid-March, is available by phone or email. Check website for exact dates.

Shinzen Japanese Friendship Garden

Woodward Park, 114 West Audubon Drive, Fresno 93720
(559) 840-1264
www.shinzenjapanesegarden.org

Four garden sections, combining plants from the East and West, highlight the separate seasons with a serenely Japanese touch. Admission fee. Call for seasonal hours.

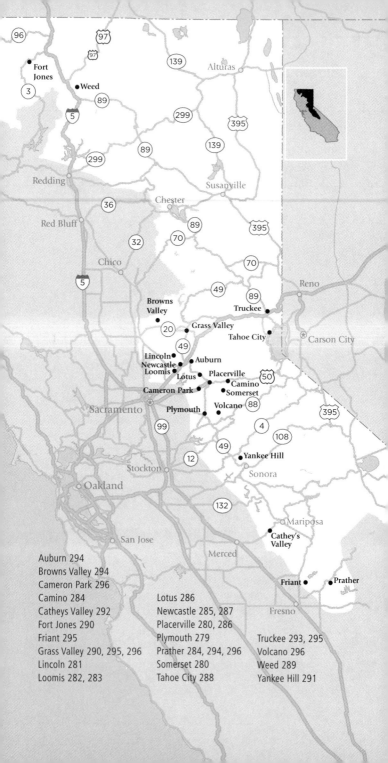

Chapter 11

Foothills and Mountains

Lilium parvum

Counties: Amador, Calaveras, El Dorado, Madera, Mariposa, Nevada, Placer, and Tuolumne in the foothills; Nevada, Placer, Plumas, Shasta, Sierra, and Siskiyou in the mountains

Elevational range: 1,000 to 5,000 feet in the foothills zone (closest to the Central Valley); 5,000 to 9,000 feet in the montane zone (dominated by conifer forests); and above 9,000 feet in the alpine zone (mostly above treeline), with Mount Whitney near Lone Pine, California, its highest peak at 14,495 feet

Sunset climate zones: 1A, 7, 9 in the foothills; 1A, 2B, 7, 9 in the mountains

Annual rainfall: foothills: 11 inches in Madera, 39 inches in Placerville; mountains: 36 inches in Yosemite, 39 inches in Redding (Shasta County)

Annual snowfall: 3 inches in Placerville, 103 inches in Mount Shasta (Shasta County), increasing in higher elevations

Winter temperatures: Foothill lows average 23°F to 9°F; mountain lows average −25°F to −50°F

Summer temperatures: Foothill highs average 85°F (Nevada City); mountain highs average 100°F mid to high 70s°F (Lake Tahoe)

Graceful sloping foothills spread out from the western flank of the Sierra Nevada mountain range (a range named in Spanish for its jagged snowy peaks) to form its base. This region lies below Sierran snow line, skirting the Central Valley.

Hot, dry summers with clear, sun-filled days start in May, with 100°F temperatures; rain seldom falls after April. Winters are cold, with occasional snow below 3,000 feet. A somewhat warmer lower thermal belt edges the Central Valley. The growing season runs 200 to 320 days, ample time to grow peaches, apples, tangerines, walnuts, pistachios, wine grapes, and Christmas trees.

Many native plants find their home in this region's quick-draining mineral soil: manzanita (*Arctostaphylos*), redbud (*Cercis*), bush anemone (*Carpinteria californica*), and wake robin (*Trillium*). Flannel bush (*Fremontodendron* or *Fremontia*) was discovered on an expedition crossing the Sierras. A rare prostrate form, Pine Hill fremontia (*Fremontodendron californicum* ssp. *decumbens*), discovered in western El Dorado County's Pine Hill Preserve, grows 2 feet high and 10 feet wide. Another California native, sky lupine (*Lupinus nanus*), a member of the scented pea family, grows freely in grasslands, where its deep blue, white-spotted flowers add delicate beauty in spring and disappear as rains cease.

Higher elevations in the Klamath Mountains, the Cascade Range, and the Sierra Nevada bring extreme winter cold, although summer temperatures are mild to hot. Temperature extremes and a short growing season of 50 to 100 days limit gardening.

Native plants—such as pines and, at higher elevations, firs and hemlocks—provide mountain forest cover. Foothill or gray pine (*Pinus sabiniana*), bird's-foot fern (*Pellaea mucronata* var. *mucronata*), and everlasting peavine (*Lathyrus latifolius*) crop up in bands at lower elevations. Another flourishing native is tiger lily (*Lilium parvum*), whose stems can reach seven feet with orange-yellow flowers mottled purple. This lily can be found from the Sierra Nevada north to Mount Shasta at elevations of 6,000 to 9,000 feet. It is particularly fond of damp stream beds and swamps.

The harsh mountain climate limits nurseries and their offerings. They stock plants suited to higher elevations, especially natives of the dogwood, currant, and pine families, and other Sierran conifers. Alpine and riparian plants all find their niche here.

Specialty Nurseries and Growers

Amador Flower Farm

22001 Shenandoah School Road, Plymouth 95669
(209) 245-6660
www.amadorflowerfarm.com
Email: deaver@daylilyfarm.com
Jeanne and Ken Deaver
Retail and mail/online order
Open every day, 9 a.m.–4 p.m.

Plant specialties: Daylilies (1,200 varieties), vegetable plants, succulents, perennials, and ornamental grasses.

History/description: Longtime gardener Jeanne Deaver got into the daylily business quite by happenstance. While buying plants at Alpine Gardens in Santa Rosa, she discovered that the business was for sale and bought it. Amador opened in 1994 as a mail-order-only business. Since 1996 the nursery, located at the edge of the foothills surrounded by vineyards (Ken is a grape grower), has been open for retail business in a big way. Four acres of gardens on themes such as fragrant, white, kitchen, cottage hill, and wine-colored, and a huge lawn with perennial beds are showstoppers that ably demonstrate the landscape use of daylilies. A gift store, a pumpkin patch, growing grounds, picnic tables, and a pond spread out over the 11-acre destination site.

Bluebird Haven Iris Garden

6940 Fairplay Road, Somerset 95684
(530) 620-5017
www.bluebirdhavenirisgarden.com
Email: mhess1863@innercite.com
Mary and John Hess
Retail and mail/online order
Open Thursday through Sunday, 11 a.m.–5 p.m., during
    bloom season (usually third weekend in April to third
    weekend in May; check website for exact dates).
    During the rest of the year, open by appointment only.

Plant specialties: Bearded iris—tall, border, and dwarf varieties, especially historic and antique varieties (2,000+ varieties total).

History/description: This garden nursery has been in its present location since 1988, although it previously existed elsewhere, primarily as a bird sanctuary. A large display garden has 4,000 varieties of irises, daffodils, and wildflowers planted among a Victorian gazebo, benches, and archways reflecting a turn-of-the-century civility. Four miles of landscaped rows containing over 100,000 irises provide a place for a pleasant stroll and can help you walk off whatever damage was done in the surrounding wine country.

Front Yard Nursery

5801 Mother Lode Drive, Placerville 95667
(530) 626-3494
www.frontyardnursery.com
Email: customerservice@frontyardnursery.com
Kristy Lamb, Richard Hosking; Wes Kohutek, manager
Retail and wholesale
Check website for seasonal open hours.

Plant specialties: Fruit trees (largest selection of both bare-root and potted fruit trees for miles around); Japanese maples, California native plants, trees, shrubs, and perennials; vegetable starts in spring and fall.

History/description: With a lifelong love of plants, in 1992 biologist Richard Hosking and his wife, Kristy Lamb, made good on their retirement dream of starting a nursery. At first their focus was on conifers and the grafting of Japanese maples, mostly for the wholesale trade, then also for retail. Over time a larger selection of plant material and nursery supplies (they are famous for a signature blend of potting soil available by the yard) were added to meet local demand. Richard retired in 2014 but still pops in to give advice. About a third of Front Yard's stock is propagated on 4.5 acres in two locations.

Gold Country Orchids

390 Big Ben Road, Lincoln 95648
(916) 645-8600
www.goldcountryorchids.com
Email: gcorchids@aol.com
Alan Koch
Retail, wholesale, and online order
Open Tuesday through Saturday, 9 a.m.–4:30 p.m.;
     wholesale by appointment only.

Plant specialties: Orchids (2,000 species), including miniature *Cattleya, Phalaenopsis,* and *Oncidium* intergenerics.

History/description: Alan Koch started a sideline orchid business with his wife, Cheryl, in 1978. Called Koch Orchids and located in Southern California, it was primarily focused on orchids that could be grown outdoors. As their attention shifted to cattleyas that required indoor space, and as collections grew and the nursery became a full-time concern, they outgrew their site. Finding these 10 acres in the Gold Country, they moved back north in 1985 and renamed the nursery Gold Country Orchids. Alan's introductions include *Sophrolaelia* 'El Dorado Sunrise', *Sophrolaeliocattleya* 'Pink Doll', and *Hawkinsara* 'Keepsake'. Alan recommends that you also visit the nearby Gladding-McBean Clayworks, purveyors of terra-cotta architectural detail to many historic buildings in California.

Golden Pond Water Plants

3275 Sierra College Boulevard, Loomis 95650
(916) 652-5459
www.goldenpondwaterplants.com
Email: goldenpondnursery@gmail.com
Sue Golden
Retail
Open April through October, Thursday
    through Sunday, 10 a.m.–4 p.m.

Plant specialties: Aquatic plants (more than 250 varieties); bog plants (including the elusive *Lysimachia ciliata, Potentilla egedii,* and *Carex nudata*); hardy and tropical water lilies (over 50 varieties); and ornamental grasses (including evergreen *Miscanthus* and *Bouteloua*).

History/description: Yet another well-trained Cal Poly graduate in landscape design, Sue Golden enjoys detailing water features and started growing aquatic plants to supply her projects. Proving successful at dividing her own stock, she started the nursery and its display ponds in 1993. She also creates miniature gardens for indoor use.

High-Hand Nursery

3750 Taylor Road, Loomis 95650
(916) 652-2065 (nursery); (916) 652-2064 (conservatory café)
www.highhand.com
nichole@highhand.com
Scott Paris
Retail
Nursery open every day, 9 a.m.–4 p.m.

Plant specialties: Trees, especially Japanese maples, and unique and unusual varieties of shrubs, perennials, succulents, and dwarf plants for container gardens.

History/description: Longtime landscaper Scott Paris bought this old fruit-packing company site in Historic Loomis in 2003 to start a nursery as a plant source for his landscape projects. His landscaping prowess has made it a pleasure garden, with paths winding through rock-bordered planting areas. The old packing shed sells flowers, art, and ironworks and a conservatory serves as a café. High-Hand propagates about a third of its plants on site. Linger a little in Loomis to visit the antique shops and Blue Goose produce stand.

High Ranch Nursery, Inc.

3800 Delmar Avenue, Loomis 95650
(916) 652-9261
www.hrnursery.com
Email: sales@hrnursery.com
John and Sarah Nitta
Wholesale and contract growing
Wholesale open Monday through Friday, 7 a.m.–4 p.m.

Plant specialties: California natives suited to the valley and foothills; native shrubs, such as wild mock orange, Western redbud, manzanitas, California wild rose, Mexican elderberry, and wild grape; oaks (12 varieties); hardy, drought-tolerant perennials and grasses, including coreopsis, buddleias, asters, penstemons, lavenders, and daylilies; the UC Davis "Arboretum All-Stars"; Mediterranean plants, shrubs, and trees, including *Lagerstroemia* 'Seminole', L. 'Cherokee', and the mildew-resistant forms of crepe myrtle, *L. indica fauriel* 'Muskogee'; and alpine and rock garden plants.

History/description: Educated at UC Davis in plant science and environmental horticulture, John Nitta got hooked on propagating and started High Ranch Nursery in 1976 on his family's 40-acre property, an old stone-fruit orchard. The nursery opened with just a few trees and then expanded to include woody ornamentals and cold-hardy perennials. Over time, the nursery grew to include a wide range of California native plants, propagated from wild-collected seeds and cuttings.

High Sierra Iris and Wedding Garden

3170 Hassler Road, Camino 95709
(530) 642-1222
www.weddingsnflowers.com
Email: nancy@weddingsnflowers.com
(530) 642-1222
Mike and Nancy Visman
Retail, wholesale, and mail order
Open every day in May, 9 a.m.–4:30 p.m.,
    or by appointment. Call for peak bloom information.

Plant specialties: Tall-bearded irises (1,500 named varieties) and daylilies.

History/description: Little did Mike Visman know what would happen when he gave his wife, the mother of his four children, an iris for a Mother's Day present in 1990. Instant infatuation led to education, collecting, and networking with breeders and iris societies, and then to the opening of this nursery. Today the nursery includes a one-acre hillside garden filled with irises. This continues the Visman family tradition of farming in the Apple Hill area since the early 1900s. Cut-your-own Christmas trees are available from the day after Thanksgiving until Christmas.

Intermountain Nursery

30443 N. Auberry Road, Prather 93651
(209) 855-3113
www.intermountainnursery.com
Email: bonnie@intermountainnursery.com
Raymond Laclergue, Bonnie Bladen
Retail, wholesale, and contract growing
Open Monday through Saturday, 9 a.m.–5 p.m.,
    and Sunday, 10 a.m.–4 p.m.

Plant specialties: California native plants from the Central Valley, foothill, and central Sierra Nevada regions; Mediterranean-climate plants, some fruit trees, and vegetable starts;

beneficial plants; and hard-to-find annuals and perennials. Erosion control and revegetation plants are also available.

History/description: After studying ornamental horticulture at UC Davis and working for the Forest Service in the Sierras, Ray Laclergue decided to open a nursery and found this property—a former bedding-plant nursery—in Prather in 1980. He was joined 10 years later by Bonnie Bladen, trained in natural resource management. They both have a strong commitment to native habitat preservation and restoration, evidenced in their community involvement, pursuit of sustainable gardening practices, and management of the 240-acre Grand Bluffs Forest. A local Mono woman taught them her ancestral ways of propagation, still pursued today. This 11-acre site includes 14 gardens to demonstrate garden uses of native plants. Visitors can picnic down by the creek, rest a spell by the fish pond, or enjoy the many hiking trails in the area. Ray and Bonnie recommend that you also visit the McKenzie Table Top Preserve and Elizabeth Miller Preserve at Black Mountain (native site of the endemic *Carpenteria californica*), both managed by the Sierra Foothills Conservancy.

Lake's Nursery

8435 Crater Hill Road, Newcastle 95658
(530) 885-1027
www.lakesnursery.com
Email: joe@lakesnursery.com
Joe and Ann Ciurej
Retail, with discounts for the trade
Open every day, 9 a.m.–5 p.m. (winter close at 4 p.m.).

Plant specialties: Japanese maples (300 cultivars); bamboo (24 varieties); conifers; and other large boxed trees. The nursery also sells perennials and shrubs.

History/description: Nurseryman Joe Ciurej bought this nursery from the Lake family in 2006, combining his interest in plants and yard art and the Lakes' collection of Japanese maples and bamboo. The plant collection, dating from 1983, continues to grow and refine itself. Today, visitors delight in the park-like grounds, Japanese garden, waterfall, koi pond, and mature groves of bamboo.

Lotus Bonsai Nursery & Gardens

1435 Lower Lake Drive, Placerville 95667
(530) 622-9681
www.lotusbonsai.com
Email: mail@lotusbonsai.com
Scott Chadd
Retail and mail order
Open by appointment only.

Plant specialties: High-evolved bonsai and stock plants (170 varieties), seeds, and accessories.

History/description: Scott Chadd's bonsai hobby started in 1972 when he met well-regarded bonsai mentor George Yamasaki. He discovered that the practice of bonsai brought solace to his frenetic life as director of public works for various cities and counties. As his collection grew, visitors from the close-knit but far-flung community of bonsai aficionados started to arrive and then wanted to buy. His five-acre site in the oak woodlands of the Sierra foothills has three acres on which grow about 200,000 trees in various stages of bonsai development.

Lotus Valley Nursery and Gardens

5606 Peterson Lane, Lotus 95651
P. O. Box 859, Lotus 95651
(530) 626-7021
Email: joebob.lvng@yahoo.com
Joe House
Retail
March through October, open Friday through Sunday, 9 a.m.–5 p.m.
    Closed November through February.

Plant specialties: Ornamental grasses (170 varieties) and drought-tolerant perennials, featuring many California native plants.

History/description: Joe House and his late partner, Robert Davenport, two delightfully compulsive gardeners, started selling just a few plants from their own rich and varied garden. Word obviously got out. The nursery has been in full-time plant production since 1988, operating in a four-acre valley near the south fork of the American River with a beautiful view of the mountains. A rock garden was created from granite blasted to prepare a building site for the original historic Wagner ranch house (which has since burned down). The beautifully tended garden features Mediterranean plants in all sorts of unusual combinations, in the ground and in a variety of unique pots. The stone sculptures throughout are cast by hand at the nursery.

Matsuda Landscape and Nursery

4888 Virginiatown Road, Newcastle 95658
(916) 645-1820
www.masteryo.com
Email: matsubonsai@sbcglobal.net
Hiroshi Matsuda
Retail
Open Thursday and Friday, 9:30 a.m.–5 p.m.;
    Saturday, 9:30 a.m.–3 p.m.; or by appointment.

Plant specialties: Bonsai stock and mature specimens of Japanese maples, elms, *Pinus thunbergii,* and other trees, including more than 500 finished bonsai and miniature landscapes. Bonsai accessories are also available.

History/description: With a degree in landscape architecture from Cal Poly Pomona, Hiro Matsuda has been a bonsai pottery importer, a landscape designer/installer, a bonsai nurseryman, a potter, an artist, and an instructor. He has introduced two new bonsai art forms: bonarte and bonniwa. Bonarte, or bonsai in a container, removes the artistic restrictions of traditional bonsai. Bonniwa, a miniature landscape in a tray, differs from other such landscapes (e.g., Saikei) in that each landscape is a complete Japanese garden, including traditional rocks, mounds, and plants, as well as a ceramic bridge, lantern, tsukabai, waterfall, and stream. Opened since 1991, the 1.5-acre nursery sells traditional bonsai, Chinese penjing, bonarte, bonniwa, Zen gardens, and Japanese painting—all the work of one remarkable man. Given the title "Bonsai Guru" by the *Sacramento Bee,* Hiro Matsuda teaches classes in bonsai and Japanese gardening. At this destination nursery, you can find Eastern artistic tradition in harmonious blend with the ruggedly Western, rolling hills of Placer County. The website features informative YouTube videos on bonsai, gardens, and other Japanese cultural topics.

McBride's Nursery/Tahoe Tree Company

401 West Lake Boulevard, Tahoe City 96145
P. O. Box 5325, Tahoe City 96145
(530) 583-3911
www.mcbridesnursery.com or www.tahoetreecompany.com
Email: mcbridesnursery@gmail.com
Leslie and John Hyche
Retail and wholesale
May through October, open Monday through Saturday, 9 a.m.–5 p.m., and Sunday, 10 a.m.–4 p.m. Closed November through April.

Plant specialties: California native plants and cold-hardy perennials, trees, and shrubs.

History/description: David and Katherine McBride started this nursery, then called Tahoe Tree Company, in 1954 as an offshoot of his tree service business, her interest in perennials and California native plants, and their combined desire to supply local gardens with healthy plants suited to the area. The second generation now directs the operation. Daughter Leslie Hyche manages the retail nursery. Leslie's husband,

John, supervises the wholesale backyard and specializes in the propagation of native plants. To honor her parents' legacy, they renamed the nursery McBride's in 2008. The 10-acre property, now sold to the Tahoe Maritime Museum but leased back to the Hyches, continues on as a nursery and includes a variety of garden displays and a large native plant propagation and growing area. They recommend Julie Carville's *Lingering in Tahoe's Wild Gardens* as a guide to nearby wildflower walks.

Menzies' Native Nursery

10805 North Old Stage Road, Weed
P. O. Box 9, Weed 96094
(530) 938-4858
www.menziesnatives.com
Email: sales@menziesnatives.com
Robert Menzies
Retail, wholesale, and contract growing
Open by appointment only.

Plant specialties: Riparian-habitat plants and 208 species of montane California native plants, specializing in conifers (40 varieties).

History/description: Robert Menzies has enviable horticultural credentials, being the nephew of Arthur Menzies (of San Francisco Botanical Garden fame) and a distant relative of the pioneer plant explorer Archibald Menzies, a Scottish physician and naturalist who accompanied George Vancouver in 1790 on an expedition to the Pacific Northwest on behalf of Britain. Robert started a nursery in Mill Valley in the 1970s and moved it to this three-acre location in Weed in 1980. An "indigenous nursery," Menzies' makes its own fertilizers and soil to maximize plant health. Robert offers botanical consultations and will contract grow for restoration projects. He and his family also operate the Rush Creek Wilderness School, which aims to reconnect people and nature. The nursery website contains a plant list of Pacific Northwest natives.

Mountain Crest Gardens

402 Bridge Street, Fort Jones 96032
(530) 468-2210; (877) 656-4035 (toll free)
www.mountaincrestgardens.com
Email: sales@mountaincrestgardens.com
Tom Jopson; Matts Jopson, vice president;
    Nora Alderson, general manager
Retail and wholesale, through phone/online order
Open Wednesday through Friday, 7 a.m.–4 p.m.

Plant specialties: Succulents, including hardy and tender varieties such as *Sempervivum* (250 varieties), *Sedum* (50 varieties), *Jovibarba* (40), *Echeveria* (50), *Crassula* (30), *Haworthia* (50), *Kalanchoe* (15), *Aeonium* (15), *Senecio* (10), and *Lewisia* (10). Also available as mixed flats and collections.

History/description: This is a complicated business. It all started in Covelo as an enterprise called Cal-Forest, which raised pine trees for government reforestation projects. Then Cal-Forest moved to a five-acre site in Etna and added wholesale bedding plants and perennials. In the mid-1990s, Jim and Irene Russ's remarkable and extensive succulent collection went on the market, and Cal-Forest snapped it up. Cal-Forest continues to grow conifers for restoration projects in Etna. The greatly expanded succulent business is now a separate division called Mountain Crest Gardens and sells mostly through website orders. Visitors are encouraged to see the plants in person and enjoy the gardens' expansive annual and perennial color. The nursery also contract grows for commercial rooftop gardens, landscapers, and wholesalers.

Peaceful Valley Farm and Garden Supply

125 Clydesdale Court, Grass Valley 95945
P. O. Box 2209, Grass Valley 95945
(530) 272-4769; (888) 784-1722 (toll free)
www.groworganic.com
Email: helpdesk@groworganic.com
Eric and Patty Boudier

Retail and mail/online order
April through October, open Monday through Saturday, 8 a.m.–6 p.m.;
    November through March, open Monday through Saturday,
    9 a.m.–5 p.m.; April through June, open Sundays 10 a.m.–4 p.m.

Plant specialties: Certified organic vegetable transplants; deer- and drought-tolerant plants; California native plants; ornamental edibles; bare-root fruit trees, berries, perennials, vines (available December through March), and potted fruit trees (olive, fig, pomegranate, and citrus). Huge assortment of seeds (vegetable, herb, wildflower, flower, bulb, cover crop, pasture, and erosion control). Peaceful Valley aims to provide "everything you need to grow organically."

History/description: What started in a garage on Peaceful Valley Road in Nevada City in 1976 now employs about 60 people and offers an encyclopedic assortment of organic gardening supplies. Despite having moved several times and having changed ownership three times, Peaceful Valley has never lost its zeal to spread the word about best garden practices—and during much of this time, words like *sustainability* and *organic* were not so bandied about. The Boudiers bought the business in 1996, moved it to this larger site in 2005, and started the retail nursery in 2008. They grow some of their plants in two large greenhouses but source most from specialty growers.

Spring Fever Nursery and Gardens

5683 Wendy Way, Yankee Hill 95965
(530) 534-1556
www.springfevergardens.com
Email: davidsspringfever@gmail.com
David and Cathy Walther
Retail
Open by appointment, Monday through Friday, 9 a.m.–4 p.m.

Plant specialties: Small lots but a huge selection of hardy perennials.

History/description: David Walther developed his lifelong love of plants as a water boy at the age of 12. By 18 he was managing a nursery; then he worked many years in the landscape business. His collection of plants began in earnest in 1994 when he bought this beautiful three-acre property in the madrone belt of the lower Sierra Nevadas. He and Cathy "vacation" by traveling to nurseries to discover new perennials, which they then test for hardiness at home. At 2,300 feet—with frost, some snow, and poor red soil with a high clay content—plants that survive here will also thrive in the valley. David and Cathy love to show off their woodland garden, but call first, as they may be at a farmers' market or on a consultation.

Superstition Iris Gardens

2536 Old Highway, Catheys Valley 95306-9738
(209) 966-6277
Facebook: @superstitionirisgardens
Email: randrcv@sti.com
Rick Tasco, Roger Duncan
Retail and mail order
Open during bloom season, usually mid-April through Mother's Day,
    Friday through Sunday, 10 a.m.–5 p.m.

Plant specialties: *Iris* (800 varieties), mostly bearded, but some beardless and species.

History/description: Rick Tasco lived at the base of the famous Superstition Mountains in Apache Junction, Arizona (40 miles east of Phoenix). He was a weekday computer programmer/analyst and a weekend iris hobbyist and breeder. He moved the garden business to a six-acre garden site in Catheys Valley in the beautiful lower foothills of Mariposa County in August 1990. The iris garden occupies two acres, with plantings being rotated on one of the acres to showcase his yearly introductions of new varieties. The American Iris Society, with permission of the British Iris Society, awards the William Rickaston Dykes Memorial Medal to only one North American–introduced iris each year. Rick has won that prestigious award twice—in 2005 for his *Iris* 'Splashacata' and in 2009 for his *I.* 'Golden Panther'.

Villager Nursery

10678 Donner Pass Road, Truckee 96161
(530) 587-0771
www.villagernursery.com
Email: info@villagernursery.com
Eric Larusson, Rob Van Dyke
Retail, wholesale, and contract growing
Open March through Christmas, weather permitting,
    Monday through Saturday, 9 a.m.–5 p.m.,
    and Sunday, 10 a.m.–4 p.m. Call first.

Plant specialties: California native plants suited to the Sierras, Great Basin, and Rocky Mountain areas; trees, shrubs, ground covers, vines, perennials, bulbs, and seed; and drought-adapted, snow-load-adapted, deacclimation-resistant, and extremely cold-hardy species.

History/description: A small florist shop, purchased in 1975, slowly evolved into a tiny retail nursery and landscape business. In the mid-1980s, the current owners, fresh from college with degrees in botany, horticulture, and ecology, as well as extensive professional botanical and horticultural experience, began tracking down and growing a wide variety of then-uncommon Sierra and intermountain native plants from everywhere they could be found or grown. The nursery grew and moved a half mile down the road to its new home in 1999. Eric and Rob continue to search the Intermountain West for seeds and cuttings of hard-to-find, interesting, and useful plants to propagate and contract grow for the nursery and clients. They also partner with growers (in slightly more growing-conducive climates) to produce a wide variety of landscape-worthy natives and cool plants from the high deserts, cold coasts, and mountain ranges around the globe. They have "killed thousands of plants in the nursery (testing and researching) so that clients won't have to do the same." Environmental education continues to be a Villager emphasis, and the nursery regularly works with schools and regional restoration groups. They encourage you to get out and hike to get to know your local ecosystems, whether they be alpine, rock garden, mixed forest, meadow, riparian, or high desert. Big sales are held in the spring and fall.

Notable Garden Centers

Bald Mountain Nursery

6195 Bald Mountain Road, Brown's Valley 95918
(530) 743-4856
www.baldmountainnursery.com

This five-acre rural nursery on an old homestead ranch has been family owned and operated since 1985, when Cecilia Rice and her husband first opened its doors. Son Jeffrey now oversees the fields of container plants, while his mother is still very involved in the office. The nursery buys liners and bare-root stock, which they grow at the nursery to large-size speci-mens so that plants are acclimated to the temperature extremes of the Sierra Nevada foothills. Open every day, 9 a.m.–5 p.m.

Eisley Nursery

380 Nevada Street, Auburn 95603
(530) 885-5163 (retail); (530) 885-0900 (wholesale)
eisleynursery.com

Earl Eisley is now in charge of this family-owned and -operated nursery that started during the Great Depression in 1932, when Lila Eisley saw an opportunity to sell pansies to gold miners on their way home from work. Earl's four children carry on this fine family tradition and all work there now. The nursery is still on their old family farm, with the retail operation occupying two acres and the wholesale growing grounds and greenhouses covering nine. It has a wide selection of plants, including a large assortment of bedding plants and vegetables, which the Eisleys buy in or propagate on site. The website lists classes offered at the nursery and a blog from the self-described "Garden Goddesses." Free popcorn. Open Monday through Saturday, 8 a.m.–5:30 p.m., and Sunday, 9 a.m.–5 p.m.

Rock and Rose, Inc. Nursery

10739 Glenshire Drive, Truckee 96161
(530) 550-7744
www.rocknrose.com

When Erik and Deanna Neu moved their landscape company to this location in 2012, the site of an old nursery, they decided to open one of their own. Rock and Rose offers a wide selection of zone-hardy shrubs, perennials, and California native plants, specializing in larger-sized trees. Bulk soils and mulches are available. Hours vary by season.

Horticultural Attractions

Bourn Cottage

Empire Mine State Historic Park
10791 East Empire Street, Grass Valley 95945
(530) 273-8522
www.parks.ca.gov

Another Willis Polk–designed mansion for mining magnate William Bourn (see Filoli Center in chapter 4). The cottage sits on 13 acres of European-style parkland in the ponderosa forest, including several noteworthy gardens of old roses and perennials.

McKenzie Table Mountain Preserve

Auberry Road between Friant and Prather
(559) 855-3473 (Sierra Foothill Conservancy)
www.sierrafoothill.org/preserves

Large basalt lava tableland, which rises above grassland and oak woodland with vernal pools. You can take the four-mile self-guided Discovery Trail or hike to the top for views of the San Joaquin River.

McLaughlin's Daffodil Hill

Rams Horn Road, Volcano
(209) 296-7048

On this bucolic four-acre farm owned by the McLaughlin family since 1887, 300,000 daffodils (300 named varieties) bloom each year, usually in March and April. The garden opens when 25 percent of the daffodils start to bloom and closes when only 25 percent remain in bloom. Call for bloom information.

Elizabeth Miller Preserve at Black Mountain

Four miles east of Prather, on Black Mountain Road
(559) 855-3473 (Sierra Foothill Conservancy)
www.sierrafoothill.org/preserves

This preserve boasts 992 acres of woody chaparral and grassland/oak woodland, home to *Carpinteria californica,* which grows in the wild only between 2,500 and 4,000 feet in central Fresno County and a small area in Madera County.

Pine Hill Preserve

Next to Cameron Park, near Highway 50,
    centered around Green Valley Road
(916) 941-3134
www.pinehillpreserve.com

This large tract of land is dedicated to the preservation of the native flora of western El Dorado County that grow on reddish gabbro soils, so named for the underlying rock. The area is host to a rich diversity of plants, containing 10 percent of all of California's native plants. Three species here are endemic to the area (*Fremontodendron decumbens, Galium californicum* ssp. *sierrae,* and *Wyethia reticulata*), while several others are threatened or endangered in the wild. The preserve offers guided tours on Saturdays in the spring, and workdays are listed on the website.

The Rose Garden at Saint Joseph's Cultural Center

410 South Church Street, Grass Valley 95945
(530) 272-4725
www.saintjosephsculturalcenter.org

A large Victorian-style garden, divided into four parts by boxwood hedgerows in the form of the Celtic harp, with many old, well-tended roses, other flowering plants, and large trees.

Deer-Resistant Gardening

Deer can be pests in suburban and rural gardens. When food grows scarce in the wild, these herbivores have been known to forage for flowers, buds, and green shoots in gardens. To curb their damage, a dual approach works best: restrict and repel.

An eight-foot-tall fence will restrict deer. Fences made from wood, iron, wire mesh, or chain link all work so long as they are tall enough. Electric fences also work, but since resourceful deer can go under or through a fence, space the electrified wires at increments off the ground. For a two-wire electric fence, space wires at 15 inches and 30 inches from the ground, and for three-wires, 10 inches, 20 inches, and 30 inches from the ground. If space permits, a double fence only four feet tall will also restrict deer; space the parallel rows of fencing about 5 feet apart.

To repel deer, gardeners draw from a wide array of remedies, including repellent sprays, baby powder, human hair, fox urine, bars of soap, moth balls in an onion sack hung at deer height from a tree, bloodmeal, feathermeal, creosote, fabric softener sheets, invisible fishing line, and more. For these repellents to work, you must routinely apply them and reapply after heavy rains. It also helps to employ several methods in rotation. If an area is known to have deer, put out repellents *before* they begin to damage plants and grow accustomed to the location.

There are plants that deer generally ignore, but no plant is totally deer proof. Many attractive trees are "deer resistant," such as Japanese maple (*Acer palmatum*), cedar (*Cedrus*), Western redbud (*Cercis occidentalis*), maidenhair tree (*Ginkgo biloba*), hawthorn (*Crataegus*), cypress (*Cupressus*), magnolia, olive (*Olea europaea*), palms, and redwoods (*Sequoia sempervirens*).

There are also many shrubs worth trying, some of them California natives: bush anemone (*Carpenteria californica*), California buckeye (*Aesculus californica*), wild lilac (*Ceanothus*), manzanita (*Arctostaphylos*), currant (*Ribes*), sage (*Salvia*), flannel bush (*Fremontodendron*), spice bush (*Calycanthus occidentalis*), and wild buckwheat (*Eriogonum*). Non-native shrubs that deter deer include glossy abelia (*Abelia x grandiflora*), barberry (*Berberis*), boxwood (*Buxus*), butterfly bush (*Buddleja*), daphne, flowering quince (*Chaenomeles*), heath (*Erica*), mahonia, rosemary (*Rosmarinus officinalis*), spiraea, and viburnum.

Since deer use scent to select tasty plants, many gardeners in deer country confound them by growing strongly aromatic plants. Some herbs with pungent leaves include anise hyssop (*Agastache*), wormwood (*Artemisia*), lavender (*Lavandula*), mint (*Mentha*), lemon balm (*Melissa*), bee balm (*Monarda*), catnip (*Nepeta*), oregano (*Origanum*), rue or herb of grace (*Ruta*), sage (*Salvia*), lavender cotton (*Santolina*), tansy (*Tanacetum*), germander (*Teucrium*), and thyme (*Thymus*).

Other perennials noted for their deer resistance are California fuchsia (*Zauschneria*), bleeding heart (*Dicentra*), trailing or creeping speedwell (*Veronica*), Jerusalem sage (*Phlomis*), beard tongue (*Penstemon*), poppy (*Papaver orientale*), and Russian sage (*Perovskia*). Ornamental Foerster's reed grass (*Calamagrostis*) is also recommended.

Other Sources

Sources of plants, seeds, bulbs, and rhizomes whose locations (mostly) cannot be visited. Available by mail, phone, fax, email, or online order.

The Arboreum Company

P. O. Box 1804, Morgan Hill 95128
www.arboreumco.com
Email: arboreum.company@gmail.com

Longtime fruit growers and members of the California Rare Fruit Growers, Todd Kennedy and Patrick Schafer have made varieties of unusual and antique bare-root fruit trees directly available to the public via their online store. The business, which started in 1983 in the Santa Clara Valley, grew out of scion exchanges. Formerly a wholesale-only business, the company's source orchards contain 800 varieties, only some of which are propagated each year, on a rotating basis.

Bay View Gardens

1201 Bay Street, Santa Cruz 95060
(831) 423-3656
Facebook: Bay View Gardens
Email: ghiobayview@att.net

Joe Ghio started collecting irises in 1953, created his first hybrid in 1954, and has been selling tall-bearded, median, spuria, Louisiana, and Pacific Coast hybrid irises since 1963. Two acres of growing grounds in Corralitos accommodate his still-growing collection. He has won the prestigious Dykes Medal for *I.* 'Mystique'. A mail-order catalog is available for three dollars.

Bountiful Gardens

1712 D South Main Street, Willits 95490
(707) 459-6410
www.bountifulgardens.org
Email: bountiful@sonic.net

A project of the nonprofit Ecology Action, Bountiful Gardens sells untreated, open-pollinated seeds for heirloom vegetables, grains, cover crops, herbs, flowers, and green manure by mail or online. Bulk prices are available.

The Cactus and Succulent Plant Mall

cactus-mall.com

A web-hosting online resource for all things related to cactus and succulent plants: specialist groups, nurseries, books, services, shows, and information about conservation, resources, and culture.

Dragonfly Peony Farm

5590 Charles Avenue, Wilseyville 95257
P. O. Box 1177, West Point 95255
(209) 293-1242
www.dragonflypeonyfarm.com
Email: dragonflypeonyfarm@gmail.com

Herbaceous, tree, and intersectional (Itoh) peonies available by mail, email, or online order. Antiques dealer and peony lover Julia Moore started her peony garden in 1998, when she bought a lovely seven-acre piece of property in the pine, cedar, and black oak–covered foothills overlooking the Mokelumne River. Today, 800 to 1,000 peonies are planted here, and some years Julia opens the garden during bloom season. Peonies are shipped from September 15 to December 15.

Easytogrowbulbs.com

(866) 725-5361

An online store of bulbs and plants for warm climates. Based near San Diego, the site was developed by folk who have worked in the flower bulb business for years. It offers a large selection of bulb varieties, including those from South Africa and the Mediterranean.

Flourishing Daylilies

315 22nd Avenue, San Mateo 94403
(510) 480-5607 (cell)
www.flourishingdaylilies.com
Email: subhana@flourishingdaylilies.com
Online order

Forever a plant lover, Subhana Ansari met Bill Maryott, who introduced her to the thrill of hybridization. Working for Bill for one season in exchange for plants, Subhana now has growing grounds at two locations in coastal San Mateo County. She specializes in modern hybrids selected for their blue tones and complex eyes.

Flowers by the Sea

P.O. Box 89, Elk 95432
(707) 877-1717
www.fbts.com

Kermit and Vikki Carter offer an extensive collection (900 species) of salvias and companion plants that are drought tolerant and attract hummingbirds, bees, and butterflies.

Forest Seeds of California

1100 Indian Hill Road, Placerville 95667
(530) 621-1551; (530) 621-1040 (fax)
Email: forestseeds@directcon.net
Retail and wholesale

Seeds of forest trees and shrubs, mostly California native and reforestation stock. Forest Seeds also does custom seed collecting and cleaning. Orders are accepted by mail, phone, and fax.

Green House Botanica

Brisbane
(650) 303-0102
www.horticopia.etsy.com
Email: scplantgeek@gmail.com

Succulents, South African and Australian protea family plants, and organic heirloom vegetables. Ten years as a professional grower and propagator for Nurseryman's Exchange encouraged Shanna Calmes to launch this online shop/site in 2009.

Greenmantle Nursery

3010 Ettersburg Road, Garberville 95542
(707) 986-7504
www.greenmantlenursery.com

Ettersburg was the private experiment station founded in 1895 by Albert Etter (1872–1950), renowned for the apple, strawberry, and chestnut varieties he developed there. In the 1970s, the area was re-inhabited by a new generation of young homesteaders. Marissa and Ram Fishman settled on their 32 acres in 1973. Ram's work as a horseshoer brought him into contact with local old-timers and their orchards. He has been involved in the task of retrieving and preserving the best Etter fruit varieties for decades, as well as collecting numerous other heirloom fruit varieties. Ram will custom bench graft your choice of rootstock. Marissa has assembled a large collection of antique roses and species, plus ornamentals of all kinds for her hillside garden. In 1983, they went into business as Greenmantle—first with a catalog and now with a website for online orders of heirloom fruit trees (including 300 varieties of apples) and old and rare roses.

Hedgerow Farms

21740 County Road 88, Winters 95694
(530) 662-6847; (530) 662-2753 (fax)
www.hedgerowfarms.com
Email: info@hedgerowfarms.com

Seeds and plugs of California native grasses, sedges, rushes, forbs, and some wildflowers. Wholesale and retail seed is available by phone, fax, or mail order. Custom growing, consulting, and seed-cleaning services are also offered. $100 minimum order.

The Heirloom Seed Store

P. O. Box 2128, Half Moon Bay 94019
(650) 726-4980
www.theheirloomseedstore.com
Email: eda@theheirloomseedstore.com

Third-generation farmers John and Eda Muller have imported heirloom Italian seeds of vegetables, herbs, and flowers since 2002 for use in their fields and by online order.

J. L. Hudson, Seedsman

Box 337, La Honda 94020
www.jlhudsonseeds.net

A "public-access seedbank" dedicated to preserving species by a wide dissemination of seeds. Huge variety of offbeat seed from around the world. Mail or online orders. Catalog online.

Kitazawa Seed Company

201 4th Street #206, Oakland 94607
(510) 595-1188
www.kitazawaseed.com
Email: seeds@kitazawaseed.com

Since 1917, the Kitazawa family has been a main source of Asian vegetable production, making mainstream such crops as edamame and daikon. 250 varieties of Asian vegetable seed are offered for retail or wholesale orders. All seed is guaranteed. Order online or by mail.

Lockhart Seeds, Inc.

3 N. Wilson Way, Stockton 95205
(209) 466-4401
www.lockhartseeds.com (coming soon)

This retail shop sells field-grown occidental and Asian vegetable seeds, including many types of onions and some flower seeds. 600 varieties of bulk seed are dispensed from old oaken drawers. Lockhart has been family owned and operated since 1935. Free catalog. Orders are currently accepted by mail and phone…and perhaps soon online.

Mistletoe–Carter Wholesale Seeds

780 North Glen Annie Road, Goleta 93117
(805) 968-4818
www.mcseeds.com

This venerable seed company has been owned by the Schaff family since 1989. It offers seeds for trees—especially palm, pines, and eucalyptus—as well as shrubs, ornamental grasses, herbs, and wildflowers. Online, mail, email, or phone orders are accepted. $100 minimum order.

Mountain Valley Growers, Inc.

38325 Pepperweed Road, Squaw Valley 93675
(559) 338-2775; (559) 338-0075 (fax)
Website: mountainvalleygrowers.com
Email: customerservice@mountainvalleygrowers.com

Mountain Valley sells organic herbs (over 400 varieties), perennials that attract bees and butterflies, and vegetables in 3-inch pots and plug trays. Retail and wholesale sales via mail, fax, phone, or online order.

Muchas Grasses

P. O. Box 683, Occidental 95465
(707) 874-1871 (phone and fax)
muchasgrasses@hotmail.com
Bob Hornback

Lecturer, educator, propagator, horticulturist, and former nurseryman Bob Hornback has a plant brokerage, design, and consultation business. His specialties include ornamental grasses, native grasses, and grass-like plants, such as phormiums.

Ornamental Edibles

5723 Trowbridge Way, San Jose 95138
(408) 528-7333; (408) 532-1499 (fax)
www.ornamentaledibles.com
Email: seeds@ornamentaledibles.com

Ornamental Edibles offers international vegetable, herb, and edible-flower seeds, as well as seeds for hydroponics specialties. It grows a large selection of salad and braising greens. Bulk sales for specialty market growers and packets for the home gardener. Order online or by phone, fax, or email.

Pacific Coast Seed Company

533 Hawthorne Place, Livermore 94550
(925) 373-4417; (925) 373-6855 (fax)
pcseed.com

Since 1985 Pacific Coast has been providing seed for wholesale distributors, both in bulk and packaged for retail outlets. The company offers native grass, turfgrass, and erosion control/revegetation grass seeds, as well as native and non-native wildflower seeds and wildflower mixes. $150 minimum order.

Palm and Cycad Exchange

www.palmandcycadexchange.com

Keith and Laurie Huber buy and sell cycads and palms via their website, which also serves as a "forum" to help palm and cycad sellers and buyers in Southern California connect with one another.

Protea Farm of California

P. O. Box 1806, Fallbrook 92088
(760) 728-4297

Australian and South African shrubs, bulbs, and perennials; epidendrums; and members of the protea family, including proteas, leucodendrons, leucospermums, and banksias. Roger Boddaert's Protea Farm has introduced yellow *Clivia* 'California Sunshine', *Haemanthus katharinae,* and the rare bulbous sea squills. All of Protea Farm's plants are drought tolerant.

Redwood City Seed Company

P. O. Box 361, Redwood City 94064
(650) 325-7333; (650) 325-4056 (fax)
www.ecoseeds.com

Open-pollinated, heirloom seed varieties of vegetables (80 peppers) and herbs can be ordered by phone, mail, or fax. Retail and wholesale sales.

Renee's Garden

6060A Graham Hill Road, Felton 95018
(888) 880-7228
www.reneesgarden.com

The founder of Shepherd's Garden Seeds in 1985, Renee Shepherd started Renee's Garden in 1997. She offers her personal selection of gourmet vegetable, kitchen herb, and cottage-garden flower seeds culled from national and international sources for the wholesale market. Retail sales through website only. A great communicator and early proponent of eating fresh and locally, Renee lectures widely and has written many articles and cookbooks.

S and S Seeds

P. O. Box 1275, Carpinteria 93014
(805) 684-0436; (805) 684-2798 (fax)
www.ssseeds.com

Seeds for California native wildflowers, grasses, and plants for reclamation, erosion control, and landscape projects. Whole-sale only.

Seedhunt

P. O. Box 96, Freedom 95019
(831) 763-1523; (831) 728-5131 (fax)
www.seedhunt.com
Email: seedhunt@cruzio.com

Ginny Hunt offers seed collected from her garden in Watson-ville and from the gardens of a host of other avid gardeners and friends. She specializes in seeds of uncommon California native bulbs and plants and of other plants suited to Mediter-ranean-type climates. Order by mail or fax.

Stover Seed Company

P. O. Box 1579, Sun Valley 91353
(213) 626-9668; (213) 626-4920 (fax)
www.stoverseed.com

A wholesale supplier since 1922, Stover Seeds offers turfgrass (many varieties), native grass, and native plant and vegetable seeds. Retail customers can shop online at www.wildflowers online.com.

Sutton's Iris Gardens

16592 Road 208, Porterville 93257
(559) 784-5107; (559) 784-6701 (fax)
www.suttoniris.com
Email: info@suttoniris.com

Over 80 acres of bearded irises, including dwarf and re-blooming varieties, the result of an uncontrollable hobby that became a business in 1983. Rhizomes can be ordered by mail, fax, or online order. The garden of 2,000 named varieties is open April and May, 10 a.m.–6 p.m.

Telos Rare Bulbs

P. O. Box 1067, Ferndale 95536
telosrarebulbs.com
Email: telosrarebulbs@suddenlink.net

Diana Chapman has been collecting bulb seed for years from other private collectors and botanical gardens, a robust hobby before it became a business. She specializes in hard-to-find bulbs from South America, South Africa, and the Western United States, and a few from the Mediterranean region. She laments that the tradition of free seed exchange between collectors is being jeopardized by import restrictions, and she hosts the Bulbmaven blog. Prepaid orders are accepted by mail or email.

Timeless Topiary

Sebastopol
(707) 861-9697
www.timelesstopiary.com
Email: sales@timelesstopiary.com

Diane and Nick Gurney, former owners of Marquardt Gardens, have been growing herbs and trees for 25 years. Since 2000, they have specialized in olive trees, citrus trees, and herb topiaries and wreaths. Phone, fax, and email orders are accepted. Custom work available.

Trees of Antiquity

20 Wellsona Road, Paso Robles 93446
(805) 467-9909
www.treesofantiquity.com

Certified organic heirloom fruit trees, with a special collection of apples but also apricots, cherries, crab apples, figs, jujubes, mulberries, nectarines, peaches, pears, persimmons, plumcots, plums, pomegranates, nut trees, and berry bushes. When the owners of Sonoma Antique Apple Nursery retired, they transferred the business to their longtime manager Neil Collins and his wife, Danielle. Mail, phone, or online orders.

William R. P. Welch

1031 Cayuga Street, Apt B, Santa Cruz 95062 (mailing address)
(831) 236-8397; (831) 426-4915 (fax)
www.billthebulbbaron.com
Email: billthebulbbaron@aol.com

William "the Bulb Baron" Welch has been selling bulbs since 1979, specializing in narcissus because they are reasonably drought tolerant and deer and gopher resistant. He has a large collection of bunch-flowered, fragrant tazetta narcissus, as well as *Amaryllis, Crinum*, oxblood lilies, and freesias. William Welch has introduced *Amaryllis belladonna* 'Welch Hybrids', *Narcissus tazetta* 'Autumn Colors Strain', and *N. t.* 'Welch's Paper White'. Email or mail order.

Wildflower Seed and Tool Company

P. O. Box 406, Saint Helena 94574
(800) 456-3359; (707) 253-2582 (fax)
www.wildflower-seed.com
Email: sales@wildflower-seed.com

Seeds of 100 varieties of wildflowers offered in various mixes, such as "California Natives," "Dry Places," "Napa Valley," and "Shady Woodland." Seeds come in 4-ounce, 8-ounce, and 1-pound packages and are available by fax, mail, or online order.

Plant Index

This index includes only those specialty nurseries and growers that specialize in one type of plant (e.g., maple) or one category of plant (e.g., California native plants).

Nursery Index

This index includes specialty
nurseries and growers and
notable garden centers.
It does not include sources
listed in the section Other
Sources, nor does it include
horticultural attractions.

Horticultural Attractions Index

About the Authors

Nancy Conner has been fascinated by coastal California horticulture since she arrived here in the early 1960s. A graduate of Wellesley College and Stanford University, she was a docent at Strybing Arboretum in the late 1970s. She cofounded the San Francisco Landscape Garden Show and was instrumental in its organization for the twelve years it was managed by Friends of Recreation and Parks in San Francisco. She has long been active in the cause for parks, serving on the boards of both the San Francisco Parks Alliance and the Presidio Trust. Her pet park projects include restoring the Conservatory of Flowers and building the underground garage in Golden Gate Park. She gardens in Inverness.

Demi Bowles Lathrop learned to garden as a young girl alongside her grandmothers and mother and carries on the tradition. Since she arrived here and earned M.A. and Ph.D. degrees in English Literature from University of California, Berkeley, her passion for gardening in California has grown. She has been a Certified Master Gardener and a contributing garden writer for the *San Francisco Chronicle* and *Pacific Horticulture* magazine. She has served as judge at the San Francisco Flower and Garden Show and as editor and contributor to various arts, design, and literary publications. HGTV's *Gardening by the Yard* featured her and her garden on a segment. In the garden community, she served on the boards of the Late Show Gardens and California Horticulture Society. She lives with her husband and children in San Francisco, where she writes and gardens.

Barbara Stevens has a proven passion for plants. A graduate of UC Berkeley, she has been very involved with the Strybing Arboretum Society and has served on its board. She was a cofounder of the San Francisco Landscape Garden Show and was its horticultural chair for twelve years. She is an active member of the California Native Plant Society, Marin and San Francisco Chapters; the California Horticultural Society; the North American Rock Garden Society; the Hardy Plant Society; and the San Francisco Parks Alliance. She has visited botanic gardens all over the world, traveling to China with the Alpine Garden Society and to Turkey, Argentina, Australia, Costa Rica, and New Zealand with the International Dendrology Society. She swims and gardens in San Francisco.

HEYDAY

About Heyday

Heyday is an independent, nonprofit publisher and unique cultural institution. We promote widespread awareness and celebration of California's many cultures, landscapes, and boundary-breaking ideas. Through our well-crafted books, public events, and innovative outreach programs we are building a vibrant community of readers, writers, and thinkers.

Thank You

It takes the collective effort of many to create a thriving literary culture. We are thankful to all the thoughtful people we have the privilege to engage with. Cheers to our writers, artists, editors, storytellers, designers, printers, bookstores, critics, cultural organizations, readers, and book lovers everywhere!

We are especially grateful for the generous funding we've received for our publications and programs during the past year from foundations and hundreds of individual donors. Major supporters include

Advocates for Indigenous California Language Survival; Anonymous (3); Judith and Phillip Auth; Carrie Avery and Jon Tigar; Judy Avery; Dr. Carol Baird and Alan Harper; Paul Bancroft III; Richard and Rickie Ann Baum; BayTree Fund; S. D. Bechtel, Jr. Foundation; Jean and Fred Berensmeier; Joan Berman and Philip Gerstner; Nancy Bertelsen; Barbara Boucke; Beatrice Bowles; Jamie and Philip Bowles; John Briscoe; David Brower Center; Lewis and Sheana Butler; Helen Cagampang; California Historical Society; California Rice Commission;

California State Parks Foundation; California Wildlife Foundation/California Oaks; The Campbell Foundation; Joanne Campbell; Candelaria Fund; John and Nancy Cassidy Family Foundation; James and Margaret Chapin; Graham Chisholm; The Christensen Fund; Jon Christensen; Cynthia Clarke; Lawrence Crooks; Community Futures Collective; Lauren and Alan Dachs; Nik Dehejia; Topher Delaney; Chris Desser and Kirk Marckwald; Lokelani Devone and Annette Brand; J.K. Dineen; Frances Dinkelspiel and Gary Wayne; The Roy & Patricia Disney Family Foundation; Tim Disney; Doune Trust; The Durfee Foundation; Michael Eaton and Charity Kenyon; Endangered Habitats League; Marilee Enge and George Frost; Richard and Gretchen Evans; Megan Fletcher; Friends of the Roseville Public Library; Furthur Foundation; John Gage and Linda Schacht; Wallace Alexander Gerbode Foundation; Patrick Golden; Dr. Erica and Barry Goode; Wanda Lee Graves and Stephen Duscha; Walter & Elise Haas Fund; Coke and James Hallowell; Theresa Harlan; Cindy Heitzman; Carla Hills and Frank LaPena; Leanne Hinton and Gary Scott; Penelope Hlavac; Charles and Sandra Hobson; Nettie Hoge; Donna Ewald Huggins; Inlandia Institute; JiJi Foundation; Claudia Jurmain; Kalliopeia Foundation; Marty and Pamela Krasney; Guy Lampard and Suzanne Badenhoop; Thomas Lockard and Alix Marduel; David Loeb; Thomas J. Long Foundation; Judith Lowry-Croul and Brad Croul; Bryce and Jill Lundberg; Sam and Alfreda Maloof Foundation for Arts & Crafts; Manzanar History Association; Michael McCone; Nion McEvoy and Leslie Berriman; The Giles W. and Elise G. Mead Foundation; Moore Family Foundation; Michael Moratto and Kathleen Boone; Seeley W. Mudd Foundation; Karen and Thomas Mulvaney; Richard Nagler; National Wildlife Federation; Native Arts and Cultures Foundation; The Nature Conservancy; Nightingale Family Foundation; Steven Nightingale and

Lucy Blake; Northern California Water Association; Panta Rhea Foundation; Julie and Will Parish; Ronald Parker; The Ralph M. Parsons Foundation, Pease Family Fund; Jean and Gary Pokorny; Jeannene Przyblyski; James and Caren Quay, in honor of Jim Houston; Steven Rasmussen and Felicia Woytak; Susan Raynes; Robin Ridder; Spreck Rosekrans and Isabella Salaverry; Alan Rosenus; The San Francisco Foundation; San Francisco Architectural Heritage; San Manuel Band of Mission Indians; Toby and Sheila Schwartzburg; Mary Selkirk and Lee Ballance; Ron Shoop; The Stephen M. Silberstein Foundation; Ernest and June Siva; Stanley Smith Horticultural Trust; William Somerville; Carla Soracco and Donna Fong, in honor of Barbara Boucke; Radha Stern and Gary Maxworthy; Liz Sutherland; Roselyne Swig; Thendara Foundation; TomKat Charitable Trust; Jerry Tone and Martha Wyckoff; Sonia Torres; Michael and Shirley Traynor; The Roger J. and Madeleine Traynor Foundation; Lisa Van Cleef and Mark Gunson; Stevens Van Strum; Patricia Wakida; Marion Weber; Sylvia Wen and Mathew London; Valerie Whitworth and Michael Barbour; Cole Wilbur; Peter Wiley and Valerie Barth; The Dean Witter Foundation; and Yocha Dehe Wintun Nation.

Board of Directors

Richard D. Baum (Cochair), Steve Costa, Don Franzen, Whitney Green, Nettie Hoge (Cochair), Marty Krasney, Guy Lampard (Chairman Emeritus), Ralph Lewin, Praveen Madan, Michael McCone (Chairman Emeritus), Alexandra Rome, Greg Sarris, Sherrie Smith-Ferri, Sonia Torres, Michael Traynor, Lisa Van Cleef, and Lucinda Watson.

Getting Involved

To learn more about our publications, events and other ways you can participate, please visit www.heydaybooks.com.